OCOMOTIVES OF THE NORTH EASTERN RAILWAY

LOCOMOTIVES
OF THE
NORTH EASTERN
RAILWAY

By

O. S. NOCK

B.Sc., M.I.C.E., M.I.Mech.E.

LONDON

IAN ALLAN LTD

By the same author:

The Locomotives of Sir Nigel Gresley.
British Locomotives at Work.
The Railways of Britain.
Kings and Castles of the G.W.R.
Scottish Railways.
British Locomotives from the Footplate.
The Great Western Railway: An Appreciation.
British Trains Past and Present.
The Premier Line.
Four Thousand Miles on the Footplate.
The Locomotives of R. E. L. Maunsell.

First Published 1954
This edition 1974

ISBN 07110 04935

Published and printed in the
United Kingdom by
Ian Allan Ltd, Shepperton, Surrey

Contents

	Preface	vii
Chapter One	1854—The Diverse Heritage	1
Chapter Two	The Line and its Gradients	8
Chapter Three	The Years of Consolidation 1854-1870 ...	18
Chapter Four	Stockton & Darlington Locomotives ...	34
Chapter Five	Fletcher, the Last Phase	44
Chapter Six	McDonnell and the Interregnum	58
Chapter Seven	Two-cylinder Compounds	73
Chapter Eight	Wilson Worsdell, 1890-1898	84
Chapter Nine	The Big-engine Era, 1899-1906	103
Chapter Ten	Transition Years—Worsdell to Raven ...	124
Chapter Eleven	Locomotive Performance, 1900-1914 ...	143
Chapter Twelve	The War and the Changing Scene ...	173
Chapter Thirteen	Another Transition: N.E.R. to L.N.E.R. ...	183
Epilogue	The New N.E.R.	193
	Index	196

PUBLISHER'S NOTE

By an unfortunate oversight the title of an existing publication by Mr. John S. Maclean was selected for this book. The publisher and author are grateful to Mr. Maclean for his co-operation in allowing them to retain it for this work with which Mr. Maclean's book has no connection.

Preface

ON whatever basis consideration is made the North Eastern must be judged one of the really great railways of pre-grouping times. Its direct descent from the earliest pioneer days of passenger transport by rail, its association with some of the earliest steam locomotives in the world, lend a rich historic colouring to its network of lines in Northumberland and Durham. Fortunately, too, the management was always historically minded, so that many relics of those early days, and many of later years have been preserved. There was a sense of continuity in its affairs, and well-cherished traditions were passed down to twentieth-century generations of railwaymen. Its first Locomotive Superintendent, Edward Fletcher, was old enough to have assisted Stephenson in the building of the *Rocket,* and one of his pupils, a clergyman's son, Vincent Litchfield Raven by name, was the last Chief Mechanical Engineer of the line. It would have been tempting to have tried to trace the whole story, not merely back to the days of the *Rocket,* but to No. 1 of the Stockton and Darlington Railway—"From *Locomotion* to the *City of Newcastle*"—or some such alluring title! But the complications of the history itself preclude any ideas of this kind, within a book of reasonable compass, and so this particular work starts at the formation of the North Eastern Railway in 1854. Even so I have not been able to deal in more than broad outline with the Fletcher days, in which the lack of uniformity in practice makes it almost impossible to do more, in two or three chapters, than indicate the general trend of design.

With the later North Eastern engines I have been most fortunate in receiving generous and comprehensive assistance from the present officers of the North Eastern Region. Mr. K. J. Cook, the Mechanical and Electrical Engineer, has made available to me the dynamometer car records kept at Darlington Works; Mr. F. H. Petty, Motive Power Superintendent, has given me much help in selecting present-day engine workings for observations, footplate passes for which have been kindly arranged by Railway Executive Headquarters in London. Then there is Mr. R. A. Smeddle, Mechanical and Electrical Engineer, Western Region, and son of Mr. J. H. Smeddle, the last Running Superintendent of the N.E.R., who has passed on to me many reminiscences of his firing days while a pupil at Darlington, and who has been so bold as to hang a beautiful painting of a "Z" Atlantic in the former Great Western C.M.E.'s office at Swindon. I have had also the utmost assistance from others not now connected with British Railways, but who know the North Eastern back to 60 years ago. Among these I must mention Mr. H. W. Davis,

M.I.C.E. of Earsdon, a former district locomotive superintendent, and later deputy Chief Mechanical Engineer of the Egyptian State Railways; Mr J. Mawson Rounthwaite, M.I.C.E., of Belford, who served under Wilson Worsdell; and Mr. John S. MacLean, whose book on North Eastern locomotives is a classic in itself. I have also referred to Mr. MacLean's book on the Newcastle & Carlisle Railway, which is a mine of historical information. The contribution of Mr. R. J. Purves towards my own book is a massive one, and in commending his beautiful photographs to the reader's study I like to look back to the many years in which we were professionally associated, he as Assistant Signal Engineer, and I on the staff of the contractors who were entrusted with so much signalling work on the North Eastern—whether as Railway, "Area", or "Region"!

In writing the present book I have made extensive references to such earlier writers as Ahrons, D. K. Clark, and the quaint little treatise on Stockton and Darlington locomotives by Theodore West. I have consulted the files of the railway and engineering periodicals, particularly *The Engineer,* with its magnificent drawings of locomotives, and I would once again, as in the case of *The Premier Line,* like to thank especially the City Librarian of Bath and his assistants for their help in looking out early volumes for me. Mr. C. R. H. Simpson, of the Locomotive Publishing Company, has given me a great deal of help with the illustrations, and I am indebted to the Stephenson Locomotive Society for the loan of certain volumes from their library.

To Olivia, my wife, I tender my very best thanks for deciphering the original manuscript, the clarity of which steadily degenerated in response to the ever-accelerating demands of Mr. Ian Allan. Of course the North Eastern gave less scope for her adroitness in the re-naming of engines than did the companion volume on the North Western; but even Crewe, with its legions of named engines, was never reduced to the straits that led the Stockton & Darlington to produce that truly comical quartet *Spring, Summer, Autumn* and *Winter!*

O. S. Nock.

Sion Hill,
Bath.
May, 1953.

Chapter One

1854—THE DIVERSE HERITAGE

A HUNDRED years ago, on the 31st July, 1854, to be precise, the Act authorising the amalgamation of three leading railway companies in North Eastern England received the Royal Assent. Those railways were the York & North Midland, the York, Newcastle & Berwick, and the Leeds Northern. The combined system took the subsequently well-known and famous name of the North Eastern Railway. It is at this stage that I take up the fascinating locomotive history of the line, and to appreciate its diversity and lack of standardisation in the early stages some reference is needed to the background of railway development, and of locomotive constructional practice in what may well be called North Eastern England. Two of the railways that were parties to the amalgamation of 1854 were themselves amalgamations or extensions of still older concerns, and although local interests were vigorously expressed in their projecting and eventual make-up, one can sense the guiding influence of George Hudson behind the gradual building up of the railway network north of the Humber. But while the York & North Midland and the York, Newcastle & Berwick were part of Hudson's grand conception of a through route from Euston to Newcastle and Edinburgh—travelling over the metals of lines in which he was personally interested, from Rugby, via Derby, Normanton, and York, the Leeds Northern, originated as the Leeds & Thirsk, had been an open rival bent, eventually, on the completion of a competitive line through to Newcastle.

In 1854 two relatively large railways in the district and many smaller ones remained outside the new combination. The Stockton & Darlington and the Newcastle & Carlisle each maintained an uneasy, if not precarious independence for several years after. Furthermore the historic partnership of the East Coast Route as we knew it in the last twenty years before "grouping" was not by any means an alliance that the North Eastern could afford to take for granted, particularly in the south where the Great Northern had been projected in direct opposition to Hudson's wishes, and built in defiance of his threats and counter manœuvres. Naturally he strove to keep as much traffic to and from the south for the Midland route, in which he was so deeply interested. In the north the strong hold upon Newcastle traffic possessed by the newly-formed North Eastern Railway was received with distaste by both partners in the West Coast Route, and various attempts at encroachment were made upon the independence of the Newcastle & Carlisle Railway. The story is a most complicated one, and involves the projecting of some further new lines in west Durham; but so far as locomotive history is concerned it had the effect of postponing the further amalgamations, and resulted in the building of still more diverse engine classes in the meantime. Thus when final amalgamation did come the combined stud was further than ever from anything approaching standardisation.

A year before the amalgamation by which the North Eastern Railway was formed the three constituent companies had entered into a working agreement for handling traffic, and Edward Fletcher had been instructed to superintend locomotive matters over all three systems. After the amalgamation he was appointed Locomotive Superintendent of the North Eastern Railway. Fletcher was a Northumbrian born and bred, as it were, among steam locomotives. Born near Otterburn in 1807, he was old enough to be serving his apprenticeship with George Stephenson at the time the *Rocket* was being built. He accompanied Stephenson to Killingworth for the engine's trials and rode on the footplate during some successful running on the colliery line before the engine left Northumberland for her triumph at Rainhill. Fletcher grew up among all the pioneer locomotive engineering centred north of the Tees, where the influence of the Stephenson's was very strong. No great locomotive engineering personality emerged from the various railways that eventually came to make up the North Eastern; the strength of the group lay in the far-sighted administration of George Hudson, and the locomotives purchased were of manufacturers' design. There was no North Eastern counterpart of Alexander Allan, at Crewe, or of Daniel Gooch, at Swindon. The great engineering personality of those early days was T. E. Harrison, who was Engineer as well as General Manager of the York, Newcastle & Berwick, and who was the guiding spirit in the amalgamation of 1854. Comment has frequently been made upon Fletcher's easy-going administration; but it was not until 1845 that he had anything of a command, and then it was no more than that of the Newcastle & Darlington Junction Railway. Major responsibility came to him relatively late in life, for railway engineers of his generation. He was 47 when the North Eastern Railway was formed.

The locomotive stock of the three original constituents totalled 387, of which 244 came from the York, Newcastle & Berwick, 114 from the York & North Midland, and no more than 28 from the Leeds Northern. By the time of the amalgamation the Y. & N.M.R. had extended far beyond its original sphere. It was projected as a vital link in the "Hudson" route to the north, diverging from the main line of the North Midland Railway near Normanton to reach York and provide connection with the one-time Great North of England Railway. But in later years the York & North Midland came to absorb the Leeds and Selby; the continuation line to Hull; the line from York to Scarborough; the Whitby and Pickering; the line northward from Hull to Driffield, Bridlington and its junction with the York and Scarborough, at Seamer; while another important through link was that between Church Fenton and Harrogate. Those 114 locomotives must have been spread very thinly over this extensive group of lines, and the majority were small and of obsolete design even for those days. The best known by far, and some of the longest lived, where eleven 2-2-2 singles built by E. B. Wilson & Co., of Leeds. These were of the famous "Jenny Lind" type, including the second of that type ever to be built. This engine, which became No. 88 of the York & North Midland, actually carried the name *Jenny Lind*. This engine survived on the N.E.R. till 1879, and two later members of the class lasted until a year later.

The backbone of motive power on the N.E.R. came originally from the York, Newcastle & Berwick, and although a miscellaneous lot on the whole the stud included some of the best express engines of the day, to which detailed reference will be made later. But on the majority of British railways express passenger running, spectacular though it may be and a creator of prestige, needs a relatively small proportion of the motive power required from day to day, and on the North Eastern that proportion came to be one of the smallest on any of the railways in Britain. In 1920, out of a total stud of just 2,000 locomotives, the North Eastern had only 332 passenger tender engines, and from these one should deduct the 17 remaining 4-2-2 singles, the 54 remaining 2-4-0s, and such essentially slow-train engines as the Class "G" "Waterbury" 4-4-0s, to gain some idea of the express passenger stud. This leaves only 241 locomotives, and even out of these the "F", "M" and "Q" 4-4-0s, totalling 87 between them, could hardly be regarded as modern main line power, even in 1920. With the addition of the five Raven Pacifics the North Eastern entered the grouping era with only 149 modern express locomotives, while by way of comparison the L. & N.W.R. out of its 3,000-odd engines included some 550 superheater express units of the 4-4-0 and 4-6-0 types.

These figures are enough to show how the character of North Eastern locomotive power developed with the years. It was primarily a freight line; the locomotive history is all the more interesting on that account, as in keeping with tradition, so many of the old N.E.R. engines are still in service today. On most British lines now very few pre-grouping passenger locomotives remain—even on the Great Western. But the freight types survive. Great Central "O4" 2-8-0s are still to be seen in their hundreds; the Crewe "Super D" 0-8-0s are still numerous, while in Scotland freight engines of Caledonian and North British design still abound. So it is also on the North Eastern. There are still more than 800 locomotives of N.E.R. design in service. and the great majority of these are working on freight.

Reverting to the year of the big amalgamation the pattern of North Eastern freight traffic development was even then apparent. As with the oldest constituent of all, the Stockton & Darlington, there was the common task of conveying coal from pits all over County Durham to the east coast for shipment, and in step with the construction of new lines of railways dock facilities were developed at South Shields, Sunderland, Hartlepool, Port Clarence, and Middlesbrough. Then followed some intense reciprocal developments in connection with the Cleveland ironstone traffic. The establishment of the great iron works of the Derwent Iron Company, at Consett, put the Stockton & Darlington Railway in a highly favourable position in having the Cleveland ores near one end of their line and the new ironworks at the other. But the increased traffic came to prove an embarrassment. Much of the coal traffic on the Stockton & Darlington in 1854 was still worked by horses, and on the steep gradients north of Bishop Auckland, and over the high moorland between Crook and Cold Rowley, rope haulage was used. The Consett works used a considerable tonnage of West Cumberland ore; this was brought to Tyneside, at Redheugh, by the Newcastle & Carlisle Railway and hauled up to Annfield over the fearsome inclines of the Stanhope & Tyne Railway, partly by horse, and partly by stationary engines. This included the crossing of Hownes Gill—down one side of the ravine at 1 in 2½ and up the other side at 1 in 3! The self-acting inclines were all very well when the loaded traffic was flowing from the high inland country to the sea, but when traffic coming up the grades grew to be as heavy, if not heavier, than that descending less primitive methods had to be introduced.

It was very largely the development of the ore traffic that led to the construction of that wild, mountain route over Stainmore summit. The South Durham & Lancashire Union Railway, as it was known, was an offshoot of the Stockton & Darlington, running via Barnard Castle and Kirkby Stephen to join the North Western at Tebay. Through ore trains were run from the Furness ironstone districts via Arnside, Oxenholme and Tebay, and in days when I first knew it Furness Railway locomotives worked over the L. & N.W.R., and handed their trains over direct to the North Eastern at Tebay. The line was opened throughout in 1861, and operated under the aegis of the Stockton & Darlington. The locomotive superintendent of the latter line, William Bouch, designed some special engines for the passenger traffic, so that when amalgamation with the N.E.R. eventually took place there were still further classes to be absorbed into the heterogeneous collection already in Mr. Fletcher's care.

The construction of the South Durham & Lancashire line was viewed with some disquiet by the Newcastle & Carlisle Railway, which latter feared a loss of their cross-country mineral traffic, and the loss of through business between Newcastle and Liverpool. The alliance between the North Eastern and the North British was a most uneasy one about this time, and the Scottish company suspected a secret alliance between the North Eastern and the Caledonian for the Newcastle-Glasgow traffic, via the Carlisle road. The North British for their part were thought to be planning a through independent route to Edinburgh from Morpeth, across country to the Border Union line, and thence via Riccarton and the Waverley route. But among this welter of rivalries and suspicions that developed about the North Eastern storm centres from 1858 onward by far the most dangerous was an apparently innocent little local scheme to make a new line from Scotswood Bridge, on the Newcastle & Carlisle, up the Derwent valley to link up with the Stockton & Darlington at Hownes Gill, a distance of less than 20 miles. The railway was to be known as the Newcastle & Derwent Valley. The North Eastern Board at once realised the gravity of this move, which was backed by no less a concern than the London & North Western. Had this small independent line been constructed, in association with the Stockton & Darlington, and with the South Durham & Lancashire, the North Western would have had a clear run to Scotswood, and nothing could then have stopped their entry into Newcastle. From such a situation it would have been no more than a natural development for Euston to secure absolute control and ownership of the entire route, and of the Stockton & Darlington itself.

At this supremely critical moment the North Eastern was fortunate indeed in the far-sightedness and sagacity of its leadership. In almost complete secrecy the Board approached the Stockton & Darlington with a proposal for amalgamation. The latter company had already begun to feel the pressure of the North Eastern competition for freight traffic, and the proposal was not unwelcome to them; terms were readily arranged, and just at the moment when the new Derwent Valley project had reached the stage of setting up a provisional committee the Stockton & Darlington, and with them the South Durham & Lancashire, declared that they would be unable to co-operate. It was not, however, until 1863 that the actual amalgamation took place; it would have been unwise to press it forward earlier, owing to the bitter resentment caused to the L. & N.W.R. and to the North British, by the defeat of the Derwent Valley scheme. Having secured this triumph the North Eastern indulged in some mild appeasement. Opposition to the amalgamation with the Newcastle & Carlisle was largely allayed by their granting the North British running powers from Hexham into Newcastle, and by granting increased traffic facilities to the North Western at Carlisle, and at other points where their interests met. The Newcastle & Carlisle amalgamation took place in 1862, and apart from one or two relatively mild flutters the North Eastern had, by the following year, secured an almost complete monopoly east of the Pennines from the Humber to the Tweed—a railway system much as George Hudson had envisaged in the "forties", and had done so much to make possible before his catastrophic fall from power.

From this reference to the build up of the railway some notes on the general operating conditions in 1854-63 will be of interest. The bulk of the freight traffic on all lines was conveyed in the old chaldron type of wagons; passenger carriages were mostly primitive four-wheelers, and luggage was conveyed on the roofs. While the main lines were operated by electric telegraph, semaphore signals were rare, and the old revolving disc type signals were still the most commonly used. On some of the old lines horse-drawn passenger coaches were still at work, while on the heavy inclines that were gravity worked descending trains of an extraordinarily mixed character were allowed to travel at surprisingly high speed. On one particular stretch these trains would consist of a dozen or more coal or coke chaldrons, one or two coaches filled with passengers and general merchandise, and the last three conveying the horses which had conveyed the empty stock up the incline! On the main line punctuality was almost non-existent and the night mails were so consistently late that a Government enquiry was in progress during the latter part of 1853.

The booked speeds were not high. The following table will give some impression of the services in operation in 1854:

Route	Distance	Express or Mail train speed
	miles	m.p.h.
Normanton—York	24½	37
York—Newcastle	81¼	39
Newcastle—Berwick	67	41
Hull—Selby	30¾	31
York—Scarborough	42¾	32

In the above table the distance from York to Newcastle is via Leamside and Felling, not by the present route through Durham. At times the running was considerably faster. Engine No. 77, the celebrated Stephenson three-cylinder "single", is credited with having worked the Royal Train from Newcastle to Berwick at an average speed of 57 m.p.h., in October, 1850. The coaching stock used was generally below the standards maintained elsewhere, and at the time of the amalgamation there were still some open third-class carriages in commission, which were pressed into service on market and other trains on which passengers were conveyed at less than 1d per mile. So far as mineral traffic was concerned, in 1854 the company possessed only three eight-ton wagons, some 2,700 six-tonners, and more than 10,000 chaldron wagons.

One incident in the year of amalgamation will serve to show something of the conditions of travel at the beginning of our story of

North Eastern locomotives. One of the major engineering works of the Leeds Northern was Bramhope Tunnel, through the high country between the valleys of the Aire and the Wharfe. Its northern entrance is distinguished by a fine circular castellated "gatehouse". In September, 1854, there was a fall of rock inside the tunnel and the Stockton to Leeds "Parliamentary" train, double-headed, ran into the obstruction. The gradient is rising at 1 in 100 throughout the tunnel in the southward direction, and alarming though it must have been in the darkness the collision would not have been serious had not the shock caused the coupling chains between the fifth and sixth carriages to break. The guard, travelling at the extreme rear of the train, was injured and it was apparently some little time before he recovered consciousness and found that the five detached carriages and his van were running backwards down the 1 in 100 gradient, with ever-increasing speed. With great courage, in face of his injuries, he managed to apply the brakes, and bring the run-away portion to rest in Arthington station. Before any passengers had time to alight yet another runaway bore down upon them from the tunnel—an open-third filled with Irish reapers—and crashed into the standing coaches. The casualty list was high, but fortunately no one was actually killed. Repairs necessary to the tunnel itself, where the roof had collapsed, were found to be extensive, and it was not until New Year's Day of 1855 that the line was opened again for passenger traffic.

Chapter Two

THE LINE AND ITS GRADIENTS

SOUTH of Newcastle the character of the East Coast main line changed considerably during the 68 years of the North Eastern Railway. At the southern end trains from the Great Northern travelled via Askern to reach the York & North Midland line at Knottingley, as the direct line from Shaftholme Junction through Heck, Selby, and Naburn was not opened until January, 1871. Even so the latter line was then referred to as the "York & Doncaster branch". North of Ferryhill the main line continued due north at what is now Tursdale Junction, through Leamside, Penshaw and Washington, to join the coast route from Sunderland at Brockley Whins. Newcastle was entered by the High Level Bridge and that famous structure continued to provide the only approach from the south until 1906, when the King Edward Bridge was opened. The present main line north of Ferryhill, via Durham and the Team Valley, was opened in 1872, and it was then possible to transfer the through East Coast passenger traffic from the heavily worked mineral line east of Durham. Today the only passenger traffic over the original line is between Leamside and Penshaw, where the line is used by the through service between Durham and Sunderland, and this is not extensive. But even after the opening of the Team Valley line in 1872 expresses from the south passed from Bensham to Gateshead and entered Newcastle Central at the east end via the High Level Bridge.

In describing the routes over which North Eastern locomotives were called upon to work there is a clear division between the main arteries of passenger traffic, which were, of course, also used by long distance freight trains, and the purely mineral lines used for conveying coal to the most convenient ports for shipment. On the East Coast main line North Eastern locomotives did not ordinarily work passenger trains south of York, whereas in the north they ran through to Edinburgh over 57·5 miles of North British metals beyond Berwick. In North Eastern days engines were always changed at Newcastle. Before the opening of the King Edward VII Bridge this was essential, as the through expresses reversed direction; but after 1906 the old arrangement persisted except on one or two special occasions. In civil engineering and signalling there was a clear-cut line of demarcation between the Northern and Southern divisions; each had their own engineer, and each used quite different patterns of semaphore signals and interlocking frames. In locomotive working at any rate in later days there was no such division, and a normal day's work for some of the crack Gateshead express engines was a run to Edinburgh and back with one crew and then a run to Leeds and back with the second.

YORK TO NEWCASTLE, WITH ALTERNATIVE ROUTES.

The opening section of this route over the 44 miles from York to Darlington is one of the finest and straightest stretches of high speed main line to be found anywhere in the British Isles. The gradient is slightly against a northbound train, after the first 12 miles which are dead level; but the average gradient from Alne to Croft Spa (30·3 miles), taking into account the slight falls as well as the rising stretches, is no more than 1 in 2,070, and I have noted average speeds of 70 m.p.h. with North Eastern Atlantics northbound over this road. The circumstances of running over this stretch have changed considerably since the grouping of the railways in 1923. Before that time North Eastern engines were starting "cold" from York, with clean fires, and with a run of no more than 80 miles ahead of them; in L.N.E.R. days, with through engine working between Kings Cross and Newcastle, the London men regarded the York-Darlington stretch as the most critical of the whole journey. If the engine was a bit shy for steam they would get a rough passage over this gradually rising stretch, where the gradient was enough to try a heavily loaded engine to the extent of losing time. Southbound, it is of course a truly glorious racing ground, and the latter chapters of this book include many high averages made between Northallerton and Skelton Junction.

Non-stopping expresses pass completely outside Bank Top station at Darlington; they have an almost straight run and the speed in both directions is usually between 65 and 70 m.p.h. From the station itself there are rather awkward starts, pulling out over the curves to regain the main line. Three-quarters of a mile out the Stockton & Darlington line is crossed on the level, and from this point the rise, now over the track of the one-time Newcastle & Darlington Junction Railway, is more pronounced, till Bradbury is passed. The adverse stretches are graded between 1 in 220 and 1 in 203, but in the 10 miles from the Stockton & Darlington crossing to the summit point north of Bradbury there is also a total of nearly 5 miles of dead level. So the line comes to Ferryhill, and beyond it, Tursdale Junction. Here the old line continues straight to the north, afterwards swinging away to pass Sherburn, some 3 miles due east of Durham. The gradients are easy, with nothing worse than 1¼ miles of 1 in 177 to Shincliffe; then after passing Sherburn there is a steady descent on gradients varying between 1 in 188 and 1 in 227 for some 5½ miles, past Leamside and Fence Houses, to the valley of the Wear at Penshaw.

Beyond this point one is introduced to the complications of early railway days in County Durham. The line to Sunderland follows the sweep of the River Wear north-eastwards, while what was once the East Coast main line follows a sharp S-alignment north-westwards to join the Pontop and South Shields line. For some six years from 1844 to 1850 the Scotch expresses of the day ran for 5 miles over what is now a purely mineral line to its intersection with the Newcastle-Sunderland line at Brockley Whins—about a mile from the present Tyne Dock. There was then no direct connection, and trains had to reverse at Brockley Whins. In 1850, however, the direct line from Washington to Pelaw was opened, for the most part over very gentle gradients, and the final stretch of 3 miles to Gateshead is on a descent of 1 in 360. Apart from the sharp S-curve between Penshaw Junction and Washington, this could be quite a fast route, though it is nowadays traversed by no regular through express passenger trains. It is heavily used for the slower classes of freight trains. During the time that this book was in preparation I *did* travel over the Leamside line, on a Sunday morning when the up "Night Scotsman" was diverted. But I was asleep at the time and did not learn of the diversion until it was too late to compile a log of the running.

The opening of the Team Valley line, in 1872, put the more populous centres of Durham and Chester-le-Street on the trunk route to Scotland. This newer line curves away westward from the Leamside route at Tursdale Junction, and dips down a beautifully wooded glen to cross the Wear on a high viaduct at Croxdale. The descent is at 1 in 150, and the rise up the far side is just as steep for nearly 2 miles, till the Durham-Bishop Auckland line is joined at Relly Mill Junction. Speed must be considerably reduced here, and still further at Durham itself, a mile farther on. The 1 in 100 gradient following the 30 m.p.h. slack through Durham is a distinct handicap to southbound trains. In North Eastern days heavy trains stopping at Durham were banked in rear up to Relly Mill Junction. From Durham the descent into the Team Valley is moderately steep, including 2½ miles at 1 in 150. At one time, moreover, the whole route from Ferryhill northward was subject to many speed restrictions due to colliery subsidences, and running times over the 36 miles from Darlington to Newcastle might be anything between 45 and 50 minutes. Today, fortunately, all the restrictions have gone, and on a fine recent run with the "North Briton" we ran from Darlington to Newcastle, in exactly 40 minutes. But whichever way one comes into Newcastle, whether from Pelaw over the High Level Bridge, or from the Team Valley line over the King Edward Bridge, the final approach is slow, and takes something away from the fine running average speeds made both in N.E.R. days and now.

Bishop Auckland.

An important secondary route, used in emergency sometimes by through expresses, is that via Bishop Auckland. The line continues south-westward from Relly Mill Junction to join the northern extension of the Stockton & Darlington Railway. From Relly Mill there is a stiff climb at 1 in 101 past Brandon Colliery and an altitude of 405 ft. above sea level is reached near Brancepeth. Thence the going is mostly downhill at 1 in 100 to 1 in 200 to the crossing of the Wear south of Hunwick, after which the line rises a little to its junction with the S. & D. at Bishop Auckland North Junction. A climb of 3 miles at 1 in 230 follows to Shildon, where the altitude is only 10 ft. below that near Brancepeth, but from Bishop Auckland southwards the mineral traffic over this route completely overshadows any value the line may have for emergency through passenger workings. From Shildon the cross-country mineral line to Thornaby and Newport-on-Tees carries a very heavy traffic, and it was indeed selected for a trial of electric traction as far back as 1916. The passenger line southward from Bishop Auckland branches away due south from the trunk mineral line at Simpasture Junction and runs roughly parallel to the East Coast main line, but about a mile away, over the remaining 6 miles into Darlington North Road station.

The Shildon and Newport line extends for about 16 miles from Simpasture Junction. The first 6¼ miles form a purely freight line on gradients descending, eastwards, at 1 in 188 to 1 in 460; but after joining the passenger line from Ferryhill at Stillington Junction the descent becomes more pronounced, and there is a stretch, among others, of nearly 2 miles at 1 in 103 from Carlton South Junction. This route provides a long trying pull for trains of coal empties, and was an excellent ground for electric traction to justify itself. But the gradients south and east of Bishop Auckland are a mere nothing compared with those of the most northerly extension of the Stockton & Darlington Railway, where the line ascends to the high mining districts of Tow Law. From Beechburn, indeed, the gradient is between 1 in 43 and 1 in 52 for 6 miles continuously save for a short easier pitch at 1 in 70. There is also a passenger service between Darlington and Tow Law.

The Great Climbs to Consett.

The Consett ironworks, perched some 900 ft. above sea level, provide some extremely stiff haulage tasks for North Eastern freight locomotives. From Ouston Junction, on the Team Valley line, the ascent to the plateau is made in just 8 miles, and most of the sustained climbing is upon grades of 1 in 50. There is a good deal of curvature, too, which can provide a terrible "grind" when working the heavy ore trains from Tyne Dock. The original Pontop & South Shields Railway went straight up the hillside from Pelton to Stanley on gradients varying between 1 in 22 and 1 in 27;

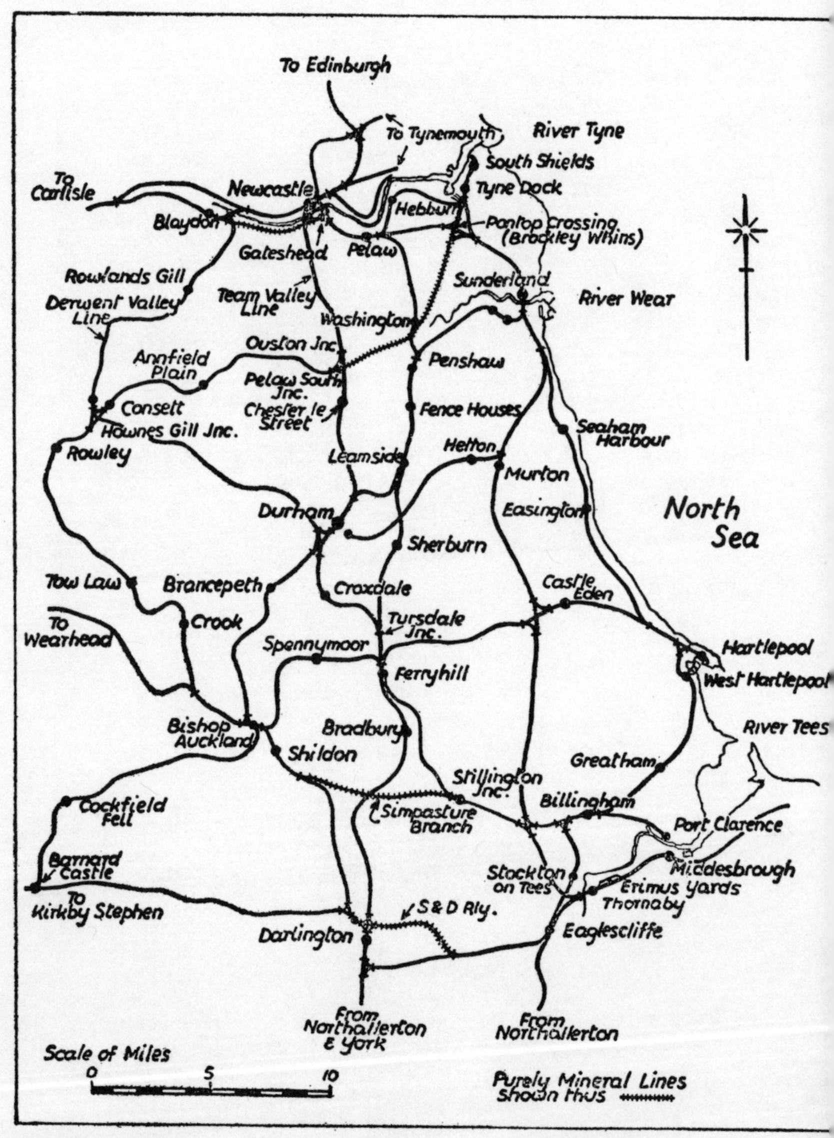

NORTH EASTERN LINES IN COUNTY DURHAM

but connection is made at Stella Gill, between Pelton and Ouston Junction, with the passenger line to Consett, and the ascending loaded ore trains from Tyne Dock transfer to the steam-worked incline at this point. The summit level is reached at Consett station, where the rails are 880 ft. above ordnance datum, after which the line dips down at 1 in 55 to its junction with the line from Blaydon a mile short of Blackhill. The latter railway is the hotly-contested Derwent Valley line, by which the London & North Western Railway hoped to gain access to Newcastle, as related in Chapter One. It diverges to the south from the Newcastle & Carlisle Railway immediately to the west of Scotswood Viaduct. Thereafter it follows the windings of the Derwent, though climbing high on to the east side of the valley. Apart from a level mile at Rowlands Gill, and very brief easings to 1 in 220 through Lintz Green, Ebchester and Shotley Bridge stations, the gradient is 1 in 66 throughout for an overall distance of 9 miles. This again is a very trying incline, and it includes a great deal of fairly severe curvature.

Main Lines from Leeds.

The old Leeds Northern is a heavy road until north of Ripon. The gradients are bad enough in themselves, but owing to the awkward locations of some junctions and curves no correspondingly high speed can be run, and the overall averages made between Leeds and Harrogate are always slow. From leaving the Midland line at Holbeck there is a heavy grind up to the south portal of Bramhope Tunnel, mostly at 1 in 100. The descent through the tunnel itself on 1 in 94 must be restrained in view of the heavy slack over the triangular junction at Arthington. Then turning across the valley of the Wharfe and climbing again at 1 in 195 the magnificent profile of Crimple Viaduct is seen ahead spanning a wide vee in the hills, and at Pannal Junction through expresses, such as the present-day "Queen of Scots" Pullman, turn rightwards from the Leeds Northern main line, which goes straight on to Starbeck, and climbing the sharply-curved connecting spur to the line from Wetherby and Church Fenton they pass slowly over Crimple Junction, and so on to the viaduct. It is a dramatically beautiful piece of railway, with the train swinging round a full right-angle in less than half-a-mile and finally pounding up the 1 in 91 gradient to the outskirts of Harrogate. On restarting, however, one can make some fine speed; the gradients are favourable to Ripon and little harder than level right on to Northallerton. Here non-stopping trains on the Leeds Northern line take the burrowing junction under the East Coast main line, but there is a severe speed restriction at Northallerton Low Junction. After that, following the gentle rise to Welbury some fast running can be made down to the Tees at Eaglescliffe, before which there is a well-aligned 3 miles downhill at 1 in 170. The coast route from Stockton, through West

Hartlepool, Seaham and Sunderland, includes no stretches of particular difficulty, excepting perhaps the northbound start from West Hartlepool up 5 miles of grades varying between 1 in 100 and 1 in 250.

The lines from Leeds to Scarborough, to Bridlington and to Hull have all been the scene of much really fast running, and in view of the performances of the older Worsdell engines to be described later in this book they are worthy of detailed attention here. All three routes have exactly the same grading characteristics at the start, for although the line to York diverges at Micklefield the descent to the dead level of the Plain of York remains at the same inclination as that of the line to Selby. Prior to this there has been a stiff climb out of Leeds; the gradient is between 1 in 280 and 1 in 230 for the first 2 miles, steepening to 1 in 160 for just over 3 miles. A level stretch is attained after Cross Gates, after which there is a racing descent of some 6 miles at 1 in 135 to 1 in 150. With York trains it is customary to ease through Micklefield, and again slightly at Church Fenton, where the main line of the York & North Midland is joined; after this the line is little removed from dead level right on through York and over the Scarborough line until the sea is neared. Scarborough station is situated high above the town, on the line of hills lying back from the shore, and in the last four miles the line ascends on gradients of 1 in 255 and 1 in 220. This uphill approach makes a grand start for westbound trains, though it is usual to ease somewhat through Seamer Junction, 3 miles out.

From the foot of the Micklefield bank, 14½ miles out of Leeds, the line onwards to Hull is virtually dead level. The severe speed restriction through Selby, prolonged by the need for caution over the swing bridge north of the station, constitutes a handicap to the running of non-stopping trains, though not so serious a one as that through York for the non-stop Scarborough expresses. The present direct line from Selby to Bridlington was not opened until a comparative late period in North Eastern development, namely 1890. Until then one travelled via Hull, Beverley and Driffield, and that roundabout route was practically level throughout. Already a branch line running virtually straight and east-north-east from Selby intersected the York to Hull branch at Market Weighton, and the new line of only 14 miles in length was constructed over the Yorkshire Wolds and heading direct for Driffield. Unlike the Scarborough main line, which has no greater inconvenience than that of severe curvature in passing through the Wolds, where it follows the deep valley of the Derwent at Castle Howard, the Bridlington line has some stiff grading between Market Weighton and Driffield. Following a severe service slack through the former station there are 3½ miles continuously at 1 in 95-100 up to Enthorpe summit, and a rather longer stretch on more broken gradients descending to the level again at Driffield. After that the line is level onwards to Bridlington.

THE TWO EAST-TO-WEST LINKS.

The Newcastle & Carlisle Railway—the first line across Britain—and the South Durham & Lancashire Union Railway had little in common save that they provided cross-country links between the East Coast and West Coast main lines, and that both originated from a need to provide better means for the conveyance of minerals. But whereas the Newcastle & Carlisle follows the valley of the South Tyne, on easily rising gradients for the first 40 miles from Newcastle, and reaches a summit level of no more than 494 ft. above ordnance datum on a plateau of dead level track 6 miles long at the crossing of the Roman Wall near Gilsland, the South Durham & Lancashire line, after moderate ascending gradients in the first 9 miles, to Gainford, climbs into some of the highest ranges of the Pennines and reaches a summit level of 1,369 ft., at Stainmore, at a distance of 30¼ miles from Darlington. Much of the ascent is on gradients of 1 in 67, 1 in 68 and so on, but this bank is a moderate one compared with the 9 miles from Stainmore down to Kirkby Stephen, mostly at 1 in 60, and over an exposed moorland at the mercy of the north and north-easterly gales in winter. From Kirkby Stephen the main route for mineral traffic climbs again to reach an altitude of 889 ft. near Ravenstonedale; but in these 5 adverse miles the worst grading is 1 in 77 and it is mostly easier than that. The last 7 miles downhill to join the West Coast route at Tebay are generally easier than 1 in 100. Here the height above ordnance datum is down to 583 ft. The continuation of the mineral train route over L. & N.W.R. metals is included in the official North Eastern Railway gradient profile sheets; but as it appears on the same drawing as the Bishop Auckland-Blackhill line, including the terrific 1 in 52 ascent from Crook to Tow Law, the Grayrigg bank looks a very modest incline by comparison.

Quite apart from the direct route up from Darlington, there is some very heavy pulling on the connecting line from Bishop Auckland to Barnard Castle, which might, with less resolute action on the part of the North Eastern, have formed part of a North Western-controlled route to Newcastle. From Bishop Auckland, after a level 2 miles, the line ascends 420 ft. near Cockfield Fell, before descending on broken grading into the Tees valley to join the main route. On the eastern side there is a climb of 4¾ miles continuously at 1 in 69-70. The connection northward from Kirkby Stephen to Penrith includes one or two stretches of 1 in 100, or so; but the traffic is relatively light and such gradients are not a handicap. As in descending westwards from Stainmore, so the western end of the Newcastle & Carlisle line includes the most trying gradients on the route, and the change in altitude from 67 ft. in Carlisle Citadel station to 494 ft. at Naworth takes place in no more than 12 miles. The most trying pitch is the 4 miles continuously at 1 in 107 which follows immediately after crossing the river Eden on Wetherall Viaduct. This incline, apart from the sharp curve at Wetherall station, includes much gradual reverse curvature, and speeds are rarely allowed to exceed 60 m.p.h. on the descent.

MAIN LINE: NEWCASTLE TO EDINBURGH.

Although the North Eastern Railway proper extended no further north than Berwick, for most of the period covered by this book all the East Coast expresses were worked through to Edinburgh by North Eastern locomotives, and it was only after grouping, in 1923, that any reciprocal arrangement came into force, whereby certain expresses were worked down to Newcastle by North British engines and men. This stretch of 124½ miles has been the scene of some of the finest speed achievements of the North Eastern; but recalling in particular the great record of 22nd August, 1895, when the average speed from Newcastle to Edinburgh was 66 m.p.h. start to stop, it must be emphasised that while much of the line is open and suitable for really fast running the curves at Morpeth, Alnmouth, Tweedmouth, Berwick and Dunbar all require some moderation of speed, and the approach to Edinburgh is relatively slow over the last 4 miles. On the racing runs of 1895 it is true that scant regard was paid to most of these curves; but that was a contest which, fortunately perhaps, has never occurred in such open and direct form since.

As to the gradients, the rising start out to Forest Hall mostly on 1 in 200, makes for a gentle beginning; but then the moderate rise and fall of the line right on to Alnmouth offers no particular hindrance. Brunel, had he been the engineer, would probably have contrived a dead level route at the expense of heavy earthworks, and avoided the sharp curve at Morpeth into the bargain; but on many a run I have timed with ex-N.E.R. engines we have bowled along between Morpeth and Alnmouth with no greater variation in speed than between 60 and 68 m.p.h. The Longhoughton bank is the first real obstacle—4 miles at 1 in 170 following the moderate slack to 60 m.p.h. or so through Alnmouth Junction; but then follows the glorious racing stretch down to the seashore at Beal, nearly 20 miles of either level or favourable road where the speeds of the faster trains lay in the "seventies" for many miles on end, and occasionally topped 80. Although it is passing well beyond North Eastern history it seems that there is no knowing what one may record on this stretch with modern Pacific engines, and I have seen at least one fully authenticated record of 100 m.p.h. here. The last miles of the North Eastern, and the most northerly of English metals, lead up at 1 in 190 to the bleak sea cliffs of Scremerston and the crossing of the magnificent Royal Border Bridge into Berwick. Then the 1 in 190 ascent is continued for 5 miles over the Border, higher and higher above the sheer black cliffs of the North Sea to Burnmouth, after which there is a respite of about 4 miles before coming to the final 6 miles or so, at 1 in 200, up to Grantshouse. This length of 23 miles, from the level dunes of Goswick up to the summit level just before Penmanshiel Tunnel, can be a most trying one, whether on a non-stop train from Newcastle to Edinburgh, or on one of those wild inclement days when a sea mist is driving in, and the rails on the 1 in 190 ascent from Berwick are slippery and even a modern Pacific cannot be kept from violent slipping.

On the southbound climb to Grantshouse the heavy going is confined to a length of 6 miles. From Innerwick, by the southern shores of the Firth of Forth, the gradient is 1 in 210 for the first 1¾ miles; but then it changes to 1 in 96, and this continues up the glen of the Pease Burn and through the short Penmanshiel Tunnel for 4¼ miles. Today, as in the days of the North Eastern Atlantics, it is rare to see an engine really pounded up this incline; drivers usually contrive to attack it at fully 60 m.p.h., and the speed at the summit was more often than not under 30 m.p.h. It is another matter with the fast, limited-load trains of the present time; but these are light in relation to engine power, compared with the East Coast expresses of the Worsdell and Raven eras. From Innerwick onwards to the outskirts of Edinburgh the line is undulating, without any long or pronounced gradients, favourable or adverse. But the final approach to Edinburgh is steeply inclined, with 1¼ miles up at 1 in 78 from Piershill Junction, past St. Margaret's engine sheds to the east end of the Calton Tunnel. With the pronounced curve at Portobello requiring some reduction of speed this last climb can, in certain conditions, be trying. In earlier days, however, and particularly in the races of 1888 and 1895 the Portobello slack was largely ignored, to the discomfiture of passengers, and the final 1 in 78 was literally charged. Even in "grouping" days there were some North Eastern drivers in whom there evidently lingered something of the racing spirit, and I remember vividly watching an "R" class 4-4-0 come tearing out of Calton Tunnel and swinging over the points into the suburban side of Waverley at what can only be called an "injudicious" speed!

Chapter Three

THE YEARS OF CONSOLIDATION 1854-1870

FOLLOWING the amalgamation of 1854 no immediate move was made to co-ordinate, still less to standardise locomotive practice on the newly formed North Eastern Railway. Each of the three constituents had its own shops: the Leeds Northern at Leeds; the York & North Midland at York; and the York, Newcastle & Berwick at Gateshead. To these was added, in 1863, the North Road works of the Stockton & Darlington Railway. From his headquarters at Gateshead Mr. Fletcher allowed each of his local superintendents almost complete freedom in the manner of dealing with the repairs and rebuilding of locomotives in their particular charge. This policy persisted for many years, even to the extent of having different colour schemes from the different works; what was obviously desirable for the Stockton & Darlington section, where the previous superintendent, William Bouch, remained in office for 12 years after the amalgamation, was permitted also at York, and for a shorter period at Leeds. Fletcher has been criticised on this account, but many years afterwards, in L.N.E.R. days, Sir Nigel Gresley did very much the same, within the more stringent conditions of the inter-war years, and many traditional Darlington characteristics from pre-grouping days were permitted on stardard locomotives such as the "D49" 4-4-0s and the "J39" goods. In Fletcher's day the North Eastern was one of the most prosperous railways in Great Britain, regularly paying a 10 per cent. dividend on ordinary shares; the local superintendents were competent, the enginemen were content, so why indulge in the upheavals of reorganisation?

With the passage of time many of the older engines, which were of private builders' design, were rebuilt in some conformity of outline with the general ideas of the shops concerned; they acquired Fletcher stove-pipe chimneys and large domes with Salter-type safety valves mounted upon them, and the local variety of the contemporary N.E.R. cab. But of *real* standardisation, of working parts and fittings, of interchangeable boilers and motion there was none. Writing of the year 1875 Ahrons comments: "The engine sheds at York, of which there were two, at the north and south ends of the station, were certainly, from a locomotive archæological point of view, the most interesting in the kingdom. I have already, in dealing with the Great Western Railway, mentioned the somewhat similar conditions at another cathedral city Chester, but, deeply interesting though the latter sheds most certainly were, they were not on the same plane at York, which was *facile princeps*. It would be absolutely impossible to give any description of all the varied locomotives stationed there such as would do justice to the subject, for at least 100 illustrations would be required". And that was in 1875, 12 years after the absorption of the Stockton & Darlington! One would find scarcely less variety at Gateshead, including many specimens quite distinct from anything to be found at York, while Leeds and Darlington would duly add their own special peculiarities.

Before referring to any of the locomotives built for the North Eastern Railway since 1854 some of the earlier engines of the constituents deserve more than a passing mention. The express engines of the York, Newcastle & Berwick were mostly of the 2-4-0 type, built variously by Stephenson's, Hawthorns or E. B. Wilson, of Leeds. There were about 60 of these, but interest seems to have centred upon the 15 or 20 single-wheelers. Among the Hawthorn types of the 2-2-2 wheel arrangement was a beautiful 7 ft. single, No. 180 *Plews,* built in 1848 and reported to have run at 70 m.p.h. on her trials; Wilson's supplied two "Jenny Lind" type singles, and a number of 2-4-0 engines with coupled wheels varying between 5 ft. 9 in. and 6 ft. 6 in.—all having that firm's classical type of boiler mountings—but by far the most intriguing of these early designs is that of the Stephenson three-cylinder 2-2-2 No. 77. This engine, as running in 1854, was a complete reconstruction of an earlier engine of the same number built by Stephenson's for the Newcastle & Darlington Junction Railway in 1847. It was originally of the long-boilered type, with the single pair of driving wheels at the rear and two separate pairs of carrying wheels—not a bogie—at the fore end. Three-cylinder propulsion was adopted in an attempt to secure steady running. As originally built the engine did some good work, including

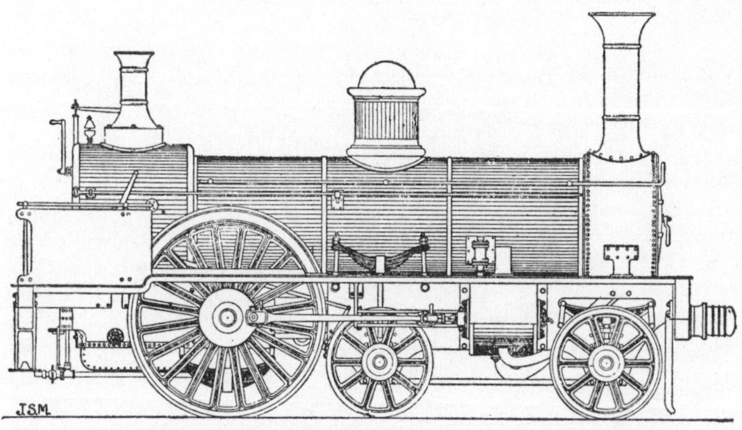

THREE-CYLINDER 2-2-2 No. 77 AS BUILT IN 1847 [*Courtesy: John S. Maclean*

THREE-CYLINDER 2-2-2 No. 77 AS RENEWED IN 1852 [*Courtesy: John S. Maclean*

the haulage of the Royal Train from Newcastle to Berwick in 1850, when Queen Victoria opened the Royal Border Bridge; but after only five years' service the engine was, to all intents and purposes, scrapped, and in 1852 a new No. 77 emerged from Stephenson's works.

This new "77" was a remarkable engine. At first glance she was like a "Jenny Lind", but with the typical Stephenson type of boiler mountings; there were outside bearings to the leading and trailing wheels, but inside bearings only to the drivers. The two outside cylinders, which were 10½ in. dia by 22 in. stroke, were very completely hidden away behind the double-framing at the fore end, while the inside cylinder was of different dimensions altogether—16 in. dia. by 18 in. stroke. Messrs. Stephenson aimed, as in the original "77", at very steady running, and in the new engine the two outside cylinders worked in unison, instead of in opposition or at right-angles. Thus any sinuous action along the track was eliminated, since there were no unbalanced lateral reciprocating forces, as between the two outside cylinders. A further point arose from this: only one set of link motion was needed to actuate the valves of the two outside cylinders, and so Stephenson's anticipated the work of Gresley, Holcroft and others, in having a three-cylinder engine with only two sets of valve gear. A traverse shaft from the valve motion transmitted the movement to the two valve rods. The inside cylinder had its crank at right-angles to the two outside ones. D. K. Clark, in his monumental work *Railway Machinery,* reports that the engine rode extremely well. From 1852 the engine was in regular service on the York, Newcastle & Berwick line, though one gains the impression that she was not so generally successful as the similar two-cylinder simple 2-2-2 No. 190, built by Stephenson's in 1849. Both engines

[Courtesy: John S. Maclean

2-2-2 No. 212, "JENNY LIND" TYPE, BUILT FOR THE YORK, NEWCASTLE & BERWICK RAILWAY

had a similar boiler, with a total heating surface of 1,046 sq. ft. and a grate area of $11\frac{3}{4}$ sq. ft. No. 190 had two cylinders 16 in. dia. by 20 in. stroke; she lasted in more or less original state until 1881, whereas No. 77 was rebuilt as a two-cylinder simple in 1860.

These two Stephenson "singles", together with the Hawthorn "seven-footer" No. 180, remained the crack locomotives of the Y.N. & B.R. almost to the time of amalgamation, but in 1853-4 three more notable 2-2-2 express engines were added to the stock. Two of these latter were actually alike, namely the "Jenny Linds" 27 and 212, from E. B. Wilson, but the third was a Hackworth engine, the *Sanspareil,* having 6 ft. 6 in. driving wheels, and cylinders 15 in. dia. by 22 in. stroke. This latter machine had some unusual features, such as wrought iron driving wheels with only ten spokes, and a dome something after the Hawthorn style placed on the forward ring of the boiler barrel and standing cheek by jowl with the chimney. She also had a special design of slide valve over which the inventor would fain have placed an armed guard. It is said that this engine was built as a direct challenge to the Stephenson No. 190. The result of the Railhill trails of 1829, in which Timothy Hackworth's original *Sanspareil* had been eclipsed by Stephenson's *Rocket,* had remained a sore point with the Shildon firm, and after delivery of the *Sanspareil* of 1854 the Hackworth's tried to persuade the N.E.R. to run a comprehensive set of comparative trials between their engine and No. 190. This, however, does not appear to have been done. But so far as the N.E.R. locomotive stock is concerned, out of six first-line express passenger 2-2-2 engines running in 1854 only two were alike; these latter, the two "Jenny's", had 16 in. by 20 in. cylinders, and 6 ft. 3 in. driving wheels. In the year of amalgamation, however, Stephenson's delivered the six 2-2-2 express engines of the "220" class—Nos. 220 to 225—bringing yet another design to the N.E.R. These were smaller engines altogether than the six "greyhounds" previously mentioned, since they had cylinders only 15 in. dia.; but in the shape of the dome, and the mounting of the Salter type safety valves on it, one saw the beginning of a prominent feature of North Eastern locomotive lineaments which was to last for the rest of Mr. Fletcher's regime. Whether it came from Stephenson's or from Fletcher himself one cannot tell.

The completion dates of the "220 class" engines throw an interesting light upon manufacturing policy of the period on the North East coast. One engine was completed in March, 1854, another in April, two in July, one in August, and one in September. Obviously they were not the only engines on the Stephenson order book at the time. They were not put through as a batch, but as individual units, since it is probable the makers were trying to satisfy several different customers at the same time. Despite their small dimensions the "220 class" appear to have done good work, and in 1872 when the Team Valley was opened, No. 224 worked the first train through—an Anglo-Scottish express. There was far more homogenity about the locomotive stock of the York & North Midland. The brunt of the passenger working on that line had, since 1848, been born by the eleven splendid little 2-2-2s of the "Jenny Lind" type. These were smaller than the two supplied to the Y.N. & B. in 1853, as they had only 800 sq. ft. of heating surface, against 1,006 sq. ft. and the driving wheels were 6 ft., except in the case of one engine, which had 5 ft. 6 in. wheels. These engines were numbered 319 to 326, and 333, 334 and 344 in the N.E.R. stock and lasted until 1878-1880. The first built of this batch, No. 88 (N.E.R. No. 319) was the *Jenny Lind* herself, and for some years carried the name on a plate mounted on the boiler barrel. No. 88 was only the second engine of the type to be constructed by Wilson's; the first of all, completed one month before No. 88, went to the Brighton Railway. Apart from one or two odd engines like the *Plews* and the *Jenny Lind* the North Eastern had no named engines until the Pacifics of 1922; on the other hand the majority of the older engines could be recognised through their successive vicissitudes of rebuilding by retaining the same numbers throughout. Furthermore the identity of those surviving was preserved during L.N.E.R. days, since the old N.E.R. kept their own numbers without any prefixes, until the entire stock was renumbered in Mr. Edward Thompson's time.

In addition to the various 2-2-2 singles, both the Y.N. & B. and the Y. & N.M. had a number of 2-4-0 express engines. I have tabulated on the opposite page a brief summary of the more important varieties.

N.E.R.: SOME EARLY 2-4-0 PASSENGER ENGINES

Original Company	Builder	Date	Coupled wheel dia.		Cylinders dia. × str.	No. built
			ft.	in.	in. in.	
Y.N. & B.	Hawthorn	1847-8	5	6	15 × 22	8
Y.N. & B.	Stephenson	1848	6	1	15½ × 22	5
Y.N. & B.	Stephenson	1853	6	2	15 × 22	3
Y.N. & B.	Wilson	1853	5	9	16 × 20	1
Y.N. & B.	Wilson	1853	6	0	15 × 22	4
Y.N. & B.	Wilson	1853	6	6	16 × 22	2 *
Y. & N.M.	Stephenson	1848	5	0	14 × 22	6
L.N.R.	Kitson	1849	6	0	16 × 22	6

*The "Big Wilsons"

The Wilson 2-4-0s of 1853 were probably the best engines on the whole line; they had the classical style of the "Jenny Linds", and for a long time after their construction they worked on the Leeds Northern Section. Like all E. B. Wilson's engines they were magnificently turned out; the boilers were lagged with strips of polished mahogany, there was a profusion of brass work, but the feature of the design that rendered them and the "Jenny Linds" so very conspicuous—the fluted dome-cover and safety valve column —was the work of a lady, Mrs. Fenton, the wife of the manager of the firm.

In the first years after the amalgamation of 1854 attention was turned mainly towards provision of a really adequate stud of main line goods engines, and in 1855 Messrs. Robert Stephenson & Co. delivered the first of a new series of 0-6-0 outside framed tender engines, having 5 ft. dia. coupled wheels and 130 lb. per sq. in. pressure. This first batch had 16 in. dia. cylinders, with 24 in. stroke, but when numerous engines of similar design were built in after years by various contractors some divergencies in dimensions were made, and later examples had enlarged cylinders 17 in. dia. The first batch by Stephenson's were known as the "390" class. They were sturdy, straightforward engines. From the outset they had Mr. Fletcher's characteristic boiler mountings except that there was not a second safety valve. They carried no more than a manhole cover on the firebox and on this cover the whistle was mounted. They had plain weather boards for cabs, with the top turned over slightly to the rearward to give a little shelter. On the buffer beams they had suspended blocks for use when running trains of chaldron wagons. Engines of this same general type were built up to a grand total of about 60 by Hawthorn's and other contractors, and about a dozen were built at various times at Gateshead. A batch was built by Messrs. Manning, Wardle & Co. in 1861; this latter firm had absorbed the business of E. B. Wilson & Co. some three years earlier, and engines Nos. 433 to 436, while generally of Fletcher's design, had Wilson chimneys and domes fluted like a "Jenny Lind" and poised on a square classical base. The manhole cover over the firebox was also square. These Manning, Wardle engines had a very scanty weather board, without any top shelter at all. The improved class which followed the "390" series was known collectively as Class "13", and although there were differences in detail between the successive batches they represented the earliest N.E.R. attempts at a standard design.

Another numerous class, of which construction was in progress in 1866-7, was an outside-framed, short-coupled 0-6-0 goods for working through mineral trains southbound from Darlington to Leeds, Doncaster and Normanton. These engines had the same basic dimensions as the "13" class, namely 5 ft. coupled wheels, 17 in. by 24 in. cylinders and 130 lb. pressure, but the rear pair of coupled wheels was set forward ahead of the firebox, as in the Stephenson "long-boilered" type. Mr. T. W. Worsdell grouped together the various engines of this general type as Class "93". This classification included some engines having coupled wheels only 4 ft. diameter, and others with 16 in. dia. cylinders. There were at least 75 engines of the group, though the various contemporary authorities, like Ahrons, who attempted to trace the complete history of the engines concerned, are by no means agreed among themselves. Morover items of "official" information gleaned from the N.E.R. by different enthusiasts conflict with each other! Here we can do little more than refer to one or two of the leading varieties. The batch numbered from 642 to 666 was very similar to the standard goods engines of the Stockton & Hartlepool Railway, and had the running plate curved

N.E.R. PASSENGER ENGINES, 1854-70

Class	Type	Cylinders dia. × str.	Driving wheel dia.	Date first one built	Remarks
		in. in.	ft. in.		
"220"	2-2-2	16×20	6 6	1854	Outside frames: coke burning.
"450"	2-2-2	16×22	6 8	1861	Outside frames.
"25"	2-4-0	16×22	6 6	1863	Double frames throughout.
Whitby bogies	4-4-0	16×22	5 0	1864	Special for Whitby line.
"544"	2-4-0	16×22	6 6	1865	Hawthorn, outside frames to leading wheels only.
"38"	2-4-0	16×22	6 0	1867	Double frames throughout.
"675"	2-4-0	15×22	5 6	1870	Inside frames throughout.
"686"	2-4-0	16×22	6 0	1870	Outside frames to leading wheels only.

Left: the *Aerolite,* as rebuilt by Fletcher in 1869.
[*Locomotive Publishing Co.*

Right: 2-4-0 No. 75 as rebuilt in 1863 from a Y.N. & B. engine of 1845: 5 ft. 6 in. coupled wheels; 15 in. by 22 in. cylinders. [*Locomotive Publishing Co.*

[*Locomotive Publishing Co.*

No. 527, built 1865 by Hawthorns, known later as Class "13": 5 ft. coupled wheels; 17 in. by 24 in. cylinders.

[*Locomotive Publishing Co.*

No. 1326, formerly Blyth and Tyne Railway, built 1865; 4 ft. 6 in. wheels; cylinders 16 in. by 24 in.

[*Locomotive Publishing Co.*

No. 1222, Stockton and Darlington Railway; built by Hawthorns 1870.

[*Locomotive Publishing Co.*

No. 326: formerly a "Jenny Lind", No. 95 of the York & North Midland Railway.

[*Locomotive Publishing Co.*

No. 451: a Fletcher engine of the "450" class, built by Hawthorns in 1861.

No. 450: as rebuilt in 1885. [*Locomotive Publishing Co.*

[*Locomotive Publishing Co.*

No. 519: built by Manning Wardle in 1864: wheels 4 ft. dia.: cylinders $16\frac{1}{2}$ in. by 24 in.

[*Locomotive Publishing Co.*

No. 1668: built by Stephensons in 1873: wheels 4 ft. dia.: cylinders $14\frac{3}{4}$ in. by 22 in.

[*Locomotive Publishing Co.*

No. 476: built at Gateshead 1875: wheels 4 ft. dia.: cylinders 18 in. by 24 in. Built for banking duties on the Redheugh incline.

slightly over the driving wheels. These engines were painted in the colours then adopted for passenger, freight and shunting engines alike —a light green—though there would be variations on this, and in the lining, according to where the engine was last sent for heavy repairs.

Between 1854 and 1870 there were built under Mr. Fletcher's superintendence no fewer than eight new types of passenger tender engines for the North Eastern Railway, quite apart from those put on the road from Darlington works, specially and exclusively for the Stockton & Darlington section. The table at the foot of page 24 sets out their salient features in the broadest outline, and the present-day reader may well wonder why so many different classes were necessary.

The varieties shown and reversions in certain cases, might well have represented the gradual evolution of design on the N.E.R., and a policy of constantly seeking improvement in design; but the building dates of these varied classes show an almost bewildering indecision—or apparent indecision—as to which classes should be built as standards for the time. But there was a tendency to build special engines for certain duties, as with the "686" class, for the Leeds Northern line, and Mr. Fletcher may have incorporated features to please the individual district superintendents concerned. The following table shows the building dates of the eight classes listed above:

Year.	"220"	"450"	"25"	"W.B."	"544"	"38"	"675"	"686"
1854	6							
1855								
1856								
1857								
1858								
1859	1							
1860								
1861		6						
1862		1						
1863	1	1	1					
1864				3				
1865			2	7	10			
1866		1	1					
1867						1		
1868			3			1		
1869			5			5		
1870						1	5	14

There are many questions one could ask about this record. Why for example, was one more "220" class "single" built at Gateshead in 1863, when the improved "450" was already at work? Why, again, were engines of the "25" and "544" classes in simultaneous production in 1865, both being 6 ft. 6 in. 2-4-0s? In 1869 engines of

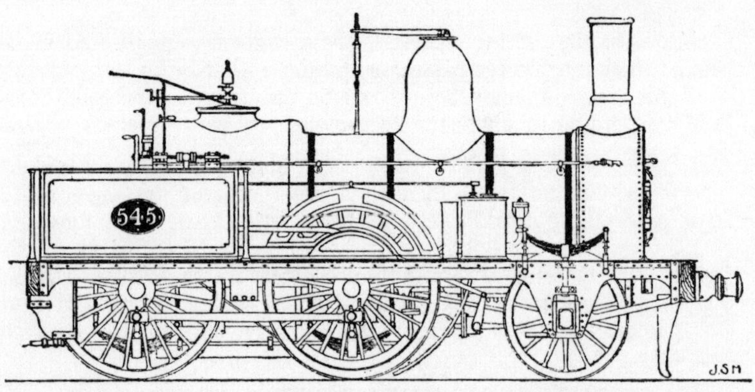

[Courtesy: *John S. Maclean*

2-4-0 EXPRESS ENGINE No. 545, BUILT BY HAWTHORN'S IN 1865. "544" CLASS

both "25" and "38" classes were built. But having once disputed the logic of the North Eastern locomotive building programme, and having looked over one's shoulder and across country to the ruthless standardisation already in full blast at Crewe, it must be admitted that to the eye of a connoisseur these North Eastern express engines were delightful to look upon, and according to contemporary reports did their work remarkably well.

The "450" class "singles" were the last 2-2-2s to be built new for the N.E.R.; three were built by Stephenson's, three by Hawthorn's, and the last three at Gateshead works. It was about this time that Mr. Fletcher took in hand the enlargement of that works in preparation for locomotive building on a bigger scale than anything hitherto undertaken by the Company. The "25" class of 6 ft. 6 in. 2-4-0 express engines were among the first fruits of this works improvement, and the thirteen engines of this class were all built at Gateshead. In 1863-66 only four were turned out, while in 1865 Hawthorn's delivered all ten locomotives of the "544" class; but in 1868-9 Gateshead completed another eight of the "25s". They were picturesque little engines, with double frames, running plate gracefully curved over the coupled-wheel axleboxes, and the Fletcher boiler mountings. These engines were later fitted with a second safety valve over the firebox, mounted on a polished brass casing almost identical in shape to that used by S. W. Johnson for so many years on the Midland Railway. At about the same time cabs were added. The accompanying line drawing, by Mr. J. S. McLean, shows the contemporary Hawthorn class, the 544-553 series. These were used turn and turn about with the "25" class on the best East Coast expresses, and did very good work. In 1869 North Eastern locomotives began working through from Newcastle to Edinburgh, and the first engine to do so was a "25", No. 468, the first of the 1868 batch. This engine was not scrapped until 1901, and indeed some of the sister engines lasted until 1905. They were all rebuilt about 1880, with new boilers and strengthened frames, and latterly, of course, they received Worsdell pattern boiler mountings. The "38" and "686" classes may be regarded as the smaller wheeled equivalents of the "25" and "544" lots, though the "686" class had some characteristics of their own and must be noticed separately.

The "Whitby Bogies" of 1864-5 were a class entirely by themselves. The line from Pickering over the Goathland moors and down into the Esk valley is heavy graded, and includes some extremely sharp curves. In the summer through carriages were run from Kings Cross to Whitby, and the Great Northern provided special four-wheeled stock as being easier than six-wheelers on the curves. These curious old 4-4-0s had the bogie set well back behind the centre line of the chimney, and with coupled wheels of no more than 5 ft. diameter they were well suited to the needs of that road. They were built by Stephenson's and had the raised firebox in which that firm then specialised, even when building to a definitely specified design. Still, Mr. Fletcher did not seem to mind, and when different batches of his locomotives were built by different contractors these firms were given considerable latitude, as we see later. The "Whitby Bogies" began life without cabs, and with a plain manhole cover over the firebox. In later years they were rebuilt with flush fireboxes, cabs, and the Johnson type of safety valve cover over the firebox. The springing of the bogie wheels was compensated, and large inverted laminated springs were fitted outside. Ten of these were built originally, Nos. 492-501; seven of them were rebuilt in 1887-9, but in their later state they lasted only a short time and the last of them were scrapped in 1893.

The "675" class, of which 34 locomotives were built at Gateshead between 1870 and 1877, were in the nature of mixed traffic units. With 5 ft. 6 in. wheels, and cylinders of only 15 in. diameter, they appear to have been destined for secondary work, including the more hilly passenger routes. But they had a relatively short existence. Much has been written elsewhere about the feebleness of the L. & N.W.R. "Samson" class 2-4-0s, as originally built; but these tiny Fletcher's, with their 15 in. by 22 in. cylinders and very small boilers, must have run them very close. Some of them worked over the Newcastle & Carlisle line, while many others operated from Hull, on slow trains to Hornsea, and through Bridlington to Scarborough. Ahrons comments: "They were quaint little machines in their original condition, and did much hard struggling with branch trains of about six or seven coaches". Struggling seems to be the word, and as those branch lines' coaches would almost certainly be four-wheelers at that time it does not need much stretch of the imagination to gauge the capacity of the engines. There were none of them left after 1890, and the latest built then had a life of no more than 13 years. On the other hand the express engines of the "25" and "544" classes had a relatively long spell of secondary work after they were displaced from the East Coast trains. They later earned a good reputation on the Leeds-Scarborough expresses.

The last "class" to be mentioned of the diverse group tabulated on page 29 was the "686" series. I have put the word "class" in quotes, because the eight engines built by R. Stephenson & Co. looked very different, externally, to those built by Beyer Peacock. They had the contemporary standard sized cylinders, 16 in. by 22 in., and 6 ft. dia. coupled wheels. The Beyer Peacock batch, Nos. 686-697, had flush top fireboxes, an additional set of safety valves between chimney and dome, a manhole cover over the firebox and a very angular and awkward looking cab. The Stephenson batch had raised fireboxes, a cab rejoicing in sweeping curves, and polished brass domes—true, they were of the Fletcher shape with Salter type safety valves on top. Further, the Beyer engines had straight running plates, and that firm's special type of builder's plate carried round the splasher, while the Stephenson's had curved running plates, and the sandboxes integral with the leading coupled-wheel splasher. But like all North Eastern locomotives of the Fletcher era they were destined to pass through several changes in external appearance. Some of them were rebuilt in McDonnell's time, and all in due course received Worsdell boiler mountings. Nine of the class were originally allocated to Leeds, and worked on the Hartlepool trains. Ahrons records that about that time Leeds had 33 passenger tender engines stationed there, made up of 13 different classes! Even with the "686" class the N.E.R. could not keep these down to one single series, for they included six of the Beyer Peacock lot and three Stephenson's. At this period there was still no sign of any settled policy towards maintenance, and if a relatively new engine went into one of the "district" works for repair it would be treated just as the local authority thought fit. Thus locomotives such as we have been discussing in these chapters would emerge with "Leeds" or "York" features, and most certainly with the local style of painting.

Green was the basic colour for all North Eastern engines, a rather light and fresh shade very similar to that of the Great Northern under Patrick Stirling, but the lining out was different at each works. The impression can best be given by tabulating the variations alongside one another.

All the North Eastern engines carried large brass number plates on the rear driving splasher, or on the lower cab panels of single-wheelers. Gateshead, Darlington and Leeds were unanimous for once in painting the backgrounds of these plates vermilion, while York

NORTH EASTERN PAINTING STYLES

Works.	*Main Colour.*	*Under frames.*	*Lining out.*
Gateshead	Light green	Red brown lined out in vermilion	Dark green and black bands, white and vermilion lines.
Darlington	Still lighter green	Dark chocolate	Ditto
York	Light green	Claret, lined with vermilion	Black bands white lines.
Leeds	Emerald green	Emerald Green	Yellow lines.

was in this respect the "odd man out", with its green background. A replica of the number plate was *painted* on the tender in all except the engines maintained at York.

And so in the later Fletcher years one could not only recognise the works affinity of a North Eastern locomotive by the style of its painting, but by its lineaments. Early 2-4-0s goods engines, "Jenny Linds" and others might be reboilered, and acquire stove pipe chimneys and Salter safety valves on their domes; but the shape of the dome, and the outline of the cab enabled one to distinguish between York and Gateshead, while the Leeds characteristics were the most distinctive of all. As for Darlington they went entirely their own way, designing new engines of their own, quite independently of Mr. Fletcher, until after 1875. The Stockton & Darlington engines deserve special mention, and are dealt with in the next chapter.

Chapter Four

STOCKTON & DARLINGTON LOCOMOTIVES

IN 1863, when the Stockton & Darlington Railway became part of the North Eastern system, that most famous of early railways owned 157 steam locomotives. The engineer was William Bouch, a brother of the Thomas Bouch who designed the first Tay Bridge, and after the amalgamation Bouch remained in charge of locomotive affairs until 1875. The line itself remained under a special committee, and Mr. Fletcher appears to have had little or no say in its affairs until after Bouch's retirement. There was much to be said for such an arrangement. The Stockton & Darlington Railway had a proud ancestry and had established an excellent tradition; the line was well managed, Bouch himself was a sound engineer, and his most celebrated design was not merely perpetuated by the North Eastern Railway, but examples survived until after the grouping in 1923. On the Stockton & Darlington the emphasis was very much on freight—more so indeed than on the North Eastern proper; and from a very early time six-coupled locomotives were practically standard for goods traffic. The works were originally at Shildon, and a number of locomotives were built there; the majority, however, came from one or other of the private builders in the district.

Of the locomotives that passed into North Eastern ownership some of the most interesting were of the old 0-6-0 mineral type, with cast iron wheels as in No. 1, *Locomotion,* and with the cylinders usually mounted high on the side of the boiler. Those wheels were of a most curious, built-up form. Presumably to avoid distortion and cracking during manufacture the wheel was cast in two pieces, a central part and an outer ring; each had half-holes cast so as to match when the two parts were put together, and oaken keys were driven in to prevent mutual rotation. A magnificent example of an old S. & D. 0-6-0 has been preserved in the *Derwent,* built by Alfred Kitching, of Darlington, in 1839, and now standing on a pedestal of honour in Bank Top station. All the old Stockton & Darlington engines, passenger and goods alike, had names, often of curious and obscure origin; these names were taken off when the locomotive stock was renumbered in the N.E.R. list about 1873. Many old veterans of the quaintest possible appearance were still running at that time, and survived to be exhibited at the Railway Jubilee celebrations at Darlington in 1875. Among these antiques were several four-wheelers. There was the *Huddersfield,* a Bury 0-4-0 of 1846, numbered 1089 by the N.E.R.; another was the *Dart,* an 0-4-0 built by Timothy Hackworth at Soho Works, New Shildon, in 1840, fitted with the old "gab" motion and having cylinders 12 in. dia. by 18 in. stroke. Theodore West, in his celebrated paper read before the Cleveland

Institution of Engineers in April, 1886, tells a good story of the Bury engines, and the recollections of an old driver. "Bury's? Oh, yes, sir", he said, "and cannie little engines they was; them little grasshoppers could switch away a tidy load behind them too; more than many folks would think, to look at 'em now." "Didn't they now and then jump off the line?" West asked the old man. "Aye, well they did now and again; you see, sir, they were so light; but bless you, if they did slip or jump off the lines they was like a nice little donkey, you could varry near get a hold of 'em by the crupper and h'ist 'em on again!" Some of the larger 0-6-0s were quite powerful engines. The "Shildon" Class of 1846 had cylinders of 15 in. by 24 in., and 4 ft. dia wheels; according to present ideas the boiler might be considered too long in relation to its diameter and to the grate area, but the six engines of this class put in over 30 years of hard mineral-train working and were all renumbered in the N.E.R. list. So far as can be traced they were the last S. & D. engines to have tender both fore and aft. The boilers were no less than 13 ft. long providing a total heating surface of 1,363 sq. ft., though the grate area was only 10 sq. ft.; the boiler pressure was 75 lb. per sq. in. and the total weight of the engine only in working order was 22¼ tons. The six engines of the class were originally named and numbered:

29 *Miner*	31 *Redcar*	33 *Shildon*
30 *Wear*	32 *Eldon*	34 *Driver*

A remarkable engine was the *Commerce,* No. 35, another 0-6-0, in which the outside cylinders were horizontal and drove on to the centre pair of coupled wheels. The connecting rod, however, was placed so close to the leading coupling rod that a large eye had to be forged integral with the connecting rod so that the latter would clear the leading crank pin. The *Commerce* also had a very long boiler, and small firebox, and together with the "Shildon" class can be regarded as something of a prototype to the famous "long-boilered goods" used on the N.E.R. for nearly 70 years. A third early variant of the "long-boiler" type was the "Priam" class of six engines built by Gilkes, Wilson & Co., of Middlesbrough, in 1848, originally for the London & Brighton Railway. Presumably the latter line could not pay for the engines, as they were never delivered, and the Stockton & Darlington purchased them in 1851. The "Priam" class were 2-4-0s with 5 ft. dia. coupled wheels, 15 in. by 22 in. cylinders and 100 lb. pressure. They were named and numbered:

65 *Stephenson*	67 *Orion*	69 *Clarendon*
66 *Priam*	68 *Brunswick*	70 *Alarm*

They all passed into North Eastern ownership, and became 1065 to 1070 inclusive.

Another class of 2-4-0 passenger engine was built specially for the S. & D. to the designs of Alfred Kitching at the Hope Town Foundry, Darlington, in 1848. Again they had the characteristic of the long boiler, but a peculiar feature was the exceptionaly close spacing of the coupled wheels; these on the majority were 5 ft. 2 in. dia., pitched at centres of only 5 ft. 4in. The cylinders were 15 in. by 20 in. stroke and a relatively high working pressure of 120 lb. per sq. in. was used. These engines, too, were long lived, and were rostered to take trains of 21 coaches without pilot assistance; as each third-class carriage included six compartments this would mean quite a heavy train, though in later years the maximum had to be reduced, since the working pressure of the boiler was reduced to 90 lb. per sq. in. They were built at intervals down to 1860; some had 5 ft. 4 in. coupled wheels, and others had 16 in. dia. cylinders. These engines were known as the "Woodlands" class, from the S. & D. name for No. 58. Their original names and numbers were:

58	*Woodlands*	100	*Stobart*	116	*Lartington*
59	*Hallgarth*	101	*Marske*	117	*Nunthorpe*
71	*Hackworth*	114	*Edward Pease*	118	*Elm Field*
98	*Piessemont*	115	*Meynell*	166	*Oswald Gilkes*
99	*Ayton*				

In 1860, as recorded in Chapter One, the South Durham & Lancashire Union Railway was opened as far as Brough, and for the passenger trains over that mountainous route Mr. Bouch put into service two 4-4-0 engines of remarkable design, the *Brougham* and the *Lowther*. Although several types of 4-4-0 tank engine had been introduced in various parts of Great Britain prior to that date these two Stockton & Darlington engines, numbered 160 and 161, were only the second design of 4-4-0 tender engine to be built for home service. The earliest were Daniel Gooch's 7 ft. 4-4-0s of the broad gauge "Lalla Rookh" class for the Great Western built in Newcastle by Robert Stephenson & Co. in 1855. The *Brougham* and the *Lowther* were true bogie engines, however, whereas the leading wheels of the Gooch machines ran in bearings carried on the main frame. The two Stockton & Darlington engines were relatively small, with cylinders 16 in. by 24 in.; 6 ft. dia. coupled wheels, and a total heating surface of 1,128 sq. ft. But the feature of these engines that immediately strikes one, after examining a photograph, is the enormous closed-in cab. Bouch no doubt had in mind the comfort of the enginemen on the exposed stretches of line over Stainmore summit, and the shelter he provided can be regarded in many respects as the prototype of the later North Eastern standard cab. But, like Patrick Stirling on the Great Nortern, Bouch was before his time; the men disliked being closed in, and on his 7 ft. 4-4-0s of 1862 he reverted to the scantiest of weatherboards.

The "Saltburn" class, as the engines of 1862 were known, created a sensation when they first appeared. Like Nos. 160 and 161 they had 16 in. by 24 in. cylinders mounted outside, but the coupled wheels were no less than 7 ft. in diameter. The boiler was very small, with 1,053 sq. ft. of heating surface and only 12¾ sq. ft of grate area. At the present time it is difficult to imagine for what purpose Bouch adopted such large wheels; it can hardly have been for high speed, as apart from the line over Stainmore the Stockton & Darlington had only the short original main line, and its eastwards extension to Saltburn. Only four of the class were built, all in the period January to March, 1862, as follows:

162 *Saltburn*	164 *Belfast*
163 *Morecambe*	165 *Keswick*

One of their most interesting constructional features was the bogie pivot; this was provided with no lateral movement, and it seems evident that little movement of the bogie was anticipated as the main frames were not cut away at all. The bogie was spherical at the top, and rested in a socket carried on the framing; the pivot was extended in the form of a screwed stem, after the style of the Gooch "bogie", and was secured by a nut below. Ahrons refers to these engines, and to Nos. 160 and 161, as "Stephenson's", rather suggesting that they were designed by the builders; whether Bouch's responsibility for them extended to much more than that of authorising their construction is a point that I can scarcely discuss here, but the plain fact remains that on a railway famed for the longevity of its locomotives, Nos. 160-165 all had very short lives. *Saltburn* was scrapped in 1879, *Morecambe,* still in its original state but without the name, ended its days as spare engine at York, being scrapped in 1888, while *Keswick* had a similar job at Scarborough.

Compared with the solid reliability of the 0-6-0 mineral engines these Stockton & Darlington excursions into the realms of spectacular passenger locomotives were peculiarly ill-starred; and when, in 1871, Bouch produced a third variety of outside cylinder 4-4-0 it seemed that he had touched rock-bottom. There are several cases in British railway history of engineers who have built simple, straightforward and wholly reliable engines, but who, towards the end of a long career, have attempted to build a "super" express engine and come an awful "cropper" in the process. Bouch's "238" Class, of which the first four came out in 1871-2, have been described as "a pot-pourri of ingenious contrivances". Unfortunately some of those contrivances were virtually untried, and gave much trouble in service. The boiler was quite orthodox, and well proportioned, and a free-running engine was envisaged by the use of coupled wheels 7 ft. 1 in. dia., and the use of piston valves instead of slide valves. The valves themselves were very large in relation to the cylinder diameter—13 in. against cylinders of 17 in.—but apparently through not appreciating the basic principles involved Bouch made the valves as solid brass discs. Furthermore the steam chests had no liners, and the result was endless trouble with valves seizing through expansion of the metal, and, when the clearances were reduced, leakage past the valves. Again something like intuition is to be seen in the use of a piston stroke of no less than 30 in. But any intentional, or unintentional steps towards the modern locomotive solution, so successively attained by Churchward more than thirty years later, in the use of cylinders long in relation to their bore, and of piston valves of large diameter, seemed to have been reached more by a process of "blind man's buff" in the Stockton & Darlington "238" Class, and their fundamental faults in other directions completely obscured any virtues they may otherwise have possessed. The boiler, though good in itself, was hopelessly small for two cylinders 17 in. dia. by 30 in. stroke. Trouble was experienced not merely with the piston valves seizing but with water becoming trapped in the valve chests; the result of this, of course, was broken pistons, and knocked-out covers.

Their famous nickname was no compliment. In the same year that they were built a Mr. Edward Jenkins, then M.P. for Dundee, had written a book on Poor Law Reform entitled "Ginx's Baby". The story, which had a strong political flavour, concerned one Ginx, who was sorely distracted at the approaching arrival of his latest offspring, so much so indeed that he told Mrs. Ginx that whether "he were twins, triplets or otherwise, he would most assuredly drown him or her or them in the water-butt and take the consequences". He did so, but the baby was rescued. As for Ginx, a herd of "Philosophers, Philanthropists, Politicians, Papists and Protestants, Poor Law Ministers and Parish Officers" descended upon him and did their best, but all to no avail. In despair he jumped over old Vauxhall Bridge into the Thames and was drowned. In the meantime, on the Stockton & Darlington line Bouch's "238" Class proved such a continuous "headache", with their piston valves, that they too were called "Ginx's Babies"; but there is no record of Mr. Bouch's having tried to jump off Deepdale or Belah Viaduct! The engine nickname has survived, and is still well known today among locomotive men, but Mr. Jenkins's book must be almost, if not completely forgotten.

So, from one cause and another, these engines needed a most inordinate amount of nursing; their troubles proved to be not merely of teething, but to be lifelong. As originally built they were designed to burn coke, and on the light passenger service of the Stockton & Darlington line they averaged about 28 lb. per mile. One of the class is reported to have run a train of 14 coaches—presumably six-wheelers—at 60 m.p.h., but any such efforts as this seems to have been mere flashes in the pan. The first engine, No. 238, was completed in December, 1871, and after certain trials three more followed from Darlington Works in August-November, 1872. These were 239-241. Mr. Bouch himself appears eventually to have been satisfied with the results, for a further six were built in 1874, Nos. 1265 to 1270; whether the faults of the earlier engines were in any way eradicated in the later ones is not known, but by that time Mr. Bouch was on the point of retirement, and within a year Mr. Fletcher had taken the "Ginx's Babies" under his own wing, at Gateshead. No. 1269 was rebuilt almost at once, as an orthodox 2-4-0. Four more were rebuilt in 1879, and before Mr. Fletcher retired in 1882 the whole class had to be so treated. From that time they became useful secondary passenger engines; they were later fitted with the Worsdell type of boiler, and in their final state lasted until 1914. But they ceased to be "Ginx's Babies" from the time of the Fletcher rebuilding.

Interesting as these curious 4-4-0 passenger engines were, freight was the life blood of the line and in coming to the later mineral engines may I quote again from Theodore West: "The Stockton & Darlington Railway, during its whole existence was one of the most prosperous and remunerative railways ever constructed. Essentially dependent upon mineral traffic, some of its branches and extensions were carried over wild moorland, secluded hills and valleys, for the valuable deposits of coal, iron ores, and limestone found in such regions. For a traffic like that power and economy in locomotive were far more the desiderata than speed or external finish. From the enormous demand for coke and ore in the prosperous times, for many years the mode of conducting the traffic with these heavy mineral trains steaming at all hours of the day and night to or from the main line, was more on the principle and motto—'Every man must look out for himself and his train'—than on the modern exactitude of published times and signals. The perpetual vigilance thus entailed worked with a remarkable freedom from serious train accidents, although, alas, hardihood and familiarity with danger led many a poor fellow among drivers and firemen to lose a limb in the usual risks of coupling and uncoupling trains".

The "1001" Class of 0-6-0 goods for the Stockton & Darlington was the final consummation of the famous Stephenson long-boilered design. Although from 1860 onwards the design was more or less standardised "Class 1001" was extended to include a number of older long-boilered 0-6-0 goods engines in much the same way as the N.E.R. Classes "13" and "93" indicated broad groupings rather than a homogeneous class of identical engines. The "1001" Class is important on account of the sterling work done by these engines and by their longevity. Some of them put in more than 50 years' service, and a fine example, engine 1275, has been preserved for posterity to admire in the Railway Museum at York. The origin of the class can be traced back to 1852 when, to the design of Mr. Bouch, the Middlesbrough firm of Gilkes, Wilson & Co. built the first two locomotives for the railway to have 17 in. diameter cylinders. These were of the long-boilered short-coupled 0-6-0 type, with 4 ft. 2½ in. dia. wheels. Eleven of this class were built in all, as follows:

Number	Name	Year built	Number	Name	Year built
56	*Towlaw*	1852	76	*Prince of Wales*	1854
57	*Shotley*	1852	77	*Alexander*	1854
72	*Peel*	1852	83	*Victoria*	1854
73	*Aberdeen*	1852	84	*Albert*	1854
74	*Emperor*	1853	85	*Hardinge*	1854
75	*Baring*	1853			

These eleven locomotives were all alike, and it is stated that the contract price for engine and tender was £2,100. Although the diameter of the cylinders was large the stroke was relatively short, only 18 in. The boilers were 13 ft. long and 4 ft. dia., and the weight of engine alone was 28 tons.

There was an apparently odd engine, No. 1141 *Excelsior* built by Gilkes, Wilson & Co. in 1859, which had an unusually large boiler; otherwise construction of the "1001" Class proper, with 17 in. by 24 in. cylinders, 5 ft. dia. wheels and 130 lb. pressure, began in 1860, the year the Lancashire & Durham Union line was opened. So far as can be traced the list of the "1001" Class engines with 5 ft. wheels was as follows:

Number	Name	Date	Builders
145	*Panther*	1860	Hawthorn's
146	*Ostrich*	1860	"
147	*Leopard*	1860	"
148	*Zebra*	1860	"
149	*Fox*	1860	"
150	*Mastiff*	1860	"
151	*Mercury*	1860	Gilkes, Wilson
152	*Venus*	1860	" "
153	*Mars*	1860	" "
154	*Jupiter*	1860	" "
155	*Saturn*	1861	" "
156	*Herschel*	1861	" "
157	*Planet*	1861	" "
158	*Lune*	1861	" "
159	*York*	1862	" "
167	*Newland*	1862	" "
168	*Clifton*	1862	" "
169	*Tufton*	1863	" "
170	*Reliance*	1864	" "
171	*Gladstone*	1863	Shildon Works
172	*Barrow*	1863	" "
173	*London*	1864	" "
174	*John Dixon*	1864	North Road Works
175	*Contractor*	1864	" " "
176	*Windsor*	1865	Stephenson's *
177	*Osborne*	1865	"
178	*Balmoral*	1865	"
179	*Edinburgh*	1865	"
180	*Dublin*	1865	"
181	*Elton*	1865	"
183	*Acklam*	1866	"
184	*Lark*	1866	"
185	*Swallow*	1866	"
186	*Union*	1865	North Road Works
187	*Iron Age*	1864	Gilkes, Wilson
188	*Lily*	1865	" "

*Built new with 17 in. by 26 in. cylinders

Number	Name	Date	Builders
189	*Spring*	1865	North Road Works
190	*Summer*	1865	" " "
191	*Autumn*	1866	" " "
192	*Winter*	1866	" " "
193	*Princess*	1866	" " "
194	*Alice*	1866	" " "
195	*Helena*	1866	" " "
200	*Eskdale*	1867	Hopkins Gilkes
201	*Carlton*	1867	" "
202	*Ireland*	1867	North Road Works
203-6	unnamed	1867-8	" " "
207-218	"	1867-8	Hawthorn *
219-220	"	1868	North Road Works

*Built new with 17 in. by 26 in. cylinders

The remainder of the class were all unnamed and were built as follows, all with 17 in. by 26 in. cylinders except as noted:

Numbers	Builders	Dates
1221-1225	Hawthorn's	1870 *
1226-1230	Hopkins, Gilkes	1870-1 †
1231-1237	North Road Works	1871-2
1242-1245	" " "	1872-3
1246-1249	Hopkins, Gilkes	1872-3
1250-1256	North Road Works	1873
1257-1264	Hopkins, Gilkes	1873-5
1271-1280	Dubs and Co.	1874
1281-1290	Avonside Engine Co.	1874-5

*17 in. × 28 in. cylinders †17 in. × 24 in. cylinders

The firm of Gilkes, Wilson & Co. must have been a versatile one, for in addition to building many of these fine mineral locomotives they built the great viaducts on the line over Stainmore, including the awe-inspiring Belah. Later, as will be seen above, the name of the firm was changed to Hopkins, Gilkes & Co.

It was on some of these engines that Bouch introduced his own form of feed water heater. The chimney was surrounded by an annular chamber, and through this space the feed pipe passed. Thus the water was warmed on its passage from the tender to the boiler. The accompanying illustration of engine No. 1222 shows one of the Hawthorn-built series of 1868 in which the feed water heating pipe was carried round the chimney at the top of the smoke box, whereas in some others, such as the Darlington-built No. 191 *Autumn,* the chimney itself was of extra girth and the pipe was apparently carried from top to bottom. As first included in the N.E.R. stock many of these engines were painted in the Gateshead style, with the number on the tender as well as on the side sheets of the cab. Some engines acquired Worsdell chimneys before general rebuilding, but the class proved so very useful, not only on the Stockton & Darlington section but in later years elsewhere, that the stud was kept in good trim for a long period, and several passed into L.N.E.R. ownership in 1923. As running after their rebuilding by Worsdell the "1001" Class had boilers 14 ft. long, with a diameter of 4 ft. 3 in.; the grate area was 13·3 sq. ft. and the working pressure 130 lb. per sq. in. The wheel base was 7 ft. 7 in. between the leading and driving wheels, and 5 ft. 3 in. from driving wheels to the trailers. The total weight of the engine in working order was 35 tons.

The provision of a very long boiler in combination with a relatively small firebox on these engines, would seem to be the very antithesis of what is now considered good practice for a locomotive designed for heavy work. But on a line like the Stockton & Darlington the occasions when a mineral train would get an uninterrupted run of any duration were rare. Long periods would be spent waiting for "line clear", and for such duty the long boiler and small firebox was ideal. The boiler itself acted as a reservoir for a large volume of steam ready for a big effort when starting a heavy train from rest. On the other hand the small grate would reduce the stand-by losses to a minimum, while a locomotive was standing, doing occasional shunting, or coasting down grade with the brakes screwed hard on. In recent years Mr. R. E. L. Maunsell exploited the same principles of boiler design very successfully on his three-cylinder Class "Z" 0-8-0 shunting tank engines for the Southern Railway.

I came across one of the old Stockton & Darlington engines in unexpected circumstances in the summer of 1922. I was on holiday with my parents at Whitby, and was enjoying the privilege of a line-side photographic permit. It would have been more enjoyable still had there been a greater variety of locomotives. It is true that 4-6-2 and 4-4-4 tanks worked over the coastal route, but on the line to Pickering there was little except the "O" Class 0-4-4 tanks. One afternoon I was prowling rather disconsolately round Whitby station yard when I was hailed by the driver of a goods engine, and was told that here, if nowhere else, was something worthy of my camera. He and his mate were a delightful pair, and though I took with a certain amount of reserve their assertion that the engine was built by George Stephenson I duly took the picture, and sent copies to them after I had returned home. Like most young enthusiasts my interests were centred upon much larger engines, and it was not until many years later than I began to appreciate and treasure the photograph I had taken that day. The engine was a "1001", one of the Dübs batch of 1874, and was, by a coincidence, the very engine chosen to be restored to her original condition for the Railway Centenary pageant of 1925. In 1922 when I saw her at Whitby she was painted plain black, beautifully clean with the Worsdell safety valve casing polished and the number, 1275, in large figures on the tender. As now preserved at York she is painted in the Gateshead passenger style of 1875, but with the number on each side of the dome in addition to appearing on the tender and on the cab sides.

After the retirement of Mr. Bouch in 1875, whereupon Mr. J. Kitching became the divisional locomotive superintendent, the few remaining passenger engines built specially for the Stockton & Darlington section partook much more of the characteristic Fletcher lines. Although no more than fourteen new passenger locomotives were constructed between 1875 and 1882, all of the 2-4-0 type, these were of three different classses as follows:

Class	Engine Nos.	Coupled wheel dia.	Cylinders dia. × stroke	Date
		ft. in.	in. in.	
"1068"	1068, 1050, 1035, 1066, 1062, 1098	6 0	17×26	1875-6
"11"	1166, 11, 1100, 1114	6 6	17×24	1877
"40"	40, 58, 1099, 1101	6 6	17×24	1882

All were built at Darlington works. The principal external difference between the "11" and "40" Classes was that the "40s" had outside bearings for the leading wheels. The "1068" and "11" Classes were rather similar in external appearance to the rebuilt "Ginx's Babies", though all of them were later fitted with Worsdell boilers similar to those put on to the Fletcher "901" Class after rebuilding. In their final state they looked rather like the "Tennant" engines, at a first glance; they all lasted well into the present century, and the last to be scrapped were the following six, all in 1912:—1166, 11, 1100, 58, 1099 and 1101. In their original condition the "1068" Class with their small wheels and large cylinder volume did well on the heavy grades over Stainmore summit, and were nicknamed by the men the "Gamecocks".

The "40" Class were the last engines to be built specially for the Stockton & Darlington, and after Mr. Fletcher's retirement at the end of 1882 the locomotive individuality of the line ended, to the great regret of most of the old employees. Not many years were to pass before the Darlington works was to be called upon to build express passenger engines for the East Coast main line, and eventually the wheel came full circle and North Road, greatly extended, came to supplant the historic birthright of Gateshead. The Stockton & Darlington contribution to the greater North Eastern Railway was massive, if for no other reason than the longevity of the "1001" Class mineral engines and the excellence of their performance.

Chapter Five

FLETCHER, THE LAST PHASE

BY the year 1870 the North Eastern was the most prosperous of all the home railways. The dividend paid on ordinary shares was no less than 10 per cent. and the trade boom which created an ever-increasing demand for Durham and Northumberland coal was intensified during the winter of 1870-1, due to the Franco-Prussian war. The fact that the North Eastern Railway had an almost complete monopoly in its own district provided an argument for those who, even in those early days, were pressing for further large scale railway amalgamations, and a Parliamentary Committee on the subject reported: "The balance of advantage to the public as well as to the shareholders may even well be thought to be on the side of amalgamation; the case of the North Eastern is a striking illustration. That railway, or system of railways, is composed of 37 lines, several of which formerly competed with one another, and before their amalgamation they had, generally speaking, high rates and fares and low dividends. The system is now the most complete monopoly in the United Kingdom; from the Tyne to the Humber, with one local exception, it has the country to itself and it has the lowest fares and the highest dividends of any large English railway company; it has little or no litigation with other companies. Whilst complaints have been heard from Lancashire and Yorkshire, where there are so-called competing companies, no witness has yet appeared to complain of the North Eastern, and the general feeling in the district it serves appears favourable to its management".

To deal with the increased freight traffic and particularly on the longer through hauls, from Newcastle and Darlington to York, and to Leeds Mr. Fletcher put on the road in 1870 a new class of main line goods engine. This Class was remarkable in that it was the first to be built in really large numbers for the North Eastern Railway, and still more so in that Robert Stephenson & Co. turned out the first 50 engines of the class within two years. The remaining 20 were built by Hawthorn's in 1872-3. Their numbers ran from 706 to 775, but for some reason they are often referred to as the "708" Class. They were sturdy excellent machines, thoroughly suited to heavy work, with 17 in. by 24 in. cylinders, coupled wheels 5 ft. diameter, and a total heating surface of 1,138 sq. ft. The boiler pressure was 140 lb. per sq. in. They had outside frames of the "sandwich" type, built up of a plank of wood sandwiched between wrought iron plates. Such frames were much favoured in early days as they imparted a certain degree of structural flexibility, without any loss of strength, at a time when permanent way was not so solid as we know it now. Mr. Fletcher retained sandwich frames in

[*Locomotive Publishing Co.*

One of the class "25" engines, used on the Newcastle-Edinburgh section.

A "Whitby Bogie", originally No. 496, after alteration in 1889. [*Locomotive Publishing Co.*

A Beyer-Peacock engine of the "901" class, No. 847. [*Locomotive Publishing Co*

No. 160 *Brougham*, with original large cab as built in 1860. [Locomotive Publishing Co.

No. 165 *Keswick*, with 7 ft. coupled wheels. [Locomotive Publishing Co.

[*Locomotive Publishing Co.*

No. 1269: one of the later "Ginx's Babies", built November, 1874.

[*Locomotive Publishing Co.*

No. 1268: a "Ginx's Baby" as rebuilt at Gateshead and decorated for the Stephenson Centenary in 1881.

No. 1050: one of the "Gamecocks", built at Darlington in 1875. [*British Railways*

No. 529: a Hawthorn engine of 1865, as rebuilt (Class "13"). [*Locomotive Publishing Co.*

No. 717: a "standard" goods of the "708" class. [*Locomotive Publishing Co.*

[*Locomotive Publishing Co.*

No. 644: a Stephenson engine of 1866, as rebuilt. Later designated "93" class.

his standard tenders, though the "708" Class were the last main line engines to be so equipped. Through their simplicity, their robust construction and solid worth, the "708" Class were great favourites with the men.

Such was the demand for freight engines in 1872 and afterwards, however, that before the later examples of the "708" Class were on the road Mr. Fletcher was building an inside-framed version of the same general design. The first of these, engine No. 398, was built at Gateshead in 1872, and no fewer than 160 were built by different contractors between 1872 and 1876. Construction was continued at intervals by the North Eastern Railway at Gateshead until a grand total of 324 engines were running; the last five were completed after Mr. Fletcher had retired, and had round-topped domes and Ramsbottom valves when new. Like the double-framed variant of the design they were excellent engines, and handled the main line goods traffic turn and turn about with the later 0-6-0s of McDonnell and Worsdell design for many years. The boiler is of particular interest, as it was used without major alteration for the well-known "Tennant" express engines of 1885. The barrel was 4 ft. 3 in. dia. and 10 ft. 7 in. long; there were 206 tubes, of 1¾ in. outside dia. providing a heating surface of 1,028 sq. ft. The firebox had a grate area of 17 sq. ft. and a heating surface of 110 sq. ft. The "398" Class goods engines had a total weight in working order, without tenders, of 37¼ tons, and 66¼ tons with their tenders. As originally built they had the elaborate colour scheme of Fletcher days, identical to that of the passenger engines, though the number was not generally carried on the tenders. In later days they received Worsdell-type boiler mountings, but could always be recognised by the characteristic Fletcher shape of their cabs. With this class a measure of standardisation had come to the North Eastern, though the usual latitude was permitted to the private builders who supplied many of these engines. Nearly one hundred of these engines were still running at the close of the year 1922, and so passed into L.N.E.R. ownership.

Stepping for a while out of strict chronological order we come next to the celebrated 0-4-4 "Bogie Tank Passenger" engines, or "BTP" Class, built with all the customary variations in detail that one expects to find in studying Edward Fletcher's locomotives. The first batch, engines 947 to 958, was built by Neilson's in 1874. Their leading dimensions were: cylinders 16 in. by 22 in.; coupled wheels 5 ft. dia., and total heating surface 1,075 sq. ft. They were finished in the ornate style of the North Eastern at that time, and had the initials N.E.R. on the running plate valence. These were followed in 1875 by another twenty, this time from Hawthorn's, numbered 1340 to 1349 and 1430 to 1439, to the same general dimensions. From this beginning the railway shops began adding to the class, and then the variations came, of the rival brands from Darlington and Gateshead. Construction continued until the year 1883, by which time there were 130 engines of the class at work. Some were built with 5 ft. 3 in. coupled wheels, others with 5 ft. 6 in. and on some the cylinders were increased to 17 in. diameter. Then there were innumerable variations in detail: in the shape of the splashers, in the design of the footstep beneath the cab, in the position of the number plate, the size of the dome, and many other items that would have driven the pundits of standardisation plumb crazy! But above all they were splendid little engines on the road, and between 40 and 50 of them passed into L.N.E.R. ownership at the end of 1922. This does not include those that were converted into 0-6-0 shunting tank engines and became the "290" Class.

One of the most interesting conversions was that of engine No. 957, one of the original Neilson batch of 1874. In 1891 this engine was chosen to haul one of the official saloons. One would have thought that a Worsdell boiler and general modernisation of appearance would have sufficed. Not a bit of it! The engine was extensively rebuilt as a single-wheeler of the 2-2-4 wheel arrangement with 6 ft. driving wheels and 17 in. by 22 in. cylinders, and became one of the most handsome tank locomotives running in the country. In due course she became L.N.E.R. Class "X2", and survived at Hull till 1937. She was really a more handsome engine than the other 2-2-4 tank, the famous *Aerolite,* on which the bunker and side tanks are, æsthetically, much too large for the diminutive boiler. The history of the latter engine extends over the entire century of this book, beginning with the tiny 2-2-2 of the Leeds Northern, built by Messrs. Kitson, Thompson & Hewitson in 1851, to the museum piece at York today. From this little mite there have been four distinct stages to the present engine, and each virtually a new machine. Fletcher's replacement, of 1869, is illustrated on page 25, but it is remarkable that the present No. 66—the sole surviving English example of the Worsdell von Borries compound system—should have been built by *Wilson* Worsdell in 1892, and not by his elder brother. The full history of this engine, or engines, is told in a beautifully illustrated article by Mr. J. M. Fleming in the *Journal of the Stephenson Locomotive Society* for September, 1951. I need only add here that the present state of the engine dates from 1902, when it was changed from the 4-2-2 to the 2-2-4 type. The nameplates were added in 1907. *Aerolite* thenceforward was used exclusively by the Locomotive Department, until 1926, when strange to say, she was transferred to the Running Department, no doubt with the idea of working out her mileage prior to scrapping. Before that evil day, however, the Railway Museum at York had been established, and after withdrawal from service in 1933, *Aerolite* went to the Museum in June of the following year.

In 1872 there was completed at Gateshead works the first of the locomotives by which Mr. Fletcher is best remembered, by the outside world at any event; this was the big 2-4-0 express engine No. 901. This engine, which was turned out in October of that year, and No. 902, which followed in December, were evidently in the nature of prototypes for trial; for the next order, for 10 locomotives of this class, was given to Beyer, Peacock & Co. and was followed by one for another ten to Neilson's. The former batch was delivered in May to July of 1873 and the Neilson lot, Nos. 924-933, arrived in November and December of this same year. Gateshead added one more, No. 903, in November, 1873, and No. 904 followed in January, 1874. Thereafter 31 more were built at Gateshead: three in 1874, nine in 1875, three in 1876, six in 1880, six in 1881, and four in 1882. But before coming to consider these very famous engines in detail it is necessary to sketch in something of the changing railway background of the "seventies" of last century, since during that decade the North Eastern suffered a considerable change in fortune.

First of all, the boom of the Franco-Prussian war years was followed by the inevitable slump, and by 1874 a considerable depression had centred upon the iron trade of the North East coast. In the following year rates were eased, in the hopes of encouraging traffic, but the decline was scarcely halted and by the winter of 1877-8 the depression which had deepened seriously was aggravated by a bitter coal strike among the Northumberland pits. Against this sombre background, however, some interesting and important engineering developments took place. Trials were made with continuous brakes in 1874. The trials were conducted on the line between Newcastle and Berwick, in the presence of Mr. Fletcher himself, and his chief assistant J. A. Haswell. One of the most impressive stops was at Longhoughton on a descending gradient of 1 in 170, in 260 yards from a speed of 50 m.p.h. Eventually on Mr. Fletcher's recommendation, the Westinghouse automatic continuous brake was adopted as the Company's standard in 1877. Moreover, the N.E.R. went further, in equipping a considerable number of the main line goods engines with the air brake, to fit them for hauling excursion and other semi-fast passenger trains when necessary; in this Fletcher was several years ahead of Webb, on the North Western, who did not begin the conversion of the Ramsbottom "DX" 0-6-0 goods to the "special" variety, equipped with vacuum brake, until 1881. The Anglo-Scottish expresses, which were then composed mainly of Great Northern six-wheeled coaches, were, from 1877, fitted with Smith's simple vacuum brake; but this was not automatic in the event of a division of the train. Its shortcomings were dramatically displayed in the terrible accident near Armagh, on the Great Northern Railway of Ireland, in 1879, and soon afterwards it was replaced on the East Coast route.

There had been an acceleration of the "Flying Scotsman" in

1872, consequent upon the opening of the Team Valley line, to an overall time of 9½ hours from Kings Cross to Edinburgh; but this train, alone among East Coast expresses, did not carry third-class passengers, and a second train leaving London at 10.10 a.m. was put on for their benefit, though taking 10½ hours for the journey. In 1873 sleeping cars were introduced on the 8.30 p.m. down from Kings Cross and on the 10.30 p.m. up from Waverley, thus adding to the weight of the night trains; but even before this working expenses had begun to rise sharply. The boom of the war years had led to an increase of wages and in prices of materials, and in July, 1872, strong representations had been made by those concerned with railway interests for increases to be made in the charges for conveyance. Thus can be noted, in these references to conditions eighty years ago, the mounting spiral of prices, wages and transport charges with which we are so painfully familiar today. It might have had the effect of causing stagnation in the policy of the North Eastern Railway had not events further west caused them to take retaliatory action.

By the opening of the year 1876 the Settle & Carlisle line of the Midland was nearing completion, and although the East Coast partners already held a considerable advantage over the West Coast in the speed of through expresses between London and Edinburgh, the Great Northern and North Eastern viewed with some concern, and not a little suspicion, the coming association of their Scottish partner with the new competitor. The outcome was a further acceleration of the "Flying Scotsman", and of the principal night expresses. After the luncheon interval at York, the Scotsman left at 2.25 p.m. and ran non-stop to Newcastle, 80½ miles in 102 min.; the 66·9 miles on to Berwick were covered in 86 min. start-to-stop, and the concluding 57·5 miles on to Edinburgh were allowed 77 min. The North Eastern engines worked through, so that in the operating of the East Coast express passenger service the North British at that time took no hand at all. At the same period the fastest night express took 105 min. non-stop from York to Newcastle, while from York to Darlington there was one train booked to cover the 44·1 miles in 53 min. In 1876-1880 all up trains called at Darlington, and relatively poor use was made of that grand line southwards to York; the fastest run—that of the up "Flying Scotsman"—was booked in no less than 54 min.

After the opening of the Midland route to Scotland the East Coast, by their accelerations of 1876, had a handsome advantage over their rivals. The overall times of the fastest trains from London to Edinburgh were: 9 hours, East Coast; 10 hours 25 minutes, West Coast, and 10 hours 45 minutes by the Midland and North British. So far as the Great Northern and the North Eastern were concerned these times remained in force until the summer of 1888. Professor

Foxwell in his classic work *Express Trains British and Foreign,* although writing in 1889, rather judges the North Eastern by its standard of speed in the early "eighties". He writes: "The North Eastern metals traverse a district ever memorable in railway history, and its main track is comparatively level; but neither easy gradients nor proud memories can prevail against an unexcitable executive and the consciousness of a safe monopoly. The company knows that it can always rely on that willing horse, the Great Northern, to do wonders south of York, so they have for years shirked their share of speed in the Scotch traffic, and the public accordingly speak of the East Coast route as 'the Great Northern route', oblivious of the fact that the larger half of the journey is run by North Eastern engines . . . No company has more powerful engines or better drivers; all that is wanting is stimulus . . ." Actually, in the early "eighties", the Great Northern's 49·2 m.p.h. from Kings Cross to Grantham with the "Flying Scotsman" was not very different from the North Eastern's 47·1 m.p.h. from York to Newcastle; but on the Leeds and Manchester services the G.N.R. then had some considerably faster trains.

Foxwell's estimate of the speed enterprise of the North Eastern, compared with that of the Great Northern, was to be completely falsified in the ensuing 30 years; but in the last days of Fletcher's superintendency there was little call for undue haste north of York, seeing that the East Coast supremacy over both their rivals was so complete. In any case the main concern of the North Eastern continued to be with freight. If by nothing else this point is borne out by the locomotive building activities between 1872 and 1882. During that time 70 new passenger tender engines were added to the stock, compared with 394 new 0-6-0 goods engines in the same period.

So we come back, at length, to the "901" Class express engines, Fletcher's masterpiece, and the consummation of his long career. The faster the years roll on, the more fortuitous it seems that the London & North Eastern Railway decided not merely to preserve, but to restore to its original condition an example of so supremely beautiful a nineteenth century locomotive design. There in the quietude of York Railway Museum stands old 910, in a splendour of brasswork and gorgeous colouring that makes the Stirling eight-footer, *Gladstone* and *City of Truro* look plain by comparison. The adjective "colourful" is now used more often in a figurative sense than literally; but letting the imagination wander from No. 910, one can picture what a kaleidoscopic array North Eastern running sheds of the "seventies" would present, when all engines, passenger goods and shunting alike were arrayed like 910, and, to judge from contemporary photographs, kept in beautifully clean condition. No. 910, as now preserved, represents the Gateshead style of painting, and the colours, although rich and varied, are not such as to be classed as gaudy. The basic green is almost exactly the same as that of the G.N.R.—a little darker in appearance than the pea-green of later N.E.R. days. It is beautifully set off by the myrtle-green surround on the tender and cab sides, and the broad dark bands on the boiler barrel are most effective. The underframes are painted claret colour. The coupling-rods, the levers to the Salter safety valves, and the reversing rod are all painted red; the last mentioned passes through the right hand driving wheel splasher and can be seen through the slotted openings on the splasher itself.

The design of the "901" Class was very sound in all respects. The basic dimensions were: coupled wheels 7 ft. dia.; cylinders 17 in. by 24 in., though the diameter in the case of engines built in 1880-2 was increased to 17½ in.; total heating surface 1,208·5 sq. ft.; grate area 16 sq. ft.; boiler pressure 140 lb. per sq. in. The slide valve dimensions, with 1¼ in. lap and 4⅛ in. travel in full gear, gave generous port openings and rendered the engines free-running, while the use of Fletcher's exhaust cocks, whereby the driver could soften the blast by diverting part of the exhaust from the blast pipe and turning it direct to atmosphere underneath the cylinders, was generally considered to play a part in reducing coal consumption. In broad principle it is something akin to the "jumper" caps fitted to modern Great Western engines except that the latter operates automatically. On the North Eastern the exhaust cocks were a widely appreciated feature, and, as will be told later, an attempt to remove them met with solid opposition. The "901" Class was massively constructed, and a study of the drawings leaves an impression of "battleship" framings and generous bearings. The leading wheels, which were 4 ft. 6 in. dia., had journals 6 in. dia. by no less than 12 in. long, and they were given side play as well. At first wooden brake blocks were used, but a sidelight upon contemporary practice is thrown by a comment in *Engineering,* upon the fitting of brakes to all the coupled wheels; this, the journal comments, is "an arrangement which deserves to be more widely adopted as it doubles the brake power under command of the driver". On the footplate the fittings are of the simplest. The inside of the cab is lined with wood that is stained and polished, and looks most handsome. The most interesting feature is the combined lever and screw reverser; this is a development of an ingenious device brought out by Messrs. Robert Stephenson & Co. in 1867. By turning the wheel the lever can be moved slowly to any desired position of cut-off, and it is possible, by manipulating the lever direct in the usual way, to change quickly from forward to reverse, or to make any other quick change desired.

As originally constructed there were considerable differences in detail between the various batches. The first four engines built at Gateshead, Nos. 901-904, had Naylor type safety valves mounted on the first ring of the boiler, between the chimney and the dome, and this arrangement was followed in the ten engines built by Beyer, Peacock & Co. There was a plain manhole cover over the firebox, but the usual Salter type valves on the dome. In her restored condition No. 910, which was built at Gateshead in 1875, has the Naylor valves, without any casing, mounted over the firebox. The Beyer, Peacock engines, with their square-cornered cabs, had a rather severe appearance. They could be distinguished also by the sandboxes being below the running plate, and by the presence of the builders' standard curved nameplate over the splashers. The Neilson batch had 1¼ in. inside frames, as distinct from the 1 in. frames of the others. The tenders of all batches were lined out in three panels. The four original Gateshead engines and the Beyer's had the engine number painted on the centre panel of the tender, while in the later batches up to 1876 the number did not appear. In the 1880-2 batch built at Gateshead the initials N.E.R. were painted in the centre panel of the tender, and in this batch too the safety valve casing over the firebox assumed the true Johnson shape, as on the Midland, encasing direct loaded valves.

Whatever their detail variations the "901" Class did excellent work on the road. Ahrons quotes the coal consumption of two links at Gateshead shed during the years 1884-5; of these No. 1 link worked entirely between Newcastle and Edinburgh, while No. 2 link worked between Newcastle, York and Leeds.

	No. 1 Link	No. 2 Link
Number of engines	13	13
Average mileage per month	4421	4412
Average coal consumption lb. per train mile	28.4	29.5
Average load tons	160	170

There were naturally variations as between one engine and another, but the highest coal consumption of any one in No. 1 link was 31·6 lb. per mile, and two engines were as low as 24·9 lb. These latter both showed mileages considerably *above* the average while their loads were above the average too. In No. 2 link individual coal consumption varied between 26·7 and 33·9 lb. These are, of course, overall consumptions covering a full month's working, and not the amount fired from start to stop on any one particular run. For comparison I may mention that present-day figures for well-designed express engines engaged in heavy work are about 45 to 50 lb. overall, thus reflecting the heavier trains of today.

The "901" Class did not remain long in their original condition. Mr. McDonnell altered No. 362 to have his particular type of chimney, round topped dome and Ramsbottom safety valves; but the form in which they became most familiar was due to Mr. T. W. Worsdell, who rebuilt them between 1885 and 1890 with new boilers, smokeboxes and plain splashers. As such they continued to do good work as secondary locomotives all over the system, and even in the twentieth century they were sometimes called upon for first-class main line work. Some of them were stationed at Darlington and of this little stud two would always be on duty as East Coast standing pilots, just as the "V" Class Atlantics did in later years, right down to the outbreak of war in 1939. No. 844, always an excellent engine, was up pilot one day in 1907 when the engine of the 1.9 p.m. "flyer" to York had to be detached, due to a hot box. No. 844 was substituted, and ran a 200-ton load to York in 47½ min. start to stop. This average of 55·7 m.p.h. with a load considerably greater than those of 1872-80 when the engines were first built was vastly better than the crack time of 1876—54 min. start to stop.

Withdrawal of these engines began in 1913, 40 years after their introduction; ten of them were scrapped in that year and 14 more in 1914. But for the onset of war the whole stud would probably have been cut up very soon afterwards, but with a serious shortage of engines developing, due to the curtailment of replacement programmes, only three more had gone by the end of 1918, leaving 28 of them still in service. Some were to be found on the East Coast lines, working into Bridlington and Scarborough, but the majority were engaged on the passenger service over Stainmore between Darlington and Penrith, and on the branch line between Kirkby Stephen to Tebay. With three-coach trains they made light of the long 1 in 60 ascents, despite their 7 ft. wheels, and with their spotless turnout and glittering safety valve casings they were an ornament to those wide landscapes over the Pennines. It was up there that I had my last sight of one of them, in unexpected circumstances. One autumn day in 1923 I had spent many hours by the West Coast main line, tramping from Tebay right down to Low Gill, back again, and then some way up Shap before the light began to fail. I came back into Tebay with one exposure left in my camera, resigned to carrying it home to Barrow unused, when at the back platform I came upon a positive apparition—a "901" on the evening train to Kirkby Stephen, superbly clean, sitting there just asking for her photograph to be taken. It was No. 367, one of the Gateshead batch of 1880, and it was the last time I ever saw one in active service.

Mr. Fletcher's last locomotive design was a small wheeled version of the "901", with 6 ft. wheels instead of 7 ft.; they were known as the "1440" Class and 15 were built between 1876 and 1882. On the steeply graded sections they did well, and it may have been due to the efforts of these engines, and the earlier 6 ft. 2-4-0s of various types that Foxwell in his work of 1889 was able to write: "The most creditable North Eastern trains are those which climb up and down the various steep branches worked by the company. Relying on the Westinghouse brake they are able to drop down steep grades at a speed otherwise inadvisable, and, as for climbing, they soar up successive miles of 1 in 40 (e.g. Whitby to Scarborough) or 1 in 60 with a lightheartedness that would scandalise the decorous companies south of Thames. The ascent from Kirkby Stephen to the summit of Stainmoor, 1,369 ft. above the sea, is a good example of these brisk cross-county performances". Nine of these smart little engines survived to pass into L.N.E.R. ownership, in January, 1923.

Chapter Six

McDONNELL AND THE INTERREGNUM

EARLY in 1883 Mr. Fletcher retired, and in April of that year Alexander McDonnell, until then Locomotive Superintendent of the Great Southern & Western Railway, took over at Gateshead. The events of the next two years will be debated as long as there are students of locomotive history. The new chief came over from Ireland with a brilliant record of achievement behind him; a native of Dublin and an honours graduate of Dublin University, he was just turned 53 years of age, and apparently in the prime of life. Far from having a purely academic outlook he had acquired a most varied practical experience of railways, before he was appointed Locomotive, Carriage and Wagon Superintendent of the G.S. & W.R. He was then no more than 35, and in a relatively short time he had produced order out of something bordering upon chaos. Modelling his practice upon that of Crewe, in standardising parts as between one engine class and another, and in effecting speed and economy in workshop practice, he laid the foundation of the noted Inchicore school of locomotive engineers, which produced such distinguished men as Sir John Aspinall, H. A. Ivatt and R. E. L. Maunsell. Indeed the famous Aspinall 4-4-0s of the Lancashire & Yorkshire, which were later developed into the great Atlantics, were based largely upon McDonnell's G.S. & W. 4-4-0 of 1877.

To McDonnell's neat and orderly mind the locomotive department of the North Eastern Railway in 1883 must have presented a very much enlarged and more complicated version of the "chaos" he found at Inchicore 18 years earlier, except that the nightmare of bad permanent way, and consequent damage to locomotive springs was not present. At Inchicore he had followed a policy of letting the oldest and most decrepit engines wear themselves out, while standardising fittings on the more serviceable ones, and making such details interchangeable with those of his own new designs. But whereas he was concerned, in Ireland, with a few hundred engines, the North Eastern stud in 1883 must have numbered about 1½ thousand, and whether he had any real appreciation of the state of affairs up and down the line before he actually took over at Gateshead is open to doubt. He came as a stranger to a strange land, and looking back to those eventful years one is curious to know what steps he took to assess the situation. Mr. John Stephenson was still at York, as Divisional Superintendent, Mr. George Graham was at Darlington, and although Wilson Worsdell had but recently gone to Gateshead there would be others born and bred on the North East coast who could have advised him. Unlike the Chief Mechanical Engineers of post-grouping days—excepting the Great Western, which was scarcely affected by grouping—the Locomotive Superintendent of McDonnell days included the running in his responsibilities, and the drivers and firemen came under his supervision.

They were a tough lot, those North Eastern enginemen of the "eighties". As Ahrons has expressed it: "The Gateshead and Newcastle 'Geordies' may be described as distinctly radical as far as politics are concerned, but in many other respects such as ingrained habits and customs, there was not a more conservative body of men in the kingdom . . . " For many years the North Eastern locomotive department had been a kind of family party; Edward Fletcher was a Northumbrian himself, and understanding his men thoroughly, he was well liked, and well respected for his personality no less than his ability as an engineer. For despite the lack of standardisation Fletcher engines ran well and economically, and the régime had, by the year 1883, gone placidly on its way for just 30 years. The majority of the men had grown up, so to speak, with Fletcher engines; they knew no others, and at the points where they came in contact with the outside world, at York, at Leeds, in Edinburgh, and at Carlisle, the latest and largest of them, the "901" Class were, without any doubt, second to none and superior to most. So why change? The fact that the new chief was a complete stranger naturally caused a good deal of comment, not to say apprehension; and when the stranger began instituting certain reforms, and there came a tightening-up of discipline the tension began to rise. It rose still further when small alterations in details were made to some of the latest Fletcher engines; but seen in the light of subsequent history the North Eastern began to experience then what the L. & N.W.R. experienced after grouping, when the Midland became the dominating partner in the L.M.S. organisation, and what Great Western men have experienced since nationalisation. But in 1883, on the North Eastern, Alexander McDonnell was playing a lone hand.

It is difficult at this stage without knowing the principal actors in the ensuing drama, to judge whether McDonnell decided at once to go ahead in the Inchicore style, and charged in regardless of opposition with the ardour of the Highland clans of Culloden, or whether he took the best advice available on the N.E.R. and then, deliberately, in face of all the known difficulties, decided to institute his reforms. Taking the long term view, there is no question but that his policy was correct; it was in his tactics that he made a serious error of judgment, so serious indeed that it ended his career as a locomotive man. Discipline and reform in the various works were ill received in themselves, but McDonnell incurred the wrath of the footplate men when he began removing the exhaust cocks from the Fletcher engines. As described in the preceding chapter, these cocks were quite a feature of the "901" Class, and may quite well have contributed to their easy and economical running. Anyway the men liked them and appreciated their points, and when McDonnell began removing them their growing resentment of the new régime, and their old loyalty to Fletcher mingled to work up a positive fury of indignation. In their view, for a stranger to dare to alter a Fletcher engine was little short of iconoclasm! The whole storm centred upon the exhaust cocks, but in face of representations, indignation meetings, and goodness knows what else, McDonnell stood firm. The exhaust cocks must go. So far the new chief had certainly shown the courage of his convictions, and he might have ridden out the storm had it not been for the shortcomings of his own express engines, the first of which were put on the road in 1884.

With one batch under construction at Gateshead works most features of the design were well known before the engines were actually completed, and many of these features merely confirmed the fear and suspicions of the footplate men that the old traditions were being swept ruthlessly away. First of all they had bogies; Mr. Fletcher had never used bogies for his main line engines, and therefore in the eyes of the men they were quite unnecessary! Another point that caused some consternation was the changeover from right hand to left hand drive. One has only to read the correspondence columns of *The Locomotive Express* prior to and immediately after the introduction of the "Britannia" Class Pacifics in 1951 to realise how sensitive enginemen can be over a change of this kind; with the "Geordies" of 1884 it added a heap more fuel to the fire, especially as it was first carried out by way of a trial on some of the Fletcher "901" Class. A final point, circulating, I believe, before the engines took the road, concerned the shape of the chimneys. The Fletcher stove-pipes were a functional design, tapering outwards in some conformity with the shape of the cone of exhaust steam ejected from the blast-pipe. McDonnell's gracefully designed cast-iron chimneys tapered the other way, externally at any rate. The men took one look at those chimneys and pronounced, once and for all, that the engines would not steam. But in spite of this mounting tide of resentment and prejudice, McDonnell had not yet lost the day, irrevocably. The "Geordies" were keen and capable men, and had the new engines proved really superior to the Fletchers in heavy express work, the unrest would probably have abated, in time. But here McDonnell's engineering judgment was at fault, and his 4-4-0s proved inferior to the "901" Class. This was the last and heaviest straw. To all the resentment and prejudice was now added the sober facts of day to day performance on the road. Whether the enginemen tried their utmost in running the new locomotives is another matter. On the basic dimensions there was little to choose between them, but the McDonnells, probably due to the valve and motion design, proved neither so powerful nor so free running.

Considered by themselves, and away from the stormy atmosphere of Gateshead in the year 1884, the McDonnell 4-4-0s were very decent, well-designed and well-constructed locomotives. They were handsome to look at, and smartly finished in dark olive green picked out with red and white lines; but the abandoning of Fletcher's colour-scheme was merely another sore point with the men. The cylinders were 17 in. dia. by 24 in. stroke, as in the "901" Class, the coupled wheels were 6 ft. 8 in. dia., the grate area was 16·8 sq. ft and the boiler pressure 140 lb. per sq. in. The total weight of engine only, in working order, was 39½ tons. The bogies were of the swing-link type, the first ever to be introduced on an English railway, and followed McDonnell's use of the same general design on his small-wheeled 4-4-0s for the Killarney branch of the G.S. & W.R. Although McDonnell's N.E.R. 4-4-0s were soon taken off the East Coast expresses they proved most useful secondary engines, and their general construction was good enough for Wilson Worsdell to fit new standard boilers to them in later years, boilers, ironically enough, that were interchangeable with the replacement boilers of the "901" Class. As such they had a slightly reduced heating surface of 1,097 sq. ft. and the grate area was reduced to 15·2 sq. ft. But they lasted a long time as light passenger engines; scrapping of them did not begin until 1914, and the last four did not go until 1920. But their initial failure on the crack trains was the final determining point in the campaign against McDonnell, and in the autumn of 1884 he resigned. He left railway work altogether, and afterwards achieved some distinction as a consultant. Of his North Eastern 4-4-0s 16 were built at Gateshead works, all in 1884, while another 12 were supplied by Hawthorn, Leslie & Co.—six in 1884 and the remainder in 1885.

McDonnell designed a class of excellent 0-6-0 main line goods engines, which were duly greeted by much the same opposition as was received by the 4-4-0s. Actually these were the first McDonnell engines to be put on the road, as the first five were turned out from Darlington works in 1883. In all 44 were built of which only the last 12 were built by outside contractors—Robert Stephenson & Co. The rest were built at Darlington. They, too, had all the features that made the 4-4-0s so disliked, except of course the bogie—left hand drive, no exhaust cocks, chimney tapering the wrong way, "unsatisfactory" colour, and so on. But after McDonnell had resigned opposition melted away like a dream, and many of the main line drivers came to consider they were the best goods engines on the line. The truth is, of course, that McDonnell in his reforming zeal had queered his own pitch with the men before his engines came out, and afterwards nothing he could do was right. It is interesting to speculate as to how far the course of North Eastern locomotive history might have been changed had he stayed. Apart from the rank and file he had two strong personalities in Wilson Worsdell and Walter M.

Smith in his immediate *entourage,* and a clash of temperaments might well have come sooner or later. It may actually have occurred in 1884 and been the final cause of his unhappy departure.

May I close this note on the McDonnell episode with a personal note? In the summer of 1920 I was on holiday with my parents at Bridlington. For one who was keen on locomotives Bridlington was then a most interesting place, where many of the old Worsdell engines were always on show. Occasionally a "T2" 0-8-0 goods put in an appearance; occasionally there came an "S" 4-6-0 in black livery, but smartly lined in red, but to a youngster with thoughts running on the larger engines there was a regrettable and total absence of Atlantics. Then one day the family made a day trip to Scarborough. Our train was hauled by the usual "F" Class 4-4-0, and interest was mild until we pulled into Seamer Junction and an up train drew in alongside hauled by one of the big "R1" 4-4-0s. Once arrived in Scarborough the family made straight for the sea; the day was brilliantly fine, and while we disported ourselves on the beach I must confess my thoughts were more often than not straying towards the railway. That "R1" had certainly whetted my appetite. Late in the afternoon, I asked parental leave to catch the penultimate train to Bridlington, but to alight at Seamer and wait for them there. A good 1½ hours of photographic time remained before sunset, and there was a chance of one or two shots. So out I went, and duly "copped" a Great Central Atlantic, of all engines, on a return excursion to Sheffield. But my principal hopes centred upon the down through express from Kings Cross. When the signals were eventually pulled off the sky was clear and the mellow evening sunshine perfect for the shot. I steadied the camera on a seat, for my hands were trembling with excitement. At last the train came into sight, and I began to stare at the oncoming engine incredulously: it was not an Atlantic or an "R1"; at best it was nothing bigger than one of the familiar "F" 4-4-0s. It proved to be not even that, but something far quainter to my eyes, and I put the camera aside in boyish disgust as the four-coach corridor express swept through Seamer behind a McDonnell 4-4-0. In my disappointment I didn't take the number; but there were only four of them left at that time—664, 1318, 1331 and 1501—and by the end of the year they had all been scrapped.

The resignation of Mr. McDonnell came at an awkward time for the North Eastern. New locomotives were needed urgently, for in the summer of 1885 the night express to Aberdeen was to be run non-stop from Newcastle to Edinburgh, 124·4 miles. At the time this was the longest non-stop run in Europe. The McDonnell engines had been intended for this, and other heavy main line jobs; but they were not powerful enough, and the situation might well have become critical had not very swift measures been taken. There could be no waiting for a new locomotive superintendent to be appointed, for him to take stock of the situation and begin designing his own engines. The General Manager, Mr. Henry Tennant, summoned the divisional locomotive superintendents to a committee over which he himself presided, and that committee worked so quickly that before Hawthorn's had delivered the last of the McDonnell 4-4-0s Darlington works had the first of the Tennant engines on the road. Mr. Wilson Worsdell, who had been assistant to Mr. McDonnell, played a leading part in the design, which could be called a model of tact, sound engineering, and real æsthetic charm. No one could have been more conscious than Wilson Worsdell of the opposition to McDonnell's practice, and in the new engines every single "bone of contention" was absent: they had no bogies, the exhaust cocks reappeared, the driving position was once again on the right hand side of the cab, and the chimney tapered outwards from the base. To the neatness of a McDonnell was restored the bright and beautiful colouring of old, while above all the pioneer "Tennant" engine immediately showed enhanced power.

The leading dimensions of the Fletcher "901" Class, the McDonnell 4-4-0s, and the "Tennants" make an interesting comparison:—

	Fletcher "901"	McDonnell	Tennant
Cylinders in.	17×24	17×24	18×24
Coupled wheels ft. in.	7 0	6 8	7 1
Total heating surface sq. ft.	1208.5	1097	1212.5
Grate area sq. ft.	16.1	16.8	18.0
Total weight of engine in working order tons	39.1	39.5	42.1

The "Tennants" at first carried the same working pressure as the McDonnell's, namely 140 lb. per sq. in., but as the dimensions suggest they were altogether more robust machines. It was significant of the gradual integration of all locomotive affairs on the North Eastern that the pioneer of the new class should have been built at Darlington; and this engine, No. 1463, was tried out in service before the remaining 19 were built. After the storm over the McDonnell 4-4-0s it is rather amusing to see that No. 1463 was sent to York, and not to Gateshead, as if to introduce the new machines by degrees. But the locomotive committee responsible for the "Tennants" need have had no fears; the engines were received by the men with enthusiasm, and remained good favourites throughout their existence, wherever they went on the system, not excepting their last days on minor branch lines. Once the pioneer engine had been tried out Darlington and Gateshead set to work simultaneously on the building of the class, and both works achieved a rate of output that would have done credit to Crewe. Darlington turned out

Nos. 1464 to 1472 in three months, while Gateshead, beginning with two per month in June and July of 1885, stepped up their output to three per month to complete the class with No. 1506 in September, 1885. The numbers of the Gateshead batch were 1473 to 1479 and 1504 to 1506. In addition to No. 1463 York had at first 1465, 1466, 1467 and 1468, while the three "1500s" went to Edinburgh; all the rest went to Gateshead shed.

As originally built there were certain differences between the Darlington and the Gateshead engines; but the most noticeable divergences from the aspect they wore in later years, when they became such familiar sights all over North Eastern England, were that the Ramsbottom safety-valve columns were at first uncovered, and that the side frames were coloured instead of black. In those early days of the class one could always distinguish a Gateshead-built from a Darlington-built member of the class—quite apart from the number—by the colour of the side frames: claret from Darlington, light red from Gateshead. Despite the speed at which they were built the workmanship put into them was first class, so that the excellent initial performance of the engines was well sustained as mileage increased. As mentioned in Chapter Five the boilers were the same as those of the Fletcher "398" Class of 0-6-0 main line goods engine, and the adoption of this undoubtedly saved a great deal of time in the design stage. The "Tennants" immediately took up the heaviest and fastest East Coast duties including the Newcastle-Edinburgh run of the down night "Tourist" express. Speeds were not high in 1885, but neither were the Kings Cross-Edinburgh non-stop runs of the "Flying Scotsman" in 1928. In the making of long non-stop runs reliability must be achieved first; acceleration can, and usually does follow. In 1885 the Newcastle-Edinburgh run of 124·4 miles was made in 173 min., an average speed of 43 m.p.h. The southern division share of the working of this same express was to run from York to Newcastle, 80½ miles, in 102 min., an average speed of 47·3 m.p.h.

In later years, when they had been transferred to lighter duties, the "Tennants" gained a reputation for rather leisurely starting. This may, of course, have been a characteristic of the drivers rather than of the engines, but all observers seem in hearty agreement that once these little "beauties" *were* going they could *fly* to some purpose. In the years immediately after the first world war I used to see them on the coast trains from Leeds, and they certainly used to whip those N.E.R. non-corridor coaches along in exhilarating style. That, however, was before my stop-watch days, and it is one of my great regrets that I did not compile any logs of their running. Fortunately there are ample records available of the work done in what may be called their "second hey-day", on the branch expresses in 1905 to 1914, and this I shall be discussing in a later

No. 362 of Fletcher's "901" class: Gateshead built. [*Locomotive Publishing Co.*

A McDonnell 4-4-0 No. 112 (with Worsdell chimney). [*Locomotive Publishing Co.*

[*Locomotive Publishing Co.*

The first of the "Tennant" 2-4-0s, No. 1463, built Darlington 1885, and now preserved.

[British Railways
Edward Fletcher.

[British Railwa
Alexander McDonnell.

[British Railways
T. W. Worsdell.

[Courtesy : John S. Maclec
Walter M. Smith.

[*Locomotive Publishing Co.*

No. 1413: a Fletcher "398" class, with Worsdell boiler mountings.

[*Locomotive Publishing Co.*

No. 657: a Stephenson 1867-built engine with Worsdell boiler, "93" class.

No. 1221: Stockton & Darlington type. [*Locomotive Publishing Co*

Above: No. 340: Class "D" 2-cylinder compound built in 1880 with Smith's piston valves.

[*Locomotive Publishing Co.*

Left: No. 367: a Fletcher "901" as rebuilt, at Tebay in 1923.

[*O. S. Nock*

Below: No. 676: Class "G" one of the Waterbury's as originally built 1887.

[*Locomotive Publishing Co.*

chapter. Some of the finest work of their "top-link" days was done in the 1888 race to Edinburgh, and as they played so prominent a part in the working of the "Flying Scotsman" during that exciting August, I am taking the race somewhat before its true chronological place in this story.

The North Eastern Railway was as slow to take up the challenge of faster running as the London & North Western. At first the pace was forced upon it by the Great Northern, and that long wait at York for luncheon tended to take a good deal of the excitement out of the race; but once the North Eastern was fully roused they put up some very fine running, in which the "Tennant" engines were well to the fore. It is most unfortunate that detailed logs of the faster journeys are not available, such as that made on the last day of the 1888 race when the train was worked from York to Newcastle in 83½ min. despite 1¾ min. standing for signals at Ferryhill and another signal check at Chester-le-Street. That was on 31st August; on the 25th, on the 29th and on the 30th the times were 80, 81 and 82 min. respectively, each time with engine No. 1475 and Driver Robson of Gateshead. The load in each case was about 115 tons. On the final day, when the overall time might have been the fastest of all, but for those signal checks, Darlington (44·1 miles) was passed in 44½ min. from York; to do that entails maximum speeds approaching 70 m.p.h. on the level at Thirsk and again after Northallerton, while on the descent into the Team Valley from Chester-le-Street four consecutive miles were run at 75½ to 76½ m.p.h. On 28th August one of the Edinburgh engines, No. 1505, ran from Newcastle to Edinburgh in the brilliant time of 127 min., though on the northern section the new Worsdell compound 4-4-0s were mostly used.

Some of the most detailed information about the "Tennant" performance and also that of the rebuilt Fletcher "901" Class is contained in a paper read before the Institution of Mechanical Engineers in 1898 by Mr. W. M. Smith, then Chief Draughtsman at Gateshead. Wilson Worsdell had borrowed the Webb dynamometer car* from the L. & N.W.R., and a series of runs were made with a fairly heavy train for that period of 186 tons between Newcastle and Tweedmouth, 65½ miles, with a "special" booked to make the run in 75 min. start to stop. Unfortunately the results so far as both "Tennants" and the "901" Class are concerned, are somewhat inconclusive. On the face of it both the engines concerned did poorly by comparison with the Worsdell "bogies", even allowing for the comparative sizes and weights of the classes in competition. But closer analysis suggests that there was some factor adversely affecting the running of the "Tennant" that is not explained by any elaborate data included in Mr. Smith's paper. This was

* See *The Premier Line* (Ian Allan).

particularly the case on the up journey. The logs of the two trials were as follows:—

TEST RUNS, NEWCASTLE–TWEEDMOUTH

	Engine No. ... ... Class	902 "901"	1472 "Tennant"
Miles		Actual time * min. sec.	Actual time * min. sec.
0.0	Newcastle	0 00	0 00
16.6	Morpeth	23 28	24 05
34.8	Alnmouth	44 04	44 02
51.6	Belford	63 30	63 23
65.7	Tweedmouth	78 55	80 08‡
0.0	Tweedmouth	0 00	0 00
14.1	Belford	17 59	20 34
30.9	Alnmouth	39 20	39 55
39.1	Morpeth	59 08	61 10
65.7	Newcastle	83 15†	83 32

*Includes allowances for signal checks as per official report
†Official net time: Actual time 87 min. 15 sec.
‡Official net time: Actual time 82 min. 25 sec.

The load was the same on both days, and there was no appreciable difference in the weather conditions to account, in particular, for the very slow return journey by No. 1472. Before discussing in more detail the actual performances of the two engines I may add that one of the big "M" Class 4-4-0s, which so distingushed themselves in the 1895 Race to Aberdeen, kept exact time on the up test run, and yet the average drawbar horsepower exerted throughout was *less* than that of the "Tennant". Despite this the one engine took 83½ min. for the journey and the other only 75!

Coming now to the details of performance by the 2-4-0 engines it should be emphasised that the "901" was not an original Fletcher, but one of the Worsdell rebuilds with a smaller boiler and cylinders bored out to 18¼ in. dia. It is clear from the coal consumption figures that both engines were being worked hard, and combustion rates of over 100 lb. per sq. in. of grate area per hour are not often sustained for any length of time. In the trials of the L. & N.W.R. 4-4-0 No. 2663 *George the Fifth* in 1910, the coal rate was about 135 lb. per sq. ft. of grate area per hour from Euston to Crewe in the making of a very fast run. Nevertheless these little North Eastern 2-4-0s must have been ably handled to burn such a volume of coal effectively on their small grates. Mr. Smith's paper states that "Towneley" coal was used, from Addison Colliery, Ryton-on-Tyne; it was of the soft Northumberland kind generally favoured for express work on the North Eastern, and well suited to burning in a thick fire. Some trouble seems to have been experienced with steaming on No. 902; while no lower boiler pressure than 110 lb. per sq. in. was recorded on the down journey, on the return trip they were down to 105 lb. by Longhoughton, and after Morpeth the needle dropped back first to 85 and then to no more than 65 lb. per sq. in. and still she managed to tie with the "Tennant"!

The slow running of No. 1472 becomes even harder to explain when the indicator records are examined and her consistently good steaming is revealed. On the return trip, except for a brief drop to 150 near the finish, the pressure was held steadily between 155 and 160 lb. per sq. in. all the way. The highest indicated horsepower recorded with No. 1472 was 665, at 60 m.p.h. with 134 lb. per sq. in. steam chest pressure. Curiously enough the maximum was handsomely beaten by the "901" in making what must have been an "all-out" start southbound from Tweedmouth; then the boiler pressure was recorded as 150, and the steam chest 145 lb. per sq. in.—both above the rated maximum—and the little engine produced 788 i.h.p. at 53 m.p.h. With direct loaded valves one can get 5 or 10 lb. per sq. in. above rated pressure when blowing off furiously; but this initial effort "winded" the engine, and by the time the next set of indicator cards were taken, at Beal, the boiler pressure was down to 118 lb. per sq. in. The slow start made from Tweedmouth by the "Tennant" makes me wonder if the brakes were dragging at some point in the train, as the speed was only 47 m.p.h. on the level between Goswick and Beal. After that No. 1472 produced a very steady output of power, and the remaining eight indicator recordings gave 656, 635, 503, 624, 646, 641, 611 and 665 i.h.p.

NOS. 902 AND 1472—DIMENSIONS COMPARED

Engine	902	1472
Cylinders dia. × stroke in.	$18\frac{1}{4}\times 24$	18×24
Total heating surface sq. ft.	1103·7	1136·2
Grate Area sq. ft.	15·0	17·0
Boiler pressure lb. per sq. in.	140	160
Average drawbar pull in tons		
Down run	1·21	1·31
Up run	1·14	1·46
Average drawbar horsepower		
Down run	360	384
Up run	321	410
Average Indicated horsepower on round trip	520	570
Coal per train mile on round trip lb.	42·21	39·46
Coal per I.H.P. hour lb.	3·94	3·33
Coal per D.H.P. hour lb.	6·02	4·77
Coal per sq. ft. of grate area per hour lb.	136·4	111
Water used per lb. of coal lb.	6·55	8·0

From the examination of individual indicator diagrams taken from engine 1472 at speeds between 50 and 60 m.p.h. it is evident that considerably more work was being done at one end of the cylinder than at the other. On any reciprocating steam locomotive the valve setting is bound to be something of a compromise due to the angularity of the connecting rod, and for express engines it was the custom generally to set the valves for equal lead at each end of the cylinder; thus, when starting, or on a heavy bank, the engine is not so strong as when set for equal cut-offs. Apart from this diagrams for the "Tennants" show a very good steam distribution—far better, in fact, than those of the big Worsdell 4-4-0s engaged in the same trials. The "Tennant" showed a surprising absence of pressure-drop from wire-drawing during the admission period, which deficiency is very noticeable in diagrams taken off No. 902, and in the "Q1" 7 ft. 7 in. 4-4-0. More of the latter engine, however, in a further chapter.

Lastly, there was the interesting item of boiler efficiency. Again the "Tennant" showed up well, coming second only to the "Q1", with an overall efficiency of 64·3 per cent. At the firing rate needed on these trials this figure compares closely with that of the 5 ft. 6 in. diameter superheater boiler used on the "V" and "Z" Atlantics, which at roughly 100 lb. of coal per sq. ft. of grate area per hour yielded an efficiency of 66 per cent. The Worsdell boiler fitted to No. 902 showed an efficiency of only 52·2 per cent., though the high firing rate of 136 lb. per sq. ft. of grate area per hour probably influenced this. In any case it would seem that both engines were working practically up to their limit on the Tweedmouth trials. Taken all round the "Tennant" Class points a locomotive moral for all time. Like the Whale "Precursors" on the North Western they were designed in an emergency, and like them they were designed by thoroughly practical men who knew exactly what was wanted to handle the traffic. There was no time for trying out fancy gadgets, no time for airing new theories; something of solid reliability was needed, "a driver's engine", and the "Tennants" certainly filled the bill. We shall meet them again in this story of North Eastern locomotives, for they lasted for more than 40 years.

Chapter Seven

TWO-CYLINDER COMPOUNDS

FOLLOWING the success of the "Tennant" engines it might have been thought a logical development for Wilson Worsdell to be appointed Locomotive Superintendent; but for the second time the North Eastern board went outside the company's service and brought in Wilson's elder brother, Thomas W. Worsdell, then Locomotive Superintendent of the Great Eastern Railway. "T.W." had certainly enjoyed a distinguished career even before he joined the Great Eastern. He was the eldest son of Nathaniel Worsdell, Carriage Superintendent of the Grand Junction Railway, who in still earlier days, with his father, had built the tender for the *Rocket*. It would seem only natural that "T.W." should spend some of his training at Crewe. But in his young days, not through any fault of his own, he was not long in any particular job, and in 1865, at the age of 27 he went to America and entered the service of the Pennsylvania Railroad. In that young country his outstanding ability found wide scope, and in a very short time he was appointed Master Mechanic at the Altoona shops—the "Crewe of the U.S.A.", as it has often been called.

But Crewe itself was to offer him still more tempting prospects. When Webb returned from Industry to succeed Ramsbottom on the L. & N.W.R. he offered T. W. Worsdell the job of Works Manager; so back to England he came, and was associated with Webb for ten years, during the eventful time that saw the building of the "Precedents" and the first experiments in compounding. Worsdell's own experiments in this direction were conducted on the Great Eastern Railway, where he was Locomotive Superintendent from 1881 to 1885, and, then, while only 47 years of age, he was appointed to the vacant chair at Gateshead. While "T.W." had shown himself a very capable works manager and administrator in two such exacting establishments as Altoona and Crewe his Great Eastern engines were generally disappointing. The "G14" 2-4-0s, which emerged from Stratford with a great flourish, were awful sluggards on the road, and his two-cylinder compound 4-4-0s, while good enough while slogging hard at low speeds, showed a poor steam distribution when running faster and were consequently sluggish. In both classes Worsdell had used the Joy valve gear, but the engine performance could hardly have been to Joy's liking. This did not sound propitious for the North Eastern; but it may be that the directors were looking to T. W. Worsdell mainly as an administrator, and reckoning that engine designing would fall mainly upon the younger brother. As it turned out the North Eastern two-cylinder compounds, when they did appear, excelled in the very feature that was so deficient in their Great Eastern forerunners—they were supremely fast, as the West Coast route was to learn in 1888.

Worsdell began modestly on the North Eastern with a most handsome design of 2-4-2 tank engine for local traffic, of which the first was completed at Gateshead in March, 1886. Crewe influences were apparent, in the use of Webb's radial axle-boxes and the Joy valve gear, but in general appearance these engines were in the tradition started by the "Tennants", except that the safety valves were encased in a tall polished brass mounting. This latter, finally enlarged to magnificent proportions on the "V" and "Z" Atlantics and on the "R1" Class 4-4-0s, became a special distinguishing feature of all new North Eastern engines for nearly 30 years. With these new 2-4-2 tanks there began the letter classification of engines; they were styled Class "A", and eventually mustered a total of 60 engines. They had 5 ft. 7 in. coupled wheels; 18 in. by 24 in. cylinders, and a working pressure of 160 lb. per sq. in. The boiler was of a new design destined to become a North Eastern standard and used on many of the smaller locomotives built in the ensuing 15 or 16 years; the tube heating surface was 994 sq. ft., the firebox 98 sq. ft. and the total 1,092 sq. ft. The total weight of the engine in working order was 52 tons. All the "A" Class engines were built at Gateshead: 20 in 1886-7, and ten in each of the years 1888, 1889, 1891 and 1892. They did excellent work on local passenger trains, and many of them were in service for more than 50 years.

The first North Eastern compound engine was completed at Gateshead works in the autumn of 1886, and, as might be expected, was a two-cylinder machine on the Worsdell-von Borries system. It was interesting, in view of comments made in the leading engineering journals about Mr. Worsdell's Great Eastern compounds, that on the North Eastern he applied the system first to an express goods engine, No. 16, the pioneer of the celebrated "C" Class of 0-6-0. As originally built the high pressure cylinder was 18 in. dia. and the low pressure 26 in. dia., the stroke of both being 24 in. The coupled wheels were 5 ft. 1¼ in. with new tyres. Joy valve gear was used, actuating slide valves with 1⅛. lap, $\frac{3}{16}$ in. lead, and a travel of 5½ in. in full gear. The boiler was an excellent one having a tube heating surface of 1,026 sq. ft.; the firebox had a grate area of 17·23 sq. ft. and a heating surface of 110 sq. ft. The boiler pressure was 160 lb. per sq. in. The spacious covered-in cab attracted much attention at the time, and it was suggested that the idea came from Mr. Worsdell's experience in America. It is ironical to reflect that when William Bouch introduced a very similar cab on his Stockton & Darlington 4-4-0s of 1860 it met with opposition from the enginemen, whereas it seems from contemporary accounts that the Worsdell cab on No. 16 was well received! In general the engine was massively built, and beautifully finished, and in 1887 *The Engineer* was moved to comment: "Even if no saving in fuel is effected the North Eastern Railway Company has obtained a splendid engine which does infinite credit to the builder as well as to the designer".

While providing an excellent shelter the cab was handsomely finished inside, with the sidesheets and roof lined with wood, painted and polished. The quality of the workmanship put into the North Eastern cab interiors was never brought home to me more forcibly than on a day in 1932 when I was browsing round the little shed at Penrith: two North Western "Jumbos" were outside, several "Cauliflowers" were there, and there was a North Eastern "C" Class goods, by that time, of course, converted to a two-cylinder simple. The contrast between the rough, stark ironmongery of the Crewe cabs and the comfort of the contemporary Gateshead engine could hardly have been exaggerated. It was on these engines that T. W. Worsdell introduced his crank axles, with circular cheeks; while providing a very robust job axles of this kind could be turned up in a lathe, thus assisting in production. This type of crank axle was used throughout the remaining 40 years of the North Eastern Railway. This first compound goods engine was stationed at Gateshead and put to work on the fast through freight services between Newcastle, York and Leeds; the average load was 40 wagons, though at times 50 were taken. At the time it was stated that the coal consumption was 6 lb. per mile less than the other engines in the link, though this comparison made against "ordinary" engines, probably older and less powerful units of Fletcher and McDonnell design, is reminiscent—unintentionally perhaps—of the claims made for modern Diesel-electric locomotives in America in contrast to earlier steam types. Comparisons or not, however, the "C" Class goods was a great success for Mr. Worsdell, and no fewer than 171 were constructed between 1886 and 1892.

Only one compound goods engine was built in 1886, and while exhaustive trials were in progress Mr. Worsdell built ten simple 0-6-0s, designated Class "C1", with two cylinders 18 in. by 24 in. but otherwise the same as the compound. But in 1887 construction of the Class "C" compounds began in earnest; 140 were built at Gateshead between 1887 and 1892, and the remaining 30 were built at Darlington. In 1894-5 Mr. Wilson Worsdell built another 20 of the non-compound series at Gateshead, and gradually the compounds were converted to two-cylinder simples. But as with the compound goods locomotives on the London & North Western, and elsewhere, they enjoyed a much longer existence as compounds than the contemporary passenger engines. Thirty-one were still running as compounds in 1910. Originally they were painted in the passenger colours, Gateshead style, with a dark green surround on the tender and the cab side sheets; they carried cast brass number plates on the cab sides, and had the initials N.E.R. on the tenders. Quite a number of these engines, as L.N.E.R. Class "J21" are still in service today—most of them with superheater boilers. Thus repaired and renewed over a period of 60 years, they still remain small excellent power units, running freely and riding well. In the summer of 1951 I had a most enjoyable trip from Penrith to Darlington on which I rode first on 65098 (old 973) and then on 65110 (old 1609). The full story has already been told*, but I shall always remember with something of a thrill how 65110 went pedalling away up the 1 in 60 from Kirkby Stephen, over Belah Viaduct and up to Stainmore summit, doing 26 m.p.h. with her load of 90 tons, and how smoothly and easily she rode at speeds up to 55 m.p.h. on the ensuing descent to Barnard Castle.

In their early days when they were the crack main line goods engines of the N.E.R., the "C" Class and the original non-compound "C1" series undertook the longer hauls, from Newcastle to York and Leeds, from Newcastle to Carlisle, and from Darlington over the Stainmore route to Tebay. Also, on account of their 5 ft. diameter wheels they were suitable for semi-fast passenger and excursion working. In many ways they were a counterpart of the famous Webb 18 in. goods of the L.N.W.R., though I have never heard of them running up to 70 and 75 m.p.h., as the old "Cauliflowers" did on oocasions. During the early years of the present century, when they had been largely displaced from the most important main line workings, they did a considerable amount of regular branch passenger working. Reverting to the time of the construction of these engines Mr. Worsdell built, concurrently, a tank engine equivalent, of which the boiler, wheels, cylinders and motion were identical to those of the "C" Class. The tank engines were of the 0-6-2 type; 51 designated Class "B", were built as compounds, and 11, Class "B1", as simples. They were used on the shorter-distance mineral workings, and today some of the survivors (L.N.E.R. Class "N8") are to be seen on the passenger workings over the extremely hilly routes from Newcastle up to Consett. A later variety similar in every way to the non-compound "B1" Class but having 19 in. by 26 in. cylinders was produced in 1893-4 by Mr. Wilson Worsdell; these engines were known as Class "N", but were actually nearly 2 tons *lighter* than Class "B1"—55¼ against 57 tons in working order. Twenty engines of this class were built, all at Darlington and will be referred to in a later chapter.

It was perhaps significant of the importance of freight traffic on the North Eastern Railway that Mr. T. W. Worsdell had progressed towards quantity-production of his new standard 0-6-0s, before his passenger engines had passed beyond the experimental form. Towards

* In *4,000 Miles on the Footplate* (Ian Allan).

the end of 1886 the first two-cylinder compound express locomotive No. 1324 was completed at Gateshead. It may have been out of deference to the McDonnell storm that the engine was built originally as a 2-4-0. The coupled wheels were 6 ft. 8 in. diameter, but while the cylinders and motion were the same as those of the Class "C" goods, the boiler provided a larger tube and firebox heating surface, and the total was 1,323 sq. ft., against 1,136 sq. ft. in the "C" Class. No. 1324 was a handsomely proportioned and beautifully finished engine, and after she had spent some three months in the main line traffic she was withdrawn in order to be exhibited, along with old *Locomotion* of the Stockton & Darlington Railway, in the Newcastle-upon-Tyne 1887 Jubilee Exhibition. That three months of running experience with No. 1324 had shown the engine to be a fast and free runner; indeed *The Engineer* reported, early in 1887, that Mr. Worsdell had found her too powerful for the work and was contemplating the use of smaller cylinders in further compound engines. She did, of course, represent an advance in tractive power over the "Tennants", having 175 lb. pressure, against 160 with the same equivalent cylinder capacity. As a 2-4-0 however she proved unsteady at high speed, probably due to the cylinders doing an unequal amount of work and thereby setting up lateral forces. When we come to the "J" Class engines reference will be made to certain experiments with the valve setting, in an attempt to secure an exactly equal horsepower from each cylinder.

T. W. Worsdell certainly seems to have used better judgment than McDonnell in planting his innovations upon the North Eastern Railway. His "A", "B" and "C" Class engines had been well received; his cabs were appreciated and when, following the experiments with No. 1324, his new standard express engines of the "F" Class came out in 1887, and had bogies, that particular feature was accepted without apparent comment. But the over-riding factor in the case of the "F" Class was that they were completely master of any main line duty that could be assigned to them, whereas in the troubled times of 1884 the McDonnell "38" Class definitely were not. Two batches of the new 4-4-0s were built in 1887, all at Gateshead works; ten were compounds with cylinders the same as in the "C" Class, and ten had two cylinders 18 in. dia. by 24 in. stroke. Mr. Worsdell, like his great contemporary at Crewe, made some show of comparing compound with simple propulsion, but as he provided his compounds with 175 lb. boiler pressure and the simples with a meagre 140 the result was a foregone conclusion! The "F1" Class, as the simples were known, had no more tractive effort than the "Tennants". Like No. 1324, the "F" Class proved to be very free-running engines, and considered in relation to their Great Eastern forerunners, which were so sluggish, one feature of their design appears to have been critical. To obtain a smooth action and free-running it was essential for the work done in the two cylinders to be as nearly equal as possible; to do this it was calculated that the cylinder volume of low pressure to high pressure should be about 2·3 to 1. This however would have resulted in a larger low-pressure cylinder than could be conveniently accommodated. Mr. Worsdell used cylinder diameters exactly the same as in his Great Eastern 4-4-0s, namely 18 in. and 26 in., but on the North Eastern engines the Joy valve gear was arranged to give a longer cut-off in the low pressure cylinder. Typical figures were: 50 per cent. H.P. and 73 per cent. L.P.; 70 per cent. H.P. and 84 per cent. L.P. This compensated for the L.P. cylinder having to be smaller than was theoretically correct. On the Great Eastern engines, by comparison, severe throttling would take place at admission to the low pressure cylinders; back pressure would set up through the receiver to the exhaust side of the high pressure cylinder, and the sluggishness in running seems readily explained thereby. Despite their freedom in running the North Eastern compounds had a harsh and noisy beat, all the more noticeable in contrast to the quiet and apparently effortless running of the "Tennants" and the "Fletchers".

The Gateshead express drivers had had time fully to take the measure of these engines when the race to Edinburgh took place in 1888, and it was with No. 117, one of the compounds, that the great Bob Nicholson made what was then the record time from Newcastle to Edinburgh—124·4 miles in 126 min. with a load of 100 tons. Nicholson was to do more brilliantly still in 1895, over the same course, but that is a story for the next chapter. The year 1888, however, witnessed an event that for the North Eastern Railway and, indeed, for British locomotive practice in general, was to prove of considerably greater significance than the Race to Edinburgh—the introduction of W. M. Smith's piston valves, on a second engine of the "D" Class of 2-4-0 compound. Now Walter M. Smith, whose second name, Mackersie, was often wrongly written as MacKenzie, was an outstanding personality; he was one of the ablest locomotive engineers ever to serve the North Eastern, and in later days he became very much the "power behind the throne". In 1887, as Chief Draughtsman, his thoughts turned to piston valves as a means of avoiding engine failures due to broken slide valves. Bouch had already tried piston valves on his "Ginx's Babies", but in such a form that failure was inevitable. Smith set out to produce a piston valve that would be free in operation, but would provide means of allowing trapped water to escape without damage to the pistons. It was on the second "D" Class engine that his first design of piston valve was tried. Why this engine, No. 340, was built as a 2-4-0 remains something of a mystery when the superiority of the "F" Class 4-4-0s had been demonstrated; but built thus she was, though readily distinguishable from the sister engine 1324 by her long extended front, covering tail rods on the pistons.

After some experience with engine No. 340, a similar type of piston valve was fitted, in 1891, to one of the "C" Class compound goods engines, No. 107, with the important difference that the valves were of the outside admission type, instead of inside admission on No. 340. From one point of view outside admission valves are to be preferred in that they make possible a shorter and more direct exhaust. On the other hand it is more difficult to keep the valve-chest covers steam tight with high pressure live steam inside, instead of exhaust steam. In spite of this the North Eastern standardised the use of outside admission valves, and many engines so equipped are still doing good service today. The performance of No. 107 was carefully watched in comparison with the eleven other engines in her link, and over a period of six months ending in December, 1891, she showed the lowest coal consumption of any, 32·05 lb. per mile. This was 3·2 lb. per mile less than the average for the remaining 11 engines, and 1·6 lb. per mile less than the lowest of any slide valve engine. For locomotives engaged in heavy freight work these were in any case excellent figures, while the mileages averaged out at about 3,100 per month. This engine, and No. 340, had 2 in. spring loaded relief valves fitted at either end of each cylinder for the purpose of allowing trapped water to escape; but it was found in practice that sometimes, with less experienced enginemen, the relief valves did not open quickly enough and cylinder covers were broken. This led Mr. Smith to the design of an improved type of valve in which relief from excessive pressure was obtained by use of segmental piston rings. This development is carrying the piston valve history beyond the day of T. W. Worsdell and we must return to the year 1888, when something of a sensation was caused in the locomotive world by the construction of a new class of 4-2-2 express locomotive at Gateshead.

At that time relations were cordial between the Locomotive Departments of the North Eastern and the Midland Railways. W. M. Smith had at one time served under S. W. Johnson, on the Edinburgh & Glasgow Railway, and in the "nineties" Derby collaborated with Gateshead in the development of Smith's piston valves. In 1888 it may well have been the success of Johnson's new "singles" on the Midland that provided the inspiration for the North Eastern Class "I" 4-2-2s. New motive power was needed for the Leeds and Scarborough expresses, and the relatively easy road and light trains doubtless underlined the view that a well-designed modern "single" would be ideal. The invention of the steam sanding gear by Mr. Holt, the Midland chief draughtsman at Derby, had obviated much of the difficulty in using "singles", due to slipping. The "I" Class engines, with driving wheels 7 ft. diameter, had what might be termed the standard North Eastern compound front end, with high pressure cylinders 18 in. diameter, low pressure 26 in. dia. and both having a stroke of 24 in.; the boiler was the same as that of the "B" and "C" and "N" Classes, and the pressure was 175 lb. per sq. in. The high and low pressure cylinders were on the same horizontal centre-line and the valves were located immediately above the cylinders. The wall of the low pressure cylinder extended through an aperture in the frame on the right hand side of the engine. Ten of these engines were built at Gateshead works: Nos. 1329 and 1330 in 1888; Nos. 1326-8 in 1889; Nos. 1527-1531 in 1890.

If the 7 ft. "I" Class engines were, from the first, intended for secondary main line work, the second Worsdell 4-2-2 series, the "J" Class, was not only a main line job, but one intended to supersede the existing 4-4-0s in the haulage of the heaviest East Coast expresses between York and Edinburgh. The driving wheels were 7 ft. 7 in. dia., the cylinders were much enlarged above those of previous North Eastern compounds, being 20 in. dia. high pressure and 28 in. dia. low pressure, both with a stroke of 24 in. The tube heating surface was no larger than that of the "I" Class but the grate area was increased from 17·2 to 20·7 sq. ft. The grate was sloping throughout. The accommodation of the huge 28 in. dia. low pressure cylinders between frames called for some ingenuity in design. It was done by placing the cylinders at a higher level, and inclined; but this device, in turn, brought the cylinder so near to the underside of the boiler that there was no room for the steam chest, and so both high and low pressure valve chests were placed *outside* the frames, and valves worked by rocking levers. The receiver was arranged very neatly as a curved tube within the narrow smoke box. Joy's valve gear was used, and after some experiments the following details were settled upon:

	High pressure	Low pressure
Lap	$1\frac{1}{8}$ in.	$1\frac{1}{8}$ in.
Travel (full gear)	$4\frac{3}{8}$ in.	$5\frac{3}{4}$ in.
Lead	$\frac{3}{16}$ in.	$\frac{3}{16}$ in.
Exhaust clearance	$\frac{1}{8}$ in.	$\frac{1}{8}$ in.

These engines were designed in anticipation of the opening of the Forth Bridge in 1890, when it was thought that heavier loads would have to be worked at higher speeds. The tenders were the largest yet built for the North Eastern, and had a capacity of 3,940 gallons of water.

These engines soon showed a remarkable ability to work heavy trains at high speed. No. 1517, the first of the class, ran a train of 32 carriages, 270 tons behind the tender, over the 66·9 miles from Newcastle to Berwick in 78 min. With a load of 18 six-wheeled coaches the same engine reached a maximum speed of 90 m.p.h. Some of the most revealing figures were obtained on some indicator trials with No. 1518, when the following results were obtained at various points between Newcastle and Berwick:

Speed m.p.h.	Cut-off (per cent.)		Indicated Horsepower
	H.P. cylinder	L.P. cylinder	
5	63	78	136
17	63	78	438
23	50	68	498
30	50	68	630
50	43	62½	662
75	47	67	1041
86	53	70	1069

The power output at 75 and 86 m.p.h. is remarkable, though from the cut-offs used it would seem that the engine was being pushed along pretty hard. It would have been interesting to know for how long such an effort could have ben sustained. The above results came from two separate trials when experiments were being made with various valve settings. With a lead of ⅛ in. for the low pressure valve more work was done in the low pressure cylinder than in the high pressure. Typical results were:

Speed m.p.h.	Indicated Horsepower	
	H.P. cylinder	L.P. cylinder
5	65	71
23	233	265
30	292	338
50	322	340

With ¼ in. lead on the low pressure valves, the following results were obtained:

Speed m.p.h.	Indicated Horsepower	
	H.P. cylinder	L.P. cylinder
17	224	214
75	546	495
86	551	518

This shows the reverse effect, and examination of the indicator diagrams concerned makes it very clear where the difference comes in. Somewhat naturally a lead of $\frac{3}{16}$ in. was finally adopted. But either set of results as tabulated above can be considered as quite good, and go a long way to explain why the Worsdell-von Borries system of compounding became so generally favoured abroad. The difficulty with so many compound locomotives was to get the low pressure cylinders to do their fair share of the work. On the L. & N.W.R. it was only with the "Teutonic" Class that Webb achieved anything near success; but T. W. Worsdell secured a real "bull's eye" with the "J" Class. Their life as compounds was, however, exceedingly short; trouble arose with the outside steam chests, and broken valves, while the complicated arrangement of rocker gear from the "Joy" motion to the outside valve spindles was another source of weakness. So it befell that within six years of their construction all ten engines of the class had been converted to two-cylinder simples. The brilliance of their work from 1894 onwards, however, belongs to Wilson Worsdell's régime.

Before closing this chapter there are one or two smaller engines to be mentioned, which, though not compounds, belong to the first Worsdell era. First among these are the "G" Class 2-4-0s, nicknamed the "Waterburys". These little branch line passenger engines are one of the mysteries set before present-day students of locomotive history; they had cylinders 17 in. dia. by 24 in. stroke, coupled wheels 6 ft. dia., and boilers of the same dimensions used on the "A" Class 2-4-2 passenger tanks. The valve gear was Joy's. Twenty of them were built, and they were sent to Leeds and Hull to work local train services. So much is plain fact. It is when one begins to enquire into their work that "the doctors differ". John S. MacLean, who knew the line intimately, and who was a personal friend of Walter M. Smith, has said: "the authorities looked with favour on these smart little engines; for their size and weight they have always been remarkably efficient . . ." Ahrons, on the other hand, writes: "The 'Waterburys' were not popular with the men. Whether they suffered from a constitutional weakness in the 'mainsprings', or had some other obscure internal complaint it is hard to say, but the fact remains that they were extremely sluggish engines". Wilson Worsdell transformed them, by rebuilding with piston valves and Stephenson link motion. The original engines were built at Darlington in 1887-8, and it rather looks as though someone came a "cropper" over the original motion design.

The remaining locomotives to be mentioned are all shunting tanks. In 1886 the "E" Class of 0-6-0 was introduced—smart little engines having 16 in. by 22 in. cylinders, 4 ft. 6 in. coupled wheels, and a boiler affording 731 sq. ft. of heating surface. No fewer than 120 of these engines were built between 1886 and 1895, and many of them are still in service today, as L.N.E.R. Class "J71". They are important as the forerunners and basis of Wilson Worsdell's "E1" Class of 1898, which became not merely the North Eastern standard shunting engine right down to 1922, but which was chosen again for further new construction after Nationalisation, in 1948! The "E1" Class have the same boiler as Class "E" but have 4 ft. diameter coupled wheels, and cylinders 17 in. by 24 in. Lastly there were the

Class "H" 0-4-0 crane tank engines of 1888, with 13 in. by 20 in. cylinders, 3 ft. 5 in. dia. coupled wheels, and domeless boilers.

And so, after a stay of only five years, T. W. Worsdell retired. His health was failing, and although he was only 53 years of age he preferred to make an end with active railway work and live quietly in the peaceful atmosphere of the English Lake District. For a time his services were retained by the North Eastern Railway as a consultant, though in view of the changes wrought by his brother one would imagine that his association in this way was a courtesy title rather than one having any practical significance. His short chieftainship had, however, left a profound mark upon North Eastern locomotive practice. Although his compound engines were rapidly converted to simples, the splendid workmanship put in their original construction enabled the rebuilt engines to work very long mileages and it was directly upon the practice of 1885 to 1890 in constructional methods that the great engines of the twentieth century were based. T. W. Worsdell lived on quietly at Arnside, Westmorland, until 1916, when he died at the age of 79.

Chapter Eight

WILSON WORSDELL, 1890-1898

THE retirement of T. W. Worsdell, in 1890, and the appointment of his younger brother Wilson to succeed him coincided, within a year, with a momentous change in top-level administration of the North Eastern Railway; for in 1891 the General Manager, Henry Tennant, retired, and was succeeded by the dynamic George Stegmann Gibb. Now Gibb was a truly great railwayman. In a very few years every department of the railway had felt the effects of his invigorating leadership, and from the state of a rich, leisured monopoly the North Eastern went forward with a big programme of improvements, accelerations, new works, and internal reform. In the Locomotive Department Wilson Worsdell must be counted as one of the most fortunate of Chief Mechanical Engineers. With a General Manager like Gibb behind him and two brilliant assistants, the way was cleared for striking progress, and progress there certainly was, seeing that in no more than ten years after the completion of the last "J" single-wheeler Gateshead was turning out the then-gigantic "S1" express passenger 4-6-0s. Vincent Raven had already shown himself a man of rare administrative ability and he was made Assistant Mechanical Engineer in 1895, while W. M. Smith continued as Chief Draughtsman. It should not be imagined, however, that Worsdell himself became a mere figurehead; far from it, for he was a first rate mechanical engineer. But by standing above the day-to-day work of his department, leaving the general administration and locomotive running to Raven, and the details of design to Smith, he was able to keep the whole rapidly changing picture in true perspective, and to guide the North Eastern through a crucial period in locomotive history with distinction and success.

Until he came to Gateshead, in 1883, it might well have seemed that Wilson Worsdell was set for a career on the North Western, rather than the North Eastern. He was born at Church Coppenhall, Crewe, but like his elder brother spent some of his early railway life in America. He was a pupil at the Altoona Works of the Pennsylvania Railroad during the time that his brother was Master Mechanic, and when "T.W." was recalled to Crewe, Wilson came also. After fulfilling various appointments he spent nine years in charge of various running sheds on the L. & N.W.R. Vincent Raven, on the other hand, had spent his whole life, since leaving school, in the service of the North Eastern Railway. He became a pupil under Edward Fletcher and was appointed Assistant Mechanical Engineer in 1895. Walter Smith's early career had been the most diverse of all. He was born at Ferry Port-on-Craig, Scotland, in 1842, and served his apprenticeship with a firm of general engineers in

No. 1531: Class "I", built 1890. [Locomotive Publishing Co.

No. 1517: Class "J", with outside steam chests. [Locomotive Publishing Co.

[Locomotive Publishing Co.

No. 779: Class "F", at Waverley, Edinburgh, showing the original style of painting, with dark green surrounds.

No. 1033: a "BTP" 0-4-4T of 1877. [*Locomotive Publishing Co.*

[*Locomotive Publishing Co.*
No. 1346: rebuilt as Class "290" at York in 1902 (L.N.E.R. Class "J77").

[*K. A. C. R. Nunn*
No. 957: rebuilt as a 2-2-4T with 6 ft. driving wheels in 1903.

[*Locomotive Publishing Co.*

No. 1638: Class "M" with outside steam chests and extended smoke box.

[*British Railways*

No. 1621: Class "M" superheated and as now preserved in York Railway Museum.

No. 1877: Class "Q" as originally built. [*W. J. Reynolds*

Class C: 2-cylinder compound No. 874, built 1889. [*Locomotive Publishing Co.*

[*Locomotive Publishing Co.*

No. 1897: Class P, 4 ft. 7 in. simple, built 1896.

No. 1678: Class P2, built 1902. [*Locomotive Publishing Co.*

Glasgow. Then, after a short time with Neilson's he joined the Edinburgh & Glasgow Railway when S. W. Johnson was Locomotive Superintendent. This early association blossomed into a lifelong friendship that came to influence profoundly the locomotive practice of both the North Eastern and the Midland Railway. When Johnson went to the Great Eastern in 1866 Smith went with him, but in 1874 at the still early age of 32 he was appointed Locomotive, Carriage and Wagon Superintendent to the Imperial Government Railways of Japan. He was one of the first British engineers to take an appointment in that country, and laid out the workshops, machinery and running sheds. In 1883, as recorded earlier in this book, he returned to England, and joined the North Eastern Railway, carrying out improvements at Gateshead works; very soon, however, he was exerting a strong influence on locomotive design. On the retirement of T. W. Worsdell in 1890 his influence became considerably greater.

In the next ten years three major points of change and development were consummated: the Worsdell-von Borries compound system was abandoned; Stephenson's link motion was used on all new engine designs, and remained the North Eastern standard down to the time of grouping, in 1922; and finally the use of piston valves was developed to a high degree of reliability by the turn of the century. Wilson Worsdell continued building Class "C" two-cylinder compound goods engines up to the end of 1892, but a further batch of main line 0-6-0s turned out from Gateshead in 1894-5 were of the "C1" Class with two 18 in. by 24 in. cylinders. One entirely new design of two-cylinder compound appeared in 1893, the big Class "M" 4-4-0 No. 1619; but before coming to Worsdell's very famous express passenger engines a brief reference is needed to some further small types to bring the chronological record of the engine classes up to date. Class "J" really marks the end of T. W. Worsdell's period, though there were some diminutive 0-4-0 shunting tanks, specially designed for working in Hull docks, built at Gateshead in 1890. They had 3 ft. 0 in. dia. coupled wheels, and cylinders 11 in. by 15 in. stroke. Five were built, Nos. 559-563, and they were designated Class "K". Then came Class "L", a more powerful edition of the standard 0-6-0 shunting tank, with 19 in. by 24 in. cylinders, and 4 ft. 7 in. coupled wheels. Ten of these engines were built, Nos. 544-553, all at Gateshead works in 1891-2.

Gateshead reached the peak of its new-engine production in 1890, with 60 locomotives built in one year, and with Darlington completing 33 in the same period the North Eastern Railway was building almost on the scale of the London & North Western, at Crewe. The years 1892-4 saw the production of the "M", "N", "O" and "P" Classes. Leaving the express passenger engines until later, the "N" Class of 0-6-2 tank was generally similar to the "B" type having the same boiler and wheel diameter; but the cylinders were increased to no less than 19 in. by 26 in. and the Stephenson link motion was used instead of Joy's gear. Twenty of these engines were built at Gateshead in 1893-4. The "P" Class goods was a smaller wheeled version of the standard main line 0-6-0, but having the smaller standard boiler, as used on the "A" Class 2-4-2 tanks, the "L" Class shunters, the "Waterbury" 2-4-0s, and which was also used on the "O" Class passenger tanks. In these days of standardisation it might be thought that there was no case for building a special design like the "P", when more "C1s" would probably have filled the need adequately. The comparative dimensions are as follows:

	Class "C1"	Class "P"
Cylinder dia. × stroke in.	18×24	18×24
Coupled wheel dia. ft. in.	5 0	4 6
Total heating surface sq. ft.	1126	1097
Grate area sq. ft.	17·2	15·2
Coal space tons	5	4
Tank capacity gallons	3038	3038
Total engine weight tons	41½	38½

The nearness of many of the collieries to the shipping ports, however, provided the North Eastern with many short-distance coal train workings, on which an engine and brake van would proceed from one of the running sheds to a nearby colliery, wait for traffic, and return with a block load. On such duty there might be a good deal of waiting, so that a locomotive with a small grate would, if carefully handled, be lighter on coal than a larger one. The tractive power made available was greater with Class "P" than with Class "C1" and the smaller engines were thus rather more suitable for getting a heavy mineral train under way. But having, by this argument, made something of a case for the building of Class "P". as a separate series, and 70 of them were built between 1894 and 1898, the ground is to some extent cut from under my feet, when I have to record that in 1898 Mr. Wilson Worsdell produced the Class "P1". These latter engines had the same chassis as the "C1" Class, with an engine wheel-base of 16 ft. 6 in. against 15 ft. 9 in. on Class "P", but the general design was in the "P" rather than the "C1" tradition, for in combination with a "C" boiler, much larger cylinders were used, 18¼ in. dia. by 26 in. stroke. One hundred and forty locomotives of Class "P1" were built in 1893-1903. Some of these latter engines are still in service today as Class "J25" in the North Eastern Region.

Turning now to the passenger tank engines, Ahrons and other locomotive historians many times discussed the divided opinions among British railway engineers of the subject of four-coupled eight-wheeled tank engines. The North Eastern Railway was a case in point. In Fletcher's day the 0-4-4 was favoured, but T. W. Worsdell, who was steeped in the traditions of Crewe, built the "A" Class 2-4-2s. Wilson Worsdell reverted to the 0-4-4, building the picturesque and handy little "O" Class; of which there were eventually 110 on the road. These engines, better known today perhaps as the North Eastern Region "G5s", are still excellent small passenger units. They are busily engaged on many local services, particularly from Sunderland and Hull, but in their prime they were among the smartest and hardest worked local passenger engines in the country. They had the standard 18 in. by 24 in. cylinders, the smaller standard boiler, as on the "A" and "P" Classses, and 5 ft. 1 in. coupled wheels, and like their counterparts on the London & South Western rode extremely well. I had the privilege of riding on some of the "O" Class engines in the early spring of 1953 in the Sunderland and Durham districts and on light trains their work was excellent. The cabs are comfortably arranged, and as we pulled out of Newcastle Central, over the High Level Bridge and down towards Pelaw, one could recapture something of the atmosphere of the North Eastern Railway. One of the delights of a small engine is of an almost perfect lookout ahead, over the top of the boiler, and with a train of four non-corridor coaches we skimmed along happily to Sunderland, running up to 45 m.p.h. between stops. This was with engine No. 1730, now British Railways No. 67257. In their early days the "O" Class had to work much harder. In addition to the suburban traffic out of Newcastle and Leeds they took the coastal trains over the very heavy route from Middlesbrough to Scarborough, and were indeed to be found at most parts of the North Eastern system. They took the local trains over the terrific gradients of the Whitby & Pickering line, and were used as pilots to express engines working through to Whitby from York or Leeds on summer holiday specials.

It was on another engine of this class, No. 67283, old 1885, that I travelled over part of the old main line to the south. It was on the 8.12 a.m. train from Sunderland to Durham, and the line following the river Wear joins the one-time East Coast main line at Penshaw Junction. In places, as in the massive station buildings at Fence Houses, there is evidence of a departed glory, but this route has nowadays the aspect of a purely mineral line—as indeed it very nearly is. It is however a regular diversion route for East Coast expresses and can take the largest locomotives. During the time I was writing this book I travelled over it on the up "Night Scotsman", though I, snugly oblivious in the seclusion of a sleeper, knew nothing of it at the time. With No. 67283 we ran non-stop over the 7 miles from Fence Houses to Durham, and on the connecting link between the past and present main lines the engine ran freely up to 50 m.p.h. at the viaduct over the Wear. The riding was very smooth and quiet, and the lever reverse very quick and easy to operate. No. 67283 was working on to Middleton-in-Teesdale, a slow and increasingly arduous run of 2¼ hours beyond Durham; but I had business in Darlington and so had to leave the train at Durham. We had run the 7 miles from Fence Houses to Durham in 14¼ minutes start to stop, including the slack to take the junction at Leamside, and a signal-delayed run in from Newton Hall Junction.

In writing of the "O" Class engines I have put my personal experience first; but I should add that they were all built at Darlington, as follows:

Year.	*Number constructed.*
1894	10
1895	10
1896	30
1897	20
1900	15
1901	25

In the years 1896 and 1901 they represented the entire new-engine output from North Road Works. In North Eastern days, they were always painted in the passenger colours, but like the "A" Class, and the various 0-6-0 goods engines, they never carried the crest. Instead they had the initials N.E.R. on the tank sides. But crest or not they were beautifully finished and beautifully kept. I saw them first at Leeds in 1917, when conditions were becoming increasingly austere; yet the "O" tanks were immaculate, with the broad brass collars at the joint of the smokebox and boiler barrel well polished and the safety valve covers glittering. But even today pride in the appearance of locomotives is not by any means a thing of the past on the North Eastern. At the time of writing there are still about a hundred of these fine little engines in service, and many are looking commendably smart in the lined-black of British Railways. Then, one brilliant day in the early spring of 1953, I happened to be at Bedlington when a positive apparition came round the curve into the station. For one moment I thought it must be a Royal special, or some other gala occasion. But no; it was merely one of the South Blyth 0-4-4s on the 1.9 p.m. stopping train to Newbiggin. These engines are allocated to regular men, and the crews are apparently in hot and constant competition as to which can make their engines look the finest! This particular one certainly looked superb, with the background to the number plate on the smokebox door painted deep crimson, and the hinge straps and "surround" of the door itself polished bright.

Now we must return to the express passenger engines of the "nineties", and in December, 1892, Wilson Worsdell completed at Gateshead the largest and heaviest express engine yet to be seen in Great Britain—the very celebrated 1620. This was the first of the "M" Class 4-4-0s, and although it bore a strong resemblance to T. W. Worsdell's "F" Class 4-4-0, there were many important differences apart from the all-round enlargement of dimensions. The cylinders were increased from the old standard 18 in. by 24 in. to 19 in. dia. by 26 in. stroke; the total heating surface was 1,341 sq. ft. and the grate area 19½ sq. ft. The coupled wheels were 7 ft. 1 in. dia. At the time some considerable surprise was caused in the engineering world by Mr. Worsdell's abandonment of compounding, particularly as the previous two-cylinder locomotives on the North Eastern appeared to be so successful. Compounding was being adopted generally on the continent of Europe and in America, and there were then at least 1,000 Worsdell-von Borries compounds in service abroad. While not exactly stigmatising Wilson Worsdell's policy as retrograde the engineering press of the day went so far as to question why it was that the British railways could not make a success of compounding. While the appearance of No. 1620 as a simple caused general surprise it must have been a particular disappointment to David Joy to see the link motion preferred to his radial gear. For the first time in England the valve chests were placed outside the frames. The slide valves working on vertical faces had a lap of 1¼ in., a travel in full gear of 4¾ in. and the lead was ⅛ in. in full gear. The arrangements of outside valve chests was fairly common in Europe at that time.

Engines 1621 and 1622 of this class had been constructed when, in May, 1893, a further example was built as a two-cylinder compound for comparative trials. This was the celebrated 1619, which had one 19 in. dia. high pressure, and one 28 in. dia. low pressure cylinder, and the stroke of both being 26 in. But although the potential cylinder capacity of No. 1619 was the same as other engines of Class "M" she carried a boiler pressure of 200 lb. per sq. in. against the 180 lb. of the simple engines. No. 1619 was followed by 16 more standard "M" Class engines, 1623 to 1638, all built at Gateshead in 1893, and it was very soon evident that they were fulfilling every expectation. With the steady increase in weight of the East Coast expresses a considerable amount of double-heading had been necessary, especially between Newcastle and Edinburgh; but with the "M" Class, any task of the day could be tackled without assistance. The last engine of the class, No. 1639, built at Gateshead in 1894, differed from the rest in having the Smith's segmental piston valves, with the valve chests *outside* the frames. These valves were the outcome of a period of careful study and development carried out jointly by the North Eastern and the Midland Railways. In referring to the earlier piston valve engines on the N.E.R., the compound 2-4-0 No. 340 and the compound goods No. 107, it was mentioned that trouble occurred with water becoming trapped in the cylinders; though the savings in coal consumed, and the increased mileage obtained from the engines so fitted encouraged further development. Mr. Johnson had obtained similar results with two Midland engines.

To overcome the practical difficulties experienced Walter Smith invented an entirely new type of valve; but in a paper read before the Institution of Mechanical Engineers in 1902 he stated: "It was chiefly due to the assistance received at Derby in carrying out experiments there, that this form of valve took a definite shape". This was the segmental valve, so designed to allow the segments to collapse inwards in case of excessive pressure and to allow trapped water to be relieved from the cylinders. Engine No. 1639 was the first to have these valves, and the results both in mileage and coal consumption, for the last six months of 1894, showed a definite superiority in favour of No. 1639. The average mileage for six months, for the eight other engines in the same link was 21,024, at a coal consumption of 34·08 lb. per mile; No. 1639 achieved a mileage of 28,890, on a coal consumption of 29·55 lb. per mile. The fitting of piston valves outside the frames, though unorthodox, was in keeping with the original design of the Class "M" engines, and the general performance details do not suggest any particular weakness from this source. Something approaching finality in the piston valve design was however reached in the conversion of the "J" Class singles from compound to simple working in 1895. Eight inch diameter piston valves were fitted, with an improved version of the segmental rings; but the valve chests were inside, and above the cylinders, and a direct drive Stephenson link motion was substituted for the complicated layout of the Joy valve gear. In 1895 these engines, despite the prowess of the "M" Class, were in many ways the pride of the line; they were highly esteemed by the running department, and took quite a big share in the Race to Aberdeen.

Before the really hectic conclusion of the Race, in late August, the North Eastern had booked the 8 p.m. from Kings Cross to cover the 80·6 miles from York to Newcastle in 92 min.—the same, within a minute, as the present schedule of the down "Aberdonian". The loads of the racing train were quite heavy, but "singles" were almost invariably used. On the night of 22nd July, 1895, for example, No. 1518 had 179 tons tare, and despite some bad delays from adverse signals kept time to Newcastle. The net time was 86 min., an average speed of 56·3 m.p.h. But when Rous Marten was on the same train a week later, No. 1522 was the engine; with a still heavier load of 195 tons she lost 6½ min. to Newcastle without any checks. Clearly something was amiss with the engine on this occasion, for on a later date, with load reduced to 134 tons she made a brilliant run, stopping dead in Newcastle in 79 min. 54 sec. from York, despite 2 min. loss by a permanent way slack near Durham. In the final week the schedule time was cut to 80 min., and for this culminating effort the "M" Class engines were brought on to the scene. North of Newcastle they had been used throughout the accelerated period, when the schedule of the non-stop run to Edinburgh was 140 min.

for 124·4 miles. With trains approaching 200 tons in weight double-heading was deemed necessary, and it had been the practice to run an "M" and a "J" single together. The trip was often made in 135 or 136 min., but on the night of No. 1522's fast trip from York to Newcastle with 134 tons, No. 1636 continued alone, and reached Edinburgh in 139 min. 21 sec. Up to this point drivers were doing no more than run to schedule, and there is every suggestion that nothing more was attempted south of Newcastle even in the final week. On the first day, No. 1624, with 105 tons, took 83 min. 24 sec. from York to Newcastle—a signal check accounted entirely for the 3½ min. lost on booked time. On the same night No. 1621 took the train on to Edinburgh in 125 min. 34 sec.

The climax, so far as the North Eastern was concerned, came on the night of 21st-22nd August, when the load was again 105 tons, and engine 1621 was used from York. The times of this run are tabulated against those of No. 1522 in the accompanying table, and strongly suggest that the big "M" Class engine was not being exerted. Among Great Northern enginemen the race was viewed with general disquiet, the more cautious spirits definitely holding their engines in, lest they should be scheduled to run at these high speeds as a regular event. It may have been the same with the crew of No. 1621, as with a heavier load the "single" almost equalled them to passing Darlington.

Whatever tongues may have been kept in their respective cheeks south of Newcastle on this last night, there is little doubt that the crew of No. 1620 were out for a record on the second stage of the North Eastern. It is a great pity Mr. Rous Marten was not a passenger on that night, as the so-called "official" record does not bear the stamp of detailed authenticity that one would like to see in the case of so obviously outstanding a run. So far as I am aware the time of 113 min. from Newcastle to Edinburgh has not been

N.E.R.: YORK—NEWCASTLE

	Engine No. ... ... Load	1522 134 tons	1621 105 tons
Distance miles		Actual min.	Actual min.
0·0	York	0	0
22·2	Thirsk	23	22½
30·0	Northallerton	30¼	29½
44·1	Darlington	42¾	42½
		P.W. Slack	—
66·1	Durham	65	66½
80·6	Newcastle	79¾	78½

Net time: 78 min.

N.E.R.: NEWCASTLE—EDINBURGH

Load: 105 tons
Engine: 1620 (Class "M")

Distance		Actual time	Average speed
miles		min.	m.p.h.
0·0	NEWCASTLE	0	—
16·6	Morpeth	18	55·3
34·8	Alnmouth	33½	70·4
51·6	Belford	48	69·6
66·9	BERWICK	60	76·5
78·1	Reston Junct.	72	56·0
95·3	DUNBAR	88	64·6
106·6	Drem	98	67·8
111·2	Longniddry	101½	78·8
117·9	Inveresk	107	73·1
121·4	Portobello	110	70·0
124·4	EDINBURGH WAVERLEY	113	60·0

eclipsed to this day, even by the "Coronation" express, though the speeds run round Morpeth, Alnmouth and Portobello curves, not to mention the interpretation of the 5 m.p.h. slack through the old station at Berwick would certainly not be tolerated in these days! Although some of the slacks were nominally severe, like the 15 m.p.h. scheduled round the S-curve of Portobello, I was amused to find in a contemporary description of a run with a new North Eastern 4-4-0 a comment on the smoothness of her riding when the Portobello curves were taken "at high speed"! Certainly there were a couple of fire-eaters on the footplate of No. 1620 in the early hours of 22nd August, 1895. The accompanying log gives the bare details of their progress. The driver, Bob Nicholson of Gateshead, had already distinguished himself with No. 117 in the race of 1888, while the fireman, Tom Blades, became one of the most famous twentieth century North Eastern drivers. He had the first Pacific, No. 2400, and worked her in the comparative dynamometer car trials against a Gresley Pacific in 1923. Still later, in 1928 and in partnership with Albert Pibworth, of Kings Cross shed, he drove the "Flying Scotsman" on the first occasion it was run non-stop from London to Edinburgh. Nicholson and Blades together certainly made a grand effort with the racing train of 1895, and their overall average speed of 66 m.p.h. was one of the finest individual feats of the whole race. It is fitting that one of these superb nineteenth century locomotives should now be preserved in the York Railway Museum. No. 1621 is not, of course, in her original condition, but in her third and final state, with superheater and chimney set forward on a different form of extended smokebox to that originally fitted. But she rests there in all the fresh beauty of the North Eastern livery, and it is with a feeling of nostalgia that one sits in her cab, so comfortable, so well arranged, and giving an excellent look out ahead: what an extraordinary contrast in cabs to that of her fellow "racer", the *City of Truro,* standing abreast of her in the Museum!

Gratifying though the work of the "M" Class must have been to all concerned at Gateshead, Wilson Worsdell laid down two new 4-4-0 express passenger designs for his 1896 programme. The first of these to be completed, the remarkable "Q1" Class with 7 ft. 7in. coupled wheels, was designed purely and simply as a "racer", to be ready for anything that might eventuate in the heat of competition for the Anglo-Scottish traffic. The "Q" was also a high-speed engine, but intended for normal express duties. It is curious, however, that both "Q" and "Q1" Classes had relatively small boilers, as will be seen from the following comparison with Class "M".

Class	"M"	"Q1"	"Q"
Coupled wheels dia. ft. in.	7 1	7 7	7 1
Cylinders: dia. × stroke in.	19×26	20×26	19½×26
Total heating surface sq. ft.	1341	1216	1212
Grate Area sq. ft.	19½	20¾	19¾
Boiler pressure lb. per sq. in.	180	180	180

For beauty of appearance the "Q" and "Q1" engines must stand second to none among nineteenth century designs. The extended smokebox fitted to the "M" Class, and which provided space for an intermediate receiver if ever they had been converted to compounds, like 1619, was not needed; the cab was improved by the fitting of a clerestory roof, and the slide valves were placed inside and above the cylinders. Apparently Gateshead were not sure enough of the segmental piston valves to incorporate them in a large new express locomotive. The "Q1" Class, with the largest coupled wheels in the world, were extraordinarily impressive engines, though as no race developed in the summer of 1896 only two of them were built. Nos. 1869 and 1870 were completed in May and June respectively; Gateshead then followed with the first ten engines of the "Q" Class, Nos. 1871-1880. In the summer of 1896 the new vestibule trains for the "Flying Scotsman" were introduced, though the timing was not severe. The night Aberdeen train was the toughest proposition, as the schedule was 92 min. from York to Newcastle with a 250-ton load. The accompanying log of the "Flying Scotsman", timed by Mr. Rous-Marten, shows a very sedate performance by the first "Q" Class engine, especially in the mediocre running between York and Darlington. The work of the "Q1" engines on the night express was more interesting, though No. 1870 on the second run was badly affected by a heavy side gale, with showers of rain. Between Newcastle and Edinburgh, however, the 8.15 p.m. "sleeper" was regularly double-headed when the load was 250 tons. The usual engines were an "M" and a "J".

Many years later, in my own journeyings on the North Eastern I came across the "Q" 4-4-0s to a greater extent than I did the "Ms",

N.E.R.: YORK—NEWCASTLE

Load: 250 tons
Engine: 1871 (Class "Q")

Distance		Actual time	Average speed
miles		min. sec.	m.p.h.
0·0	YORK	0 00	—
11·2	Alne	14 53	45·1
22·2	Thirsk	27 43	51·5
30·0	Northallerton	37 00	50·5
38·9	Dalton Junct.*	47 24	51·2
44·1	DARLINGTON	52 41	59·0
57·0	Ferryhill	69 00	47·5
66·1	DURHAM	79 17	52·4
70·0	Plawsworth	84 37	43·9
71·9	Chester-le-Street	86 30	60·4
74·7	Birtley	89 14	61·3
76·3	Lamesley	90 51	59·5
78·9	Bensham	93 38	56·1
80·0	Gateshead	95 16	—
80·6	NEWCASTLE†	96 31	—

*Now Eryholme †Via High Level Bridge

THE 8.15 p.m. KINGS CROSS TO ABERDEEN

Engine No.		1869		1870	
Engine Class		"Q1"		"Q1"	
Load, tons tare		245		244	
Distance		Actual	Speeds	Actual	Speeds
miles		min. sec.	m.p.h.	min. sec.	m.p.h.
0·0	York	0 00	—	0 00	—
11·2	Alne	13 55	48·3	14 41	45·8
22·2	Thirsk	26 14	53·6	26 42	55·0
30·0	Northallerton	34 58	53·5	35 16	54·7
44·1	DARLINGTON	49 59	56·4	50 29	55·2
57·0	Ferryhill	65 46	49·0	67 11	46·3
66·1	DURHAM	76 54	48·4	77 56	50·8
70·0	Plawsworth	82 03	45·5	83 07	45·2
74·7	Birtley	86 08	69·0	87 35	63·2
80·6	NEWCASTLE *	92 00	—	94 39	—

*Via High Level Bridge

L.N.E.R.: (N.E. Area) YORK—LEEDS

Load: 403 tons tare, 425 tons full
Engine: Class "Q" 4-4-0 No. 1875

Distance		Actual	Speeds *
miles		min. sec.	m.p.h.
0·0	YORK	0 00	—
2·0	*Chaloners Whin Junct.*	5 05	—
7·7	Bolton Percy	12 55	47½
10·8	Church Fenton	16 45	50
14·0	*Milepost 14*	21 45	30
15·8	Micklefield	25 50	25
16·6	Ridge Bridge	28 00	21½
18·2	Garforth	31 30	—
24·0	*Neville Hill Junct.*	40 10	—
—		sig. stop	
25·5	LEEDS	45 20	—

*Maximum and minimum by stop watch. Net time 43½ min.

and had several trips behind them as recently as 1938 between Selby and Hull. But the journey I shall always remember came one Sunday afternoon in the early autumn of 1930 when I was travelling from York to Leeds. I arrived at the station to find extensive marshalling in progress in which extra vehicles for a theatrical party were being added to the normal rake. Eventually the load totalled up to 403 tons tare, and to haul this to Leeds, including the ascent of Micklefield bank, one Class "Q" engine was provided, No. 1875. Comparison of the log with that of No. 1871 on the "Flying Scotsman" in 1896, shows that the honours rest with No. 1875. On the dead level out to Church Fenton speed was worked up to 50 m.p.h. and then the 7·0 miles of ascent to beyond Ridge Bridge, graded at 1 in 145-133-146-150, were cleared in 13¼ min., an average of 31½ m.p.h. No fast running was made down the bank from Garforth and although time was lost—and lost to the extent of 8½ min. net—the performance of so relatively small a locomotive was excellent. The log is tabulated on the opposite page.

In their hey-day, when the 92-min. timing of the 8.15 p.m. "sleeper" from Kings Cross was the fastest run of the whole 24 hours between York and Newcastle, the "Q" Class engines did excellently, despite their small boilers, and twenty were more of them were built at Gateshead in 1897. Their numbers were 1901-1920 and 1921-1930. In using small boilers and larger cylinders Gateshead may have been animated by the ideas of S. W. Johnson, at Derby, who did the same in order to make it virtually impossible for drivers to thrash their engines, and thus work uneconomically.

Reference has been made in the chapter dealing with the "Tennant" 2-4-0 engines to the trials carried out in October and November, 1896 with five different classes of express passenger engines between Newcastle and Tweedmouth. The results with the Fletcher "901" Class, and with the "Tennant" have already been discussed in some detail; the modern engines concerned were a "J" 4-2-2, with piston valves, a "Q1", and a standard original "M" with outside valve chests and extended smokebox. Owing to the varying conditions prevailing on different days one cannot place too great a reliance upon the figures obtained. We know only too well from the experience of the recent interchange trials on British Railways how relatively small circumstances can alter the test results obtained, but in the North Eastern trials of 1896 a remarkable feature was the excellent performance of the "single", despite the worst weather conditions of the whole series. Very complete details of the working were given in a paper read before the Institution of Mechanical Engineers in October, 1898, by Mr. Smith, and from these details I have prepared the accompanying summary. The coal consumption of the "single", in pounds per train mile, was naturally affected by the bad weather conditions; but in his later paper, describing the development of the segmental ring piston valves Mr. Smith said, in respect of the "J" in the 1896 trials: "This engine was in every respect well in advance of the others. It did not show any signs of weakness". Seeing that the "others" included such engines as the "M" and the "Q1" this was praise indeed for the "single".

1896 TRIALS, NEWCASTLE—TWEEDMOUTH AND BACK: 131 MILES

Engine Class		"J"	"M"	"Q1"
Load behind tender	tons	187	187	187
Actual average speed m.p.h. ...	DOWN	46·5	50·9	48·7
	UP	54·2	51·8	51·2
Net average speed m.p.h.	DOWN	50·9	52·7	50·5
	UP	54·2	52·4	52·4
Weather conditions		Heavy N.E. gale and rain	Calm, fine	Calm, fine
Average I.H.P. (round trip)		692	603	558
Coal used per mile	(lb.)	43·35	37·26	37·33
Coal per I.H.P. hour	(lb.)	3·28	3·25	3·44
Coal per sq. ft. of grate area per hour ...	(lb.)	109·6	99·9	90·8
Evaporation, water per pound of coal ...	(lb.)	7·97	7·70	8·45

While quoting the drawbar horsepower corresponding to each of the indicator diagrams, Mr. Smith's paper does not give the average drawbar horsepower for the complete journeys. It was largely as a result of these trials that Mr. Worsdell decided to incorporate the segmental ring piston valves in the "R" Class express passenger 4-4-0 engines, the first of which was turned out at Gateshead works in August, 1899.

As the nineteenth century drew to a close North Eastern locomotive affairs were in state of swift evolution, and the new "big" engines of 1898 and 1899 will come into the next chapter. In passing, however, and to exemplify once again the staple needs of North Eastern motive power, it may be stated that in the eight years 1891 to 1898 a total of 454 new locomotives were added to the stock; yet of these only 54 were for the main line express passenger work. At the same time a good deal was being done to render the older engines more suitable for changing conditions. Many of the various types of Fletcher 2-4-0 received boilers like those fitted to the "901" Class; the one-time "Ginx's Babies", the small-wheeled "1440" Class, and others partook of an appearance something like a "Tennant', so far as boiler mountings were concerned, and these latter engines were equipped with the handsome Worsdell safety valve casing, and in consequence became even more pleasing to the eye. But one of the most interesting "rebuildings" carried out at this time—not only in itself, but in the subsequent history of the engines concerned—was that of the conversion of a number of Fletcher 0-4-4 tank engines into 0-6-0 side-tank shunters. The first to be done was No. 290, and the work was carried out in the York shops. Despite the legend on the works plates, which has been perpetuated on the plates to be seen today, one must be pardoned for doubting if there was very much of the old engines used, save for a few fittings, when it is recalled that a 5 ft. 6 in. 0-4-4 tank was converted into a 4 ft. 1 in. 0-6-0! The cylinders were, however, of the same dimensions—17 in. dia. by 22 in. stroke—and may possibly have been used. But converted, renewed, or whatever else one may call the transformation, the 0-6-0s proved excellent little engines—so good that 38 of the original 50 are still in service today. It *is* service, too; real honest-to-goodness revenue earning, and not merely playing out time.

In the course of writing this book I was privileged to make a visit to Blyth, and there I saw these tough little "290" Class (now Class "J77") pushing the huge loaded hopper wagons up to the staiths. These tall gantries, beside the estuary of the river, are constructed entirely of timber and the "290s" are the heaviest engines permitted on the staiths themselves. Three of them are stationed at South Blyth, for pushing up to the "new" staiths, and six of them are at the north shed, for the heavy work up to the north and west staiths. At Links Road box, whence they push up to the new staiths, I saw No. 68431 (old 151) at work; the maximum load up the 1 in 60 gradient is eleven 20-ton wagons, about 300 tons. At the north staiths the "push" is rather longer, and includes an awkward curve right on the heaviest gradient. Here the maximum load for one engine is 15, equal to about 450 tons, but there is a considerable length of rising approach before passing on to the staiths, and a second engine is used while the track is on dry land. Here I rode on the footplate of No. 68417 (old 607), and with both engines literally going all-out the pandemonium was terrific, and reminiscent of two L.M.S. 0-6-0 tanks banking a heavy express up the Lickey Incline. But on a boisterous March day, with the sea below us on the left, and the 50-year-old engine working like a Trojan, this short run up to the north staiths was as thrilling an experience as one could wish for. Just as we came down on to the worst piece, round the curve at the beginning of the timber gantry, the second engine dropped off, and No. 68417 roared away on her own while the timber work swayed slightly beneath us, after the fashion of the old Brunellian viaducts in Cornwall.

The first two "J77s" on which I rode at Blyth had the rounded cab roofs of engines rebuilt at York shops; but some were rebuilt at Gateshead, and these had the normal square-cornered cabs. It was on one of these latter, No. 68397 (old 1342) that I rode while banking a train up the longer, though more gradual incline to the west staiths. Here the maximum load permitted is eighteen 20-tonners, about 550 tons, and with this full load it was again a case of "all-out" the whole way. These shunting engines are modestly designated "pilots"; but there are few pilots anywhere on British Railways that have to work so hard as these old worthies. Before leaving Blyth I was shown round the North shed, a typical N.E.R. roundhouse; it is, moreover, a depot where, so far, there are stationed no locomotives except of North Eastern origin. Besides the veteran 0-6-0 shunters there are many of the Wilson Worsdell big "P2" and "P3" 0-6-0 goods, though I shall have more to say about those fine engines in the next chapter. When it comes to longevity, however, the "290" Class 0-6-0s (L.N.E.R. "J77") will almost certainly be eclipsed by the "E1" Class tanks (L.N.E.R. Class "J72"), first introduced in 1898, having 4 ft. 1 in. dia. wheels and cylinders 17 in. by 24 in. Twenty were built at Darlington in 1898-9, and another 55 were built during Sir Vincent Raven's time. Ten more were added to the L.N.E.R. stock after grouping, in 1925, and these were not built in North Eastern shops at all, but at Doncaster! The limit was finally reached when another batch, of 28, was built at Darlington, *after nationalisation,* in 1949-51. In the last group, Nos. 69001-69028, all the old N.E.R. characteristics were faithfully reproduced, including the shapely Worsdell safety valve casing.

Chapter Nine

THE BIG-ENGINE ERA, 1899-1906

IN the first eight years of Wilson Worsdell's superintendence events had certainly moved fast in the locomotive department. New engine designs, as represented by Classes "E1", "L", "M", the compound 1619, "N", "O", "P", "P1", "Q" and "Q1", had all been put into service. But from 1899 the emergence of new designs continued even more rapidly for a time, and testified to an exceptional fertility of ideas, and to an exceptional output of work from the Gateshead drawing office under W. M. Smith's leadership. The following constitutes a bare record of developments from 1899:

Year	Class	Description
1899	R	4-4-0 express passenger
	S	4-6-0 mixed traffic
1901	S1	4-6-0 express passenger
	T	0-8-0 heavy mineral
1902	T1	0-8-0 heavy mineral
	U	0-6-2T heavy mineral
1903	V	4-4-2 express passenger
1904	P2	0-6-0 mineral
1906	4CC	4-4-2 compound express passenger
	P3	0-6-0 mineral
1907	W	4-6-0T heavy passenger tank
1908	R1	4-4-0 express passenger
1909	X	4-8-0T humping engine

With additions to existing classes, and construction of the above, the combined new engine output of Gateshead and Darlington works was 474 in the eleven years 1899-1909.

The year 1898 had seen both works engaged in building freight and shunting engines. Thirty-two "P1" 0-6-0s represented the total output from Gateshead, while Darlington turned out 10 "E1" shunters, and 17 Class "P" goods. From Gateshead, however, came one further engine, strictly speaking a rebuild, that might have been a curtain raiser to the entire twentieth century locomotive policy of the North Eastern Railway. The two-cylinder Worsdell-von Borries compound No. 1619 was completely redesigned by Mr. Smith, and came out as a three-cylinder compound with one high pressure cylinder inside and two low-pressure cylinders outside. This arrangement, which was patented by Mr. Smith, was as logical as F. W. Webb's arrangement was the reverse! Instead of two small high pressure cylinders and one enormous low pressure, the three cylinders in Smith's system were all much the same size. Through its adoption on the Midland Railway, and subsequently on the grand scale by the

L.M.S., the Smith compound system is so well known as to need no detailed description here. In its original form, however, and as first used by Mr. Johnson on the Midland, the engines were provided with a changeover valve by which the driver could, if necessary, admit a certain amount of live steam direct to the low pressure cylinders so as to develop increased power on a heavy gradient. This is sometimes termed semi-compound, or reinforced compound working. A similar control is provided on all the famous de Glehn compounds in France, and as on those latter engines the original Smith compound had independent valve gears for the high and low pressure cylinders. This called for intelligent work on the driver's part, and on the North Eastern No. 1619 certainly did well.

Apart from the arrangement of cylinders—high pressure, 19 in. by 26 in.; low pressure 20 in. by 24 in.—there were certain interesting details in the design. The high pressure cylinder had a segmental ring piston valve, but the outside cylinders had ordinary slide valves. The boiler was new, and differed from any other on the N.E.R. A much larger fire grate was adopted, with an area of 23 sq. ft.; the total heating surface was 1,328 sq. ft. and boiler pressure 200 lb. per sq. in. A novel feature was the use of cross water tubes in the firebox, to improve the circulation of water and to increase the heating surface; this device was invented and patented by Mr. Smith, though it is of course best known through its adoption by Dugald Drummond on the London and South Western Railway. On No. 1619 when first turned out as a three-cylinder compound there was no outward sign of these water tubes, and what was more important, no means of removing the tubes without complete shopping of the locomotive. In August, 1900, a new firebox was fitted with outside covers for providing access to the tubes, and it is in this latter form that No. 1619 is illustrated on page 127 hauling a down East Coast express. At the time of this change a tender with increased coal space was attached to the engine, carrying 5 instead of 4½ tons, and from that time the total weight of engine and tender in working order was 94½ tons. No. 1619 proved master of any task allotted to it; it was naturally under close scrutiny from headquarters at Gateshead and handled by regular crews, but nevertheless in the first four months 21,000 miles were covered on top-grade express duty. The enginemen concerned acquired the necessary technique of manipulating the independent reversing gears, and the change valve when necessary, and it might indeed have seemed that here was the prototype of the future North Eastern express locomotive.

But Wilson Worsdell proceeded with some caution. Those controls on No. 1619 were decidedly more than enginemen had been expected to understand and operate in the past. New engines were needed at once, as the rapid increase in East Coast loads was making it necessary to double-head the "M" and "Q" Class engines north of

No. 674: Class "A" 2-4-2T introduced in 1886. [*Locomotive Publishing Co.*

No. 304: Class "E" 0-6-0T introduced in 1886. [*Locomotive Publishing Co.*

No. 1779: Class "O" 0-4-4T introduced 1894. [*Locomotive Publishing Co.*

[*L. & G.R.P. 21898*

Whitby shed in 1895. Engines in the foreground are: left to right: 0-6-0 No. 659 ("93" Class); 2-4-2T No. 1602 (Class "A"); and 0-6-0T No. 1763 built Hawthorns 1866.

[*O. S. Nock*

Tweedmouth roundhouse. Engines, left to right, are 2349 (P3), 483 (A), N.B.R. 0-6-0, Class "A" 2-4-2T, and a Class "E" 0-6-0T.

[*L. & G.R.P. 21897*

Whitby shed in 1895, showing engines 958 0-4-4 BTP, and 1667 long-boilered 0-6-0, with McDonnell 4-4-0 No. 664 behind.

Class "V", Atlantic No. 532. [*W. J. Reynolds*

[*W. J. Reynolds*

Class "S", 4-6-0 No. 2003 as originally turned out in green livery.

Class "S1", 6 ft. 8 in. 4-6-0 No. 2113. [*Locomotive Publishing Co.*

[Locomotive Publishing Co.

York Station, south end. Engines, left to right, are N.E.R. 0-6-0; Midland "Belpaire" 4-4-0; N.E.R. "S1" No. 2114; G.N.R. 4-4-0 No. 1332; a Midland engine behind; a G.E.R. 2-4-0, and G.N.R. No. 1334 (Ivatt 4-4-0).

Newcastle, and, with the results of the Tweedmouth trials of 1896 in mind, he decided upon a greatly enlarged two-cylinder simple 4-4-0. In comparison with the previous three classes, "M", "Q" and "Q1" the changes in basic dimensions were significant. After increasing first to 19½ and then to 20-in. cylinders, a reversion was made to 19 in. for the new "R" Class, while on the other hand the boiler was much enlarged, to provide a total heating surface of 1,527 sq. ft. The grate area was 20 sq. ft., and the boiler pressure 200 lb. per sq. in. But apart from the large boiler the outstanding feature of the new engines was the use of Smith's patent piston valves, beneath the cylinders but not on the same vertical centre line. Direct-action Stephenson link motion was used, in a very simple and straightforward layout. The valves themselves were no less than 8¾ in. diameter, and provided a large port area for inlet and exhaust from the cylinders. Like the previous locomotives with Smith's piston valves the "R" Class had outside admission, which became the accepted North Eastern standard practice. It was followed right down to the grouping.

Engine No. 2011 was the first of the "R" Class to be constructed, in August, 1899, and she was the subject of very special attention. Unlike North Eastern express locomotives of the day, and unlike the rest of the class she was double-manned, and ran daily from Newcastle to Edinburgh and back, following this with a second round trip from Newcastle to Leeds and back. This daily mileage of 455, made six days a week, was continued with scarcely a break for over two years, with the result that the engine had reached the exceptional, and perhaps unbelievable mileage of 284,000 before her first visit to the shops for general overhaul. Of course, No. 2011 was under very close observation, and there is little doubt that her two regular drivers entered into the spirit of this marathon trial and did their best to create an out-and-out record. The remaining engines of the first batch, 2012 to 2020, averaged 163,000 miles between heavy repairs, and with them, not making such long daily rounds as No. 2011, these mileages represented as much as 3½ years' service! They were all kept in beautiful condition, and the regular enginemen, not having to share them with even one other crew, took great pride both in their appearance and their working efficiency. Many minor adjustments and repairs would be done by the drivers and firemen, without the "booking" of such defects at the shed, and the men naturally grew to know the individual peculiarities of their own engines, and could make allowance for them when running their trains. But having taken all this into consideration there is no doubt that the Class "R" engines were outstanding in their general reliability, and when Mr. Smith read his paper on piston valves before the Institution of Mechanical Engineers in July, 1902, many contributors to the discussion spoke appreciatively of them.

At the turn of the century the East Coast service did not include any fast schedules. It was a case of steady uniform running with heavy trains—even then beginning to exceed 300 tons in weight—and the "R" Class proved as reliable in timekeeping as they were reliable mechanically. For the work done they were economical engines in their day; the average coal consumption of those stationed at Gateshead was at first about 45 lb. per mile. This, of course, was an overall figure, including lighting up, light mileage, and days spent as standing pilots at Newcastle. The average train load was then a little over 200 tons. Fortunately, by the kindness of various friends, I have been able to collect together a considerable amount of performance data covering this most interesting period in North Eastern locomotive history. I have grouped together the runs over various sections of the main line, and included these logs and the relevant descriptions in a separate chapter, so that the work of different classes of engines can be readily compared. These logs taken in ordinary day-to-day running are supplemented by details of trial runs made with the dynamometer car. So far as the "R" Class engines are concerned, ten more were built at Gateshead in 1900, Nos. 2021-2030 inclusive, and another ten, Nos. 2101-2110, followed in 1901.

Shortly after the introduction of the "R" Class Mr. Rous-Marten clocked No. 2011 on a day when the up "Flying Scotsman" was made up to a load of 320 tons behind the tender. From an account written at the time it seems evident that this was something of a "show" run. Certainly the start out of Newcastle was extremely fast, with speed rising to 60 m.p.h. soon after Low Fell and a splendid climb of Plawsworth bank. Average speeds over five successive miles from Birtley were 50, 47, 45, 42 and 40 m.p.h., and the minimum on the 2½ miles of 1 in 150 from Chester-le-Street was 37½ m.p.h. Between Aycliffe and Darlington a maximum speed of 70 m.p.h. was attained. The run from Darlington to York would be considered sluggish today, though time was well in hand on the contemporary schedule. The complete log is tabulated opposite. A run clocked about the same time by Mr. Norman D. McDonald, also from Darlington to York, showed that the "R" Class engines could run fast, though not at this early stage in their career displaying anything superior to what the "M" Class engines had done in the Race to Aberdeen.

Although the next new design to be considered, Class "S", follows logically after Class "R", the first two engines to be completed, Nos. 2001 and 2002, actually preceded the record-breaking No. 2011 by two months. Although the "R" was destined to prove far more useful in express traffic, and to have a much longer life, it was perhaps only natural that Class "S" created infinitely more of a stir in 1899, not only from its size and handsome appearance but from its pioneer position as the first passenger 4-6-0 in the British

N.E.R.: UP "FLYING SCOTSMAN" IN 1900

Load: 15 vehicles, 320 tons tare
Engine: Class "R" 4-4-0 No. 2011

Distance		Actual	Average speed
miles		min. sec.	m.p.h.
0·0	NEWCASTLE	0 00	—
0·6	Gateshead	2 10	—
1·7	Bensham	3 56	37·4
3·0	Low Fell	5 29	50·3
4·3	Lamesley	6 45	61·6
5·9	Birtley	8 33	53·4
8·7	Chester-le-street	11 59	48·8
10·6	Plawsworth	14 32	44·7
14·5	DURHAM	20 01	42·8
18·7	Croxdale	25 19	47·5
23·6	Ferryhill	30 59	51·9
26·3	Bradbury	34 01	53·3
31·1	Aycliffe	38 39	62·1
36·5	DARLINGTON	44 41	—
0·0		0 00	—
2·6	Croft Spa	5 01	—
5·2	Dalton Junct.*	8 07	50·3
6·9	Cowton	9 58	55·2
10·4	Danby Wiske	13 44	56·0
14·1	Northallerton	17 52	53·8
21·9	Thirsk	25 54	58·4
26·1	Sessay	30 04	60·5
28·0	Pilmoor	31 56	61·1
30·7	Raskelf	34 35	61·1
32·9	Alne	36 37	64·4
34·4	Tollerton	38 01	64·3
38·6	Beningbrough	42 10	60·8
44·1	YORK	48 29	—

*Now Eryholme

Isles. It is, however, most interesting to compare the dimensions of the two classes.

On the first engines of Class "S" Mr. Worsdell reverted to ordinary slide valves placed vertically inside the frames and actuated by direct Stephenson's link motion. The valves had $1\frac{1}{8}$ in. lap and

N.E.R.: DARLINGTON—YORK

Load: 117 tons tare
Engine: Class "R" No. 2020

Distance		Actual	Average speed
miles		min. sec.	m.p.h.
0·0	DARLINGTON	0 00	—
3·1	Milepost 41	4 58	—
6·1	„ 38	7 57	60·3
7·1	„ 37	8 52	65·4
11·1	„ 33	12 18	69·8
		p.w. slack	—
14·1	„ 30	15 44	52·5
16·1	„ 28	17 38	62·1
21·1	„ 23	21 48	72·0
26·1	„ 18	25 59	71·7
29·1	„ 15	28 28	72·4
34·1	„ 10	32 25	76·0
39·1	„ 5	36 30	73·5
42·6	„ $1\frac{1}{2}$	39 23	72·9
44·1	YORK	41 25	—

The net time on this smart run was 40 min.

COMPARATIVE DIMENSIONS—CLASSES "R" AND "S"

Description		Class **"R"**	Class **"S"**
Cylinders dia. by stroke	in.	19×26	20×26
Coupled wheels dia.	ft. in.	6 10	6 1
Boiler			
Tubes	number	255	204
Outside dia.	in.	1¾	2
Length between tubeplates	ft. in.	11 10⅛	15 4⅛
Heating surfaces			
Tubes	sq. ft.	1383	1639
Firebox	sq. ft.	144	130
Total	sq. ft.	1527	1769
Grate Area	sq. ft.	20	23
Boiler pressure	lb. per sq. in.	200	200
Blast pipe			
Inside dia. of nozzle	in.	5	5
Adhesion weight	tons	35¼	46¼

⅛ in. lead, as in the piston valves of Class "R", but the valve travel in full gear was a fraction longer, $4\frac{21}{32}$ in. against $4\frac{11}{32}$ in. The boilers of both the "R" and "S" engines steamed well in heavy working conditions, but an anomaly is to be seen in the use of the same blastpipe orifice on both classes. Unless a locomotive is to be worked with a greater back pressure than is economical the diameter of the blast nozzle is *the* limiting factor of the entire performance, and it should be proportional, in some measure, to the steaming capacity of the boiler. But, as will be seen from the comparative table, although the "S" Class engines were given a greater heating surface and a larger grate area the blast nozzle was the same as that of the Class "R".

Technicalities apart, however, the Class "S" locomotives when they first appeared in 1899 were impressive beyond measure. Their beautiful lines were marred a little, at first, by the short cab fitted to engines 2001, 2002 and 2003 so that the engine could be accommodated on a 50 ft. turntable. At the time of their construction the North Eastern had no experience of such a long engine, and trouble arose from inadequate side clearances in coupled-wheel journals and on the rods. The driving wheels had flangeless tyres, so that the curves at Newcastle and York might be negotiated more readily, but for some time the class as a whole was a bit "touchy" so far as the running gear was concerned. As motive power units the Class "S" engines were designed to eliminate double-heading on the Newcastle-Edinburgh section with the heavy East Coast expresses. One would imagine that the original intention was to use the "S" engines, north of Newcastle, and the "R" Class on the southern division. It did not work out quite that way, for while the "Rs" were singularly free from trouble, the original "S" Class was rarely out of it. When a trial run was made in the summer of 1899 with a 350-ton train from Newcastle to Edinburgh, No. 2001 had to be held in severely over long stretches of the road as an eccentric was tending to heat. This test was made with a "special", run at "Flying Scotsman" timings, and the accompanying log was compiled by Mr. Rous-Marten. The make-up of the train—25 six-wheeled coaches—was such as to involve a considerably higher resistance in pounds per ton than that of the modern 350-ton "North Briton", and this should be taken in account when studying the details of the performance. The eccentric showed signs of heating at an early stage in the run, and in consequence no very high speeds were attempted.

N.E.R. 25-COACH "SPECIAL"—NEWCASTLE TO EDINBURGH

Load: 25 six-wheelers, 352 tons tare
Engine: Class "S" 4-6-0 No. 2001

Distance		Actual	Average speed
miles		min. sec.	m.p.h.
0·0	NEWCASTLE	0 00	—
		sig. stop	
1·7	Heaton	11 48	—
5·0	Forest Hall	17 59	32·0
7·7	Annitsford	21 59	40·5
9·9	Cramlington	25 03	43·1
11·5	Plessey	27 03	48·0
13·9	Stannington	29 56	49·9
16·6	Morpeth	33 08	50·6
20·2	Longhirst	37 26	50·2
23·2	Widdrington	40 59	50·7
25·6	Chevington	43 52	50·0
28·5	Acklington	47 16	51·2
31·9	Warkworth	51 14	51·3
34·8	Alnmouth	54 42	50·2
37·5	Longhoughton	57 58	49·6
39·4	Little Mill	61 06	36·4
43·0	Christon Bank	65 40	47·4
46·0	Chathill	68 39	60·2
49·2	Lucker	72 14	53·8
51·6	Belford	74 59	52·3
54·9	Smeafield	78 36	54·8
58·6	Beal	82 20	59·3
60·8	Goswick	84 47	53·9
63·5	Scremerston	88 17	46·3
		sigs.	
66·9	BERWICK-UPON-TWEED	95 15	—
0·0		0 00	—
5·6	Burnmouth	12 43	26·4
7·2	Ayton	15 04	40·9
11·2	Reston Junction	20 00	48·7
16·3	Grantshouse	27 24	41·4
21·0	Cockburnspath	33 06	49·5
23·7	Innerwick	35 46	60·8
28·4	DUNBAR	40 56	54·6
34·1	East Linton	47 39	51·0
36·7	East Fortune	50 52	48·6
39·7	Drem	54 27	50·4
44·3	Longniddry	60 28	46·0
48·0	Prestonpans	64 56	49·8
51·0	Inveresk	68 12	55·2
52·8	New Hailes	70 20	47·9
54·5	Portobello	72 20	51·0
		sigs.	
57·5	EDINBURGH (WAVERLEY)	79 09	—

Net times: Newcastle-Berwick, 85 min. Berwick-Edinburgh, 77 min.

Even taking the most charitable view of it one can hardly regard this trial run with No. 2001 as a very inspiring effort. How far that eccentric was really troubling them it is difficult to say. Rous-Marten made light of it, and wrote up the day's round in a most enthusiastic vein, even though they decided to return with no more than half the load. It is recorded that the engine was blowing off hard during the ascent of Longhoughton bank; the maximum speeds were 63½ m.p.h. at Beal and 65 down the Cockburnspath bank. On the return journey a maximum speed of 67 m.p.h. was attained at one point.

Engines 2004 to 2010 were completed at various dates between December, 1899 and June, 1900. No. 2006 was sent to the Paris Exhibition of 1900, and gained a gold medal; Nos. 2009 and 2011 were used for Royal train workings between York and Newcastle in the same year. Nevertheless, the class as a whole was not shaping as well as had been hoped and in December, 1900 the first engine of Class "S1" appeared, No. 2111. This could be described as a 6 ft. 8 in. version of Class "S", though on the larger variety Smith's patent piston valves were used again, and there were certain changes in the boiler. The distance between the tube plates was 16 ft. 2⅝ in., and fewer tubes were used—193 against 204 in Class "S". The total heating surface remained the same at 1,769 sq. ft. and the grate area was the same, namely 23 sq. ft. Again the diameter of the blast nozzle was 5 in. For the year 1900 the "S1" was a huge engine, and at the same time a most graceful one; in favourable conditions the five engines of this class proved very free runners. Rous-Marten compiled a number of logs with them, and on one of these a 300-ton train was taken up to Berwick in 66 min. 23 sec. from Newcastle start-to-stop, or 63 min. net, while on the moderate descending gradients of this route speeds exceeding 80 m.p.h. were reached. On the 1 in 170 gradient of Loughoughton bank the speed was sustained at 52½ m.p.h. Another interesting trial was made between Darlington and York with the up afternoon "Scotsman" when a load of 260 tons was run from the Darlington start to a signal stop at Waterworks Box—just outside York—in 40 min. 51 sec. start-to-stop. The distance is 43·9 miles, so that the engine made the notable average speed of 64·4 m.p.h. There was no exceptional maximum, but the generally high speed was well sustained throughout at 68 to 72 m.p.h.

The remaining four engines of Class "S1", Nos. 2112-5, were built at Gateshead in the summer of 1901, but No. 2115 was scarcely completed when No. 2116 came out, in August, the pioneer of the 0-8-0 heavy mineral engines. The "big-engine" spirit had certainly gripped the North Eastern locomotive department in earnest by this time, though with the enormous mineral traffic of the line there was ample justification for something larger than the "P1" 0-6-0. By 1901, it should be recalled, the London & North Western had been building 0-8-0 mineral engines for more than eight years. No. 2116 was the first of Class "T". One might have thought there was a case for some degree of standardisation of boilers between the "S" the "T" Classes; but while the boiler barrel was the same, with a distance of 15 ft. 4⅛ in. between tube plates, the "T" had the tube arrangements of the "S1", namely 193 tubes of 2 in. outside diameter. The firebox was smaller, with a grate area of 21·5 sq. ft.; this with the reduced number of tubes brought the total heating surface of the "T" down to 1,675 sq. ft., against 1,769 in the "S" The cylinders were 20 in. dia. by 26 in. stroke, with the Smith segmental-ring piston valves, 8¾ in. dia., and the diameter of blast nozzle was the usual 5 in. The coupled wheel diameter was 4 ft. 8 in. In outward appearance the original "T" Class were surely the most ornate mineral locomotives ever to be built in twentieth-century England. They were bedecked in the full passenger livery—like all other N.E.R. engines of the day—with brass-capped chimneys, polished brass safety-valve covers, and coat-of-arms on the sand boxes, and the deep brass collar at the join of the boiler and smoke box. Possibly they may have been equalled in splendour of appearance by the Churchward "28XX" 2-8-0s on the Great Western, after those engines received copper-capped chimneys, and the gartered coat-of-arms was put on to the tenders; but they can never have been surpassed, and with the co-operation of the Locomotive Publishing Company's artist, Mr. V. Welch, we have made No. 2122 the subject of the frontispiece plate, as a joint tribute to the North Eastern pre-eminence in mineral traffic and as a reminder of what a British heavy freight engine could look like 50 years ago.

The "T" Class 0-8-0s were grand engines. Some of their earliest duties lay in working coal trains from Stella Gill to Tyne Dock, over the Pontop and South Shields line. At the turn of the century the Stella Gill district, lying about a mile north-west of the main line at Chester-le-Street, was a concentration point for coal traffic brought down the various gravity operated inclines, and from Pelaw Colliery Junction it is a fairly level run of 11 miles to Tyne Dock. Towards the northern end the line begins to assume a gradually descending character, on a 1 in 250 for 2 miles, and there is an abrupt fall at 1 in 47 into the dock sidings. Over this route the "T" Class engines handled loaded trains of 1,200 to 1,300 tons. Being almost exclusively a mineral line, apart from the intersection with the Leamside route at Washington and the level crossing with the Newcastle-Sunderland line at Pontop Crossing, the coal trains usually got a good road, and on a typical run made in 1902, a train of 1,326 tons was worked from Stella Gill to Tyne Dock in 52 min., an excellent *average* speed of 21 m.p.h. In the reverse direction the "T" Class handled 60 empty coal wagons up the initial 1 in 47 out of Tyne Dock, and if wagons were available the empty trains were made up to 80 wagons before leaving for Stella Gill. Ten locomotives of Class "T" were built in 1901, their numbers being 2116-2125. These engines were followed by a series, otherwise identical, but with ordinary slide valves, built at Gateshead between March and June, 1902. These were known as Class "T1", and the numbers of the first ten were scattered, as follows: 130, 527, 1002, 1320, 1700, 1704, 1708, 1709, 1717, 1729. A further 30 of the piston valves engines were built in 1902-1904. This temporary hesitation in the use of the segmental-ring piston valves for all large North Eastern Locomotives is interesting, because after the dynamometer car was built one of the first series of tests carried out with it in July and August, 1906 was to determine the relative efficiency of the "T" and "T1" Classes in heavy mineral working between West Auckland and Tebay. In these trials the slide-valve engine had considerably the better of it.

The eight-coupled engines were put on to the heavy road over Stainmore in the summer of 1902, and by their introduction it was found that trains of 40 loaded coke wagons, with two brake vans, could be taken unassisted throughout to Tebay. Although it is stepping a little out of chronological order it will be of interest to refer at this stage to the dynamometer car trials of 1906, the results of which I have been privileged to examine by the courtesy of the Railway Executive. The engines concerned were the first "T1" to be built, No. 130, and a "T" of the first batch, No. 2125, and great care was taken to ensure that the two engines were in good and comparable condition. Five return trips were made with each engine; the load on the outward journey was 25 loaded coke wagons, one 20-ton brake van, and the dynamometer car, while on the return 36 empty wagons were hauled. The overall results were as follows:

TRIALS OF 0-8-0 MINERAL ENGINES

Engine number ... ... Engine class ... ... Type of valves	2125 "T" Smith's piston	130 "T1" Slide
Length of each return trip, miles	95½	95½
Average speed, m.p.h.	16·3	16·9
Average speed on rising gradients m.p.h.	13·8	14·0
Coal consumption lb. per mile	81·1	72·8
Evaporation lb. of water per lb. of coal	7·55	7·66
Engine mileage from general repair to start of test	10,113	15,924

In actual work done the road performance of the two engines was practically identical, except that the slide valve engine ran more freely downhill due to the valves lifting from their seats. To show something of the actual work done on the road I have prepared the diagrams on page 117, showing the performance between West

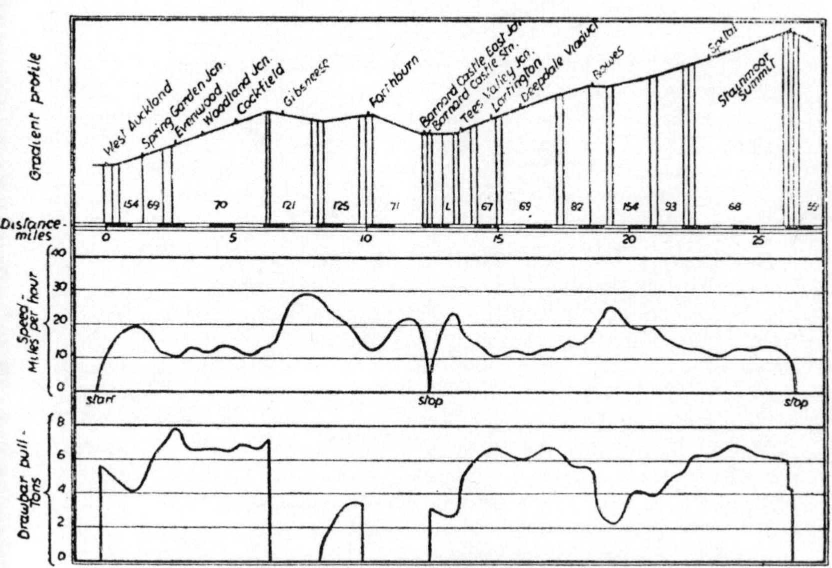

Test run with N.E.Rly. Engine Nº 2125, class "T", 8 coupled mineral type fitted with piston valves
Load:- 25 laden coke wagons, 20T. van, & dynamometer car.
Direction of run:- Westward from West Auckland to Stainmoor Summit.

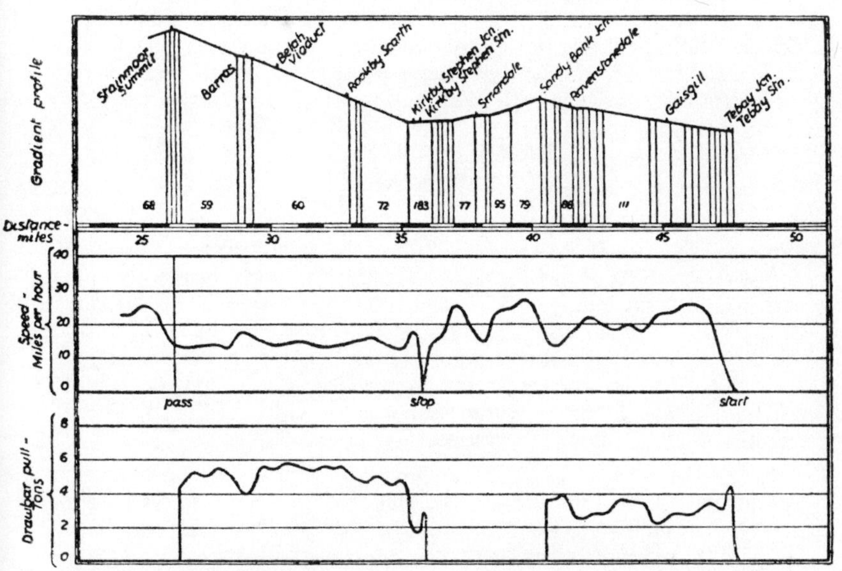

Test run with N.E.Rly. Engine Nº 130, class "T1", 8 coupled mineral type fitted with slide valves
Load:- 36 empty coke wagons, 20T. van, & dynamometer car.
Direction of run:- Eastward from Tebay to Stainmoor Summit.

Auckland and Stainmore on a typical west bound run, and between Tebay and Stainmore on the return trip. Following these trials it was perhaps only natural that slide valves were used on future engines of this type. Twenty more "T1" Class were built in 1907-8 and a further 20 in 1911, both batches at Darlington works. Thus of the non-superheater 0-8-0s there were eventually 40 with piston valves and 50 with slide valves.

In October, 1901, the General Manager of the N.E.R., Mr. George S. Gibb, with four senior officers of the company, sailed for the U.S.A. on a tour studying American railway methods. Apart from Philip Burtt, the Superintendent of the Line, all Gibb's associates on this tour were engineers: T. M. Newall, the Docks Engineer; C. A. Harrison, the Chief Engineer, designer of the coal loading staiths at Dunston and Blyth, and later, of the King Edward Bridge at Newcastle; and lastly Wilson Worsdell. Now Gibb was one of the most energetic, progressive and unorthodox of railway managers. In days when most of his contemporaries were inclined to stand aloof from public relations and to ignore criticism Gibb cultivated the friendship of serious-minded students of railway affairs like Sir William Ackworth, and enthusiasts like Norman D. Macdonald. There must have been times when Gibb had doubts about his "public relations" policy, for Macdonald had all the white-hot enthusiasm of his race combined with the persistence of an advocate—which indeed he was, practising brilliantly in Edinburgh. He had his own ideas on locomotive design, so much so that Gibb, in a moment of exasperation, once retorted: "When Macdonald providentially dies you will find big red letters of blood branded deep into his back:

BIGGER BOILERS
BETTER BRAKES".

Well, Gibb and Wilson Worsdell must have seen many big boilers during their tour of American railways, and it is said that Worsdell himself was very much impressed with the performance of the Atlantic type engines on the Reading Railroad, working the Atlantic City Flyers. When they returned, and Worsdell began to work up his impressions into a design for a "super" express passenger engine that should be the largest so far constructed in England, he would no doubt have found a ready supporter in Gibb, if for no other reasons than for those of prestige.

While the work of the "S1" engines had been good, and at times spectacular there is no denying the fact that for their size they were inferior to the "R" 4-4-0s; and for the speeds of that day the "Rs" were still adequate, even with the maximum loads. But it was certainly time to look ahead, and it so happened that when authority was given to proceed with the new "super" engines W. M. Smith, the Chief Draughtsman, was away ill, and not expected back for some little time. And so concerning the design of the new engines there has been handed down one of those stories that are inevitably connected with men of strong personality; it may be entirely apochryphal, but it is certainly amusing, and may have some foundation in fact. When he returned, so the story goes, the design of the new Atlantics was complete, and work was advanced in the shops; but Smith was strongly critical of many points, and Wilson Worsdell had some very difficult days! It is somewhat significant that when Smith himself was given authority to design some further Atlantics engines the result was very different. But whatever internal strains may have been set up within Gateshead offices and works during the building of the new engines of 1903—if indeed there were any—the outcome, so far as size and appearance went, was indeed magnificent. The first "V" Class Atlantic, No. 532, was completed in November, 1903, and was one of those rare locomotives in which a huge boiler is poised so as to give an appearance of elegance rather than an effect of mere, massive bulk. Whatever W. M. Smith thought, N. D. Macdonald must have rubbed his hands in delight at 532, on which the total heating surface was increased from the largest N.E.R. boiler so far, the "S1", with 1,769 sq. ft., to no less than 2,455 sq. ft., with a grate area of 27 sq. ft. The length between the tube plates was 16 ft. $2\frac{5}{8}$ in., as on the "S1" Class, but within a barrel 5 ft. 6 in. dia. there were 268 tubes (against 193), and the tube heating surface alone was 2,275 sq. ft. The cylinders remained 20 in. dia. but the stroke was increased to 28 in. The segmental ring piston valves were used, $8\frac{3}{4}$ in. dia., and the valve setting was the same as on the "S1" and "T" Classes. Again the blast nozzle was 5 in. dia. The weight of the engine alone in working order was 72 tons.

The completion of engine No. 532 was followed by an event of great importance and significance to the North Eastern locomotive department. It happened that Wilson Worsdell was a great personal friend of G. J. Churchward, and at that time the Great Western were busily engaged in testing the prototypes of their new standard engines. One can imagine that Worsdell was anxious to test the performance of his new Atlantic, and so on Saturday, 21st November, 1903 the Great Western dynamometer was attached to the 2.20 p.m. "Scotsman" from Kings Cross. H. A. Ivatt took advantage of this circumstance to secure a test record with his "magnum opus", and over the Great Northern line the train was worked by the pioneer large Atlantic, No. 251. The outcome of this northern visit was that the North Eastern built a dynamometer car of their own, a fairly close copy of the Great Western car, and from 1906 onwards a number of interesting tests were carried out. It was in this car, many years later, that the world record speed for steam traction was registered, the 126 m.p.h. of *Mallard* on Sunday, 2nd July, 1938.

Although scattered, and filling blank spaces in the locomotive lists, the numbers of the ten "V" Class Atlantics are known almost as well as if they had been names. After No. 532 they were completed at Gateshead works between January and October, 1904, in the following order: 532, 649, 784, 295, 1680, 742, 1753, 1776, 1792, 1794. Their performances will be discussed in the next chapter.

Two more freight designs come next for consideration. Class "U" is the tank engine equivalent of the "P1" goods: a 0-6-2 with 18¼ by 26 in. cylinders, 4 ft. 7 in. coupled wheels and the "C" Class boiler. As the designation suggests, the first engines of the class preceded the "V" Atlantics. Class "U" consisted of no more than 20 units, built at Darlington in 1902-3. A development of considerably greater importance followed in 1904 when Wilson Worsdell produced the "P2" Class of 0-6-0 tender engine. A further result of the visit to America in 1901 led to a general increase in the net loads conveyed on freight trains. The General Manager was anxious to use larger wagons; the 20-tonner became the North Eastern standard for mineral carrying, and although the process of development had necessarily to be a gradual one the gross freight train load increased from 276 tons in 1903 to 402 tons at the time of grouping. These were, of course, all-line averages. To be ready for heavier loads the "P2" goods engine of 1904 was given an enormous boiler, 5 ft. 6 in. dia., with a tube heating surface of 1,531 sq. ft.; the grate area was 20 sq. ft., and the working pressure originally 200 lb. per sq. in. The coupled wheels were 4 ft. 7 in. as in Class "P1" and the cylinders 18¼ in. by 26 in. With the safety valve columns arranged in a group of four, and encased in a huge brass mounting, they were "stocky" workmanlike engines. The boiler is pitched relatively low, and one hardly realises its girth until seeing a "P2" head-on. It is the only 5 ft. 6 in. boiler that I know of where the look-out from the cab is over the top!

Fifty engines of Class "P2" were built in 1904-5, 30 at Darlington and another 20 at Gateshead. Then in 1906 came a modified version, in which the cylinders were enlarged to 18½ in. dia. and the pressure lowered to 180 lb. per sq. in. This series, beginning with a batch of 20 built at Darlington in 1906, was designated Class "P3". Classes "P2" and "P3", as L.N.E.R. "J26" and "J27", are still at work in large numbers today. At the time of writing all 50 of the "P2" Class survive, and there are 115 of Class "P3". The last 35 of Class "P3" were built from 1921 onwards with superheaters and piston valves, but in many of these latter the superheaters have now been removed. Quite recently I had an opportunity of seeing at first hand the way these engines handle the local coal traffic into Blyth. From the north shed there I joined engine No. 65886, old 2384, one of the very last batch, built in 1923, and still retaining a superheater. With a brake van attached we went out tender first, past

Cambois Colliery and then westwards to join the passenger line to Newbiggin at Marcheys House just before reaching North Seaton. Thence we pushed on, in the face of an icy wind (!) to Ashington; then passing on to the metals of the Ashington Colliery Railway we drove northwards to Ellington Colliery, abreast of the East Coast main line between Longhirst and Widdrington stations. This outward run, of about 6 miles, was made in just half an hour. On arrival at Ellington our load was not quite ready, and some time was spent in marshalling; but after a stay of only half an hour we restarted for North Blyth with a substantial train of twenty 20-ton hopper wagons, five 10-tonners and the 20-ton brake van—a load of approximately 700 tons behind the tender. Over a route including several sharp rising gradients the engine handled this load most competently, without one single slip. On the grade past the colliery workings at Ashington she was going hard, with the lever one notch from full gear—about 60 per cent. cut-off—and the regulator full open. Naturally the exhaust was loud and fierce, but she was dead on her beat, and boiler pressure was well sustained. In spite of adverse signals, which nearly stopped us at Ashington station, we passed Marcheys House Junction, 4·6 miles from the start, in 22¾ min.; but immediately afterwards we were stopped at Winning Colliery Crossing. In general the coal trains get a fairly clear road and follow each other in close succession—all worked by "P3" Class engines. Short though it was this out-and-home trip was a most interesting example of present-day work of the class, though when first introduced the "P2" and "P3" engines took a big share in the long distance mineral workings, and in the main line freight traffic. A dynamometer car record of a "P3" on the Newport-Shildon line is discussed in Chapter Twelve.

The year 1906 was a momentous one for the North Eastern. It began with the resignation of Sir George Gibb, who left York to become Deputy Chairman and Managing Director of the London Underground railways; it later witnessed the death of W. M. Smith at the early age of 64. Smith died in harness, but not before he had produced his locomotive masterpiece. In addition to his pioneer engine No. 1619, "Smith compounds" were at work on the Midland and on the Great Central; but his two four-cylinder North Eastern Atlantics, 730 and 731, must be regarded as the finest of them all. Although the boilers were no more than 5 ft. diameter these engines were slightly heavier than Class "V" in total weight, and the nominal tractive effort was slightly greater too. The cylinder arrangement was the same as in Webb's "Jubilees" and "Alfreds" on the L. & N.W.R. with the high pressure cylinders outside—14¼ in dia. by 26 in. stroke, and the low pressure cylinder inside, and having the large diameter of 22 in., also with 26 in. stroke. It is interesting to compare the proportions of the boiler with that of the "V" Class:

N.E.R.: BOILERS OF ATLANTIC ENGINES

Class	V	4CC
Dia. of barrel	5 ft. 6 in.	5 ft. 0 in.
Type of firebox	round topped	Belpaire
Tubes, number	268	242
outside dia.	2 in.	2 in.
length between tubeplates	16 ft. 2⅝ in.	14 ft. 7¼ in.
Heating surface ... ... sq. ft.		
tubes	2275	1782
firebox	180	209 *
total	2455	1991
Grate Area... ... ... sq. ft.	27	29
Boiler pressure lb. per sq. in.	200	225

* Including 29 sq. ft. from cross water tubes.

Although the total heating surface was less in the case of the compounds the shorter length of tube would be an advantage in steaming, and the grate area was larger. In tests made with the dynamometer car between Newcastle and York the compounds proved markedly superior to the Class "V" engines. Piston valves were used for both high and low pressure cylinders, 7½ in. and 10 in. diameter respectively, and the valve gear for the high and low pressure cylinders was combined. The valve spindles were driven through rocking levers, and although the cranks for each high and low pressure pair on each side of the locomotive were diametrically opposite the valves moved in unison. This was made possible by the ingenious device of using inside admission for the high pressure cylinders, and outside admission for the low pressure. This provided the usual very direct exhaust passage from the low pressure cylinders to the blast pipe, and an equally direct passage from the high pressure exhaust to low pressure admission. The blast nozzle was 5½ in. diameter. Engine No. 730 had Stephenson's link motion, and 731 had Walschaerts gear—the only North Eastern engine to be so equipped. Engines 730 and 731 were also alone among the N.E.R. stud in having Belpaire fireboxes. The safety valve casing was strongly reminiscent of the earliest Midland compounds, being extended to include a third valve column.

These two engines were in very truth masterpieces of locomotive design: extremely powerful, as the dynamometer car records included in Chapter Eleven will show, and graceful to a high degree from whatever angle they were viewed. Yet, they were hardly completed before their famous designer was seized with a fatal illness, and he did not live to learn of their magnificent achievements on the road. It is no disparagement to the memory of Wilson Worsdell to say that with the passing of Walter Smith an era of North Eastern locomotive history came to an end. Clear thinking and forthright, it was once said of him, and rather quaintly, by the Minister of Jesmond Presbyterian Church, that his reports and engineering treatises were as good as a theological discourse for brilliance of reasoning. He will always be remembered by the Smith compounds, yet at the time of his death it could hardly have been foreseen that 190 more of the Midland version would be built twenty years later.

Chapter Ten

THE TRANSITION YEARS—WORSDELL TO RAVEN

IN the year 1906, apart from the two experimental compound Atlantics the North Eastern Railway had no more than 15 large express locomotives: ten "V" Class 4-4-2s and the five "S1" 4-6-0s. The brunt of the East Coast working was being borne by the 30 "R" Class 4-4-0s, so successfully that in 1906-7 a further 30 were constructed at Gateshead. Their numbers were:

Built 1906		Built 1907			
476	712	1026	1184	1217	1236
592	713	1042	1206	1223	1258
707	723	1051	1207	1232	1260
708	724	1078	1209	1234	1665
711	725	1147	1210	1235	1672

It would seem that Wilson Worsdell had not decided what his standard large engine was eventually to be, and like Churchward in his experimental days on the G.W.R., he built a well-tried moderate-powered design for general service while tests of larger engines continued. In this way the running department was furnished with a stud of wholly reliable engines, the road performance of which is well illustrated by the many logs tabulated in Chapter Eleven.

At the same time the original "S" Class, with certain modifications, was chosen as a standard for mixed traffic and express goods workings; 30 more were built at Gateshead in 1906-9, of which the first ten had wide splashers and were painted green. The last 20 had narrow splashers, and a raised running plate extending from the cab to the cylinder casings. The numbers of the "S" Class engines were as follows:

1900	**1906**	**1907-8**	**1908-9**
2001	726	738	750
2002	740	739	751
2003	756	741	752
2004	757	743	753
2005	760	744	754
2006	761	745	755
2007	766	746	756
2008	768	747	758
2009	775	748	759
2010	1077	749	762

[*R. J. Purves*

The 9.50 a.m. from Kings Cross to Edinburgh picking up water at Lucker troughs. Engine: 4-cylinder compound No. 731.

[R. J. Purves

10.0 a.m. Newcastle-Liverpool express (via Sunderland) near Pelaw, hauled by Class "R" 4-4-0 engine No. 1217.

[R. J. Purves

Eastbound train of coke empties near Stainmore summit: Class "P1" 0-6-0 No. 2068 banked in rear.

[Rev. T. B. Parley

3-cylinder compound No. 1619 on down Flying Scotsman near Benton Quarry.

[F. E. Mackay

12.30 p.m. Newcastle-Liverpool express on Wiske Moor troughs hauled by Class "V1" 4-4-2 No. 698.

Class "W" 4-6-2T No. 689 at Scarborough [*P. Ransome Wal*

Class "X" 3-cylinder 4-8-0T No. 1354. [*Locomotive Publishing Co.*

Class "Y" 3-cylinder 4-6-2T No. 1113. [*Locomotive Publishing Co.*

The final batch from 750 onwards had Westinghouse brake only, whereas the others were equipped for passenger working and were consequently dual fitted. It was on the last two batches that Worsdell tried the variable blastpipe and ash ejector used on several subsequent classes of North Eastern locomotive. This device was under the control of the driver, who could increase the blastpipe nozzle diameter when working heavily, and so reduce the draught on the fire. This was intended to lessen the amount of fire throwing, and waste of fuel; but from all accounts the ash ejecting part of the apparatus, although designed to break up any accumulation into the finest particles, did land the North Eastern in trouble from crops set on fire! The variable blastpipe and ash ejector first fitted experimentally to No. 1042 (Class "R") was fitted to several other engine classes when new, including the "Whitby tanks" and the "R1" express 4-4-0s; but it was not used after 1910.

The first five of the "Whitby tanks" were built at Gateshead in 1907. They were designed to cope with the very heavy gradients of the coastal route between Middlesbrough and Scarborough, where among other exceptional inclines there is the climb from Fyling Hall to Ravenscar, 3 miles at 1 in 39. These engines were originally built as 4-6-0s with 19 in. by 26 in. cylinders; 5 ft. 1 in. coupled wheels; a total heating surface of 1,312 sq. ft. and a working pressure of 170 lb. per sq. in. At first they were equipped with small coal bunkers having a capacity of no more than 2¼ tons; this proved inadequate, and at a later date was increased to 3½ tons and the locomotives were changed to the 4-6-2 wheel arrangement. They were appropriately Class "W", and their numbers ran from 686 to 695 inclusive. They had a monopoly of the passenger service over the coast line northwards from Scarborough for many years, and in 1920 and 1921 I used to see them pounding away up the banks with trains of four and five flat-roofed bogie coaches. Then they were well past their hey-day, and a Darlington driver who had sampled the Raven 4-4-4 tanks once remarked that the "W" Class were "more like dredgers than engines!". Nevertheless they served a useful purpose in their day, and at the time of writing the last survivor is still in service as station pilot at Hull Paragon.

A Worsdell tank engine design of more lasting significance was the Class "X" three-cylinder 4-8-0 introduced in 1909 for heavy shunting duties, in the hump yards alongside the river Tees between Thornaby and Middlesbrough, at Hull, and elsewhere. The possibilities of a three-cylinder simple engine of high tractive effort for this class of work had been demonstrated on the Great Central Railway, at Wath, where the huge Robinson 0-8-4 banking engines had been in use since 1907. But although producing an extremely powerful engine the North Eastern did not consider it necessary to have so large a boiler, and the Class "X" 4-8-0s had 67½ tons of adhesion weight against 77 on the Great Central 0-8-4s. On the Class "X" engines (L.N.E.R. Class "T1") the cylinders are 18 in. by 26 in.; coupled wheels 4 ft. 7 in. dia. and the boiler pressure 175 lb. per sq. in., giving the high nominal tractive effort, at 85 per cent. working pressure, of 34,080 lb. The moderate-sized boiler provides a total heating surface of 1,310 sq. ft. and the grate area is 23·65 sq. ft. Originally these engines had the variable blast pipe and ash ejector. As distinct from the Class "W" Whitby tanks, on which the springing of the coupled wheels was compensated throughout, to suit the very difficult running conditions of the coastal route, the coupled wheels of the "X" Class were fitted with uncompensated plate springs to all axles. One most interesting constructional feature of the "X" Class shunting engines was that the three cylinders and their associated valve chests were contained in a single casting, so foreshadowing the "monobloc" construction used many years later by Sir Nigel Gresley for his "V1" and "V3" 2-6-2 tanks, and for the "V2" heavy mixed traffic 2-6-2 tender engines. In those L.N.E.R. types, however, not only were the three cylinders and their valve chests cast integrally, but the smoke-box saddle was included as well. Wilson Worsdell did not go so far as this in his Gateshead-built engines of 1909. Six of the Class "X" 4-8-0s were built in 1909 and another four in 1910; their numbers were 1350 to 1359 inclusive. There is however a melancholy note about these engines, in that they were the last to be built new at Gateshead works. Owing to the limited space available, between the main line and the river, extensions to that historic works were not practicable, and as the space for extension *was* available at Darlington it had been decided to transfer all new construction from Gateshead. The last N.E.R. express engine to be constructed in the old works was the Class "R" 4-4-0 No. 1672, and she, appropriately enough, held for many years the record for the Darlington-York run—44·1 miles in 39 min. 34 sec., 67 m.p.h. average. The Class "X" engines proved most successful, and a further five were built by the L.N.E.R. at Darlington in 1925, Nos. 1656-1660. Thirteen of the class are still in service today as British Railways Nos. 69910 to 69922.

In the spring of 1953 I was privileged to see something of the present-day work of these historic engines, still engaged upon the very duties for which they were first designed 44 years ago. At the time of writing three of them are stationed at Stockton and eight others are at Newport; it was in the Erimus hump marshalling yards, alongside the river Tees and abreast of Newport shed, that I saw several of them hard at work. Normally there are four in continuous humping duties, two at the outward, and two at the inward hump. These directions relate to the flow of traffic into and out of Middlesbrough. Each engine is in continuous service for 24 hours at a stretch, and their bunker capacity of 3 tons of coal carries them "twice round the clock", save in exceptional circumstances during the winter months, when to help things out it is usually the practice to top the bunker up after the fire has been made up, and just before they leave the shed. Even after 24 hours' working they are not in the shed for more than 6 hours; more often than not, in keeping with the very smart shed working practice of the North Eastern Region, they are out again in not more than 2 hours.

The actual work they do on the humps is remarkable seeing that neither of the Erimus yards is mechanised to any extent. All point operation is by hand and the wagons are braked by shunters running alongside. Yet on a general average about 2,200 wagons are propelled over each hump in every 24 hours. Individual trains are mostly between 40 and 50 wagons, and the speed of humping is approximately 2 m.p.h. At the outward yard the reception roads are on a curve, and the steady performance of the 4-8-0 tank engines in starting their loads and maintaining the requisite humping speed without any slipping was impressive to see. Today, after more than 40 years' service, they are still giving an excellent account of themselves, in freedom from casualty, light repair costs, and long periods between successive shoppings. They remain non-superheated, though the variable blastpipe with which they were originally fitted has long since been removed.

From this point onwards in the story the emphasis so far as new construction is concerned naturally moves to Darlington. In 1907-8 four more of the Class "290" tank engine conversions were carried out, from 0-4-4 to 0-6-0, and in 1908 also a single conversion to the same class was done at Gateshead; but Darlington was mainly concerned with new freight engines in 1907-8, building 14 "P3" 0-6-0s, and 20 "T1" 0-8-0s in those two years. Principal interest, however, developed towards the end of 1908 when, for the first time since the "Tennants", Darlington was concerned with a new main line express engine, the "R1" Class 4-4-0. After the experiments with 4-6-0s and Atlantics the reversion to the 4-4-0 type was interesting and in many ways a confirmation of the outstanding success of the "R" Class. It is true that the 1906 trials with the dynamometer car had shown off the remarkable capacity of the compound Atlantics; but these latter were large and expensive engines, and it was perhaps only natural that Wilson Worsdell should be tempted to try a "super" "R". The cylinder and coupled wheel dimensions were the same in both the "R" and "R1" Classes, but the "R1" was provided with a 5 ft. 6 in. diameter boiler, a grate area of 27 sq. ft. and a working pressure of 225 lb. per sq. in. This increased the nominal tractive effort from 17,025 lb. to 21,900 lb., though the potential capacity of the "R1", with its much larger grate was more than the tractive effort might suggest. The "R1" Class had the variable blastpipe by which the orifice could be increased from 4¾ in. dia. to 7½ in., at the driver's judgment. The piston valves were no less than 10 in. dia. but fitted with the more modern spring rings, as in the "X" Class 4-8-0s, instead of the Smith segmental type. The valves themselves were above the cylinders, instead of below as in Class "R", but the drive was still by direct Stephenson's gear without the interposition of any rocking levers.

As originally built the engines were not superheated. The boiler barrel was relatively short, with a distance of only 11 ft. $3\frac{1}{8}$ in. between tubeplates, and with the tubes themselves 2 in. outside diameter, as in the much longer boilers of the "V" Atlantics, the steaming would naturally be very free. There was no lack of heating surface in spite of the short barrel. The 254 tubes contributed 1,579 sq. ft., and the firebox 158 sq. ft., making a total of 1,737 sq. ft. —nearly as large as that of the "S1" 4-6-0s. The grate was level at the back, and sloping at the front, after the Great Western fashion. That the "R1" Class was designed for hard work with the heaviest East Coast expresses, rather than high speed running with light trains, is suggested by the valve setting, arranged for equal cut-offs at either end of the cylinder as against equal leads. In a high speed engine the lead, with its effect upon "cushioning" at each end of the stroke, is the important factor; but one cannot have it both ways, and for getting away with heavy trains, and in climbing banks like Cockburnspath a greater power output is obtained by setting for equal cut-offs. The "R1s" had $1\frac{1}{8}$ in. lap, $4\frac{3}{32}$ in. travel in full gear, and in full forward gear the lead was $\frac{3}{16}$ in. on the fore port and $\frac{1}{16}$ in. on the back port. A final point about these remarkable engines, emphasising still further the kind of work they were expected to do, was the adhesion weight of *42 tons*. Wilson Worsdell evidently intended to have no trouble with slipping!

Technicalities aside, the "R1s" were, above all, superb looking engines. Although built at Darlington the second of the class, No. 1238, posed for the official photograph on the banks of the Tyne, as so many Gateshead-built engines had previously done; and in producing one of his delightful oil paintings Mr. F. Moore departed for once from his characteristic parkland setting, and gave us instead a distant view of the Newcastle quays. We are fortunate in being able to reproduce this beautiful picture as a frontispiece, and no further words of mine are needed in describing the appearance of the engine. I need only add that No. 1237-9 were completed at Darlington in 1908, and the remainder of the ten in 1909. They were put to work on the heaviest East Coast trains between York and Edinburgh, and took loads of over 400 tons unassisted between Newcastle and Edinburgh. Writing in the *Railway Magazine* for April, 1910, Mr. J. F. Gairns commented: "Since their introduction they have as nearly monopolised the principal Scotch traffic as their numbers would permit". Schedules were not fast by later standards. The down

"Flying Scotsman" was allowed 98 min. for the 80·1 miles from York to Newcastle and 149 min. for the 124·4 miles on to Edinburgh, where the working time of arrival was 6.8 p.m. against the public time of 6.15. On a particular run, No. 1239, with a gross load of 365 tons, left York 2¾ min. late and reached Newcastle on time despite a permanent way slack at Birtley. Then with a reduced load of 330 tons No. 1237 kept almost exact time to Edinburgh, arriving a few seconds before 6.8 p.m. A log of this run is tabulated herewith:

N.E.R.: THE "FLYING SCOTSMAN"

Load: 317 tons tare, 330 tons full
Engine: 4-4-0 No. 1237, Class "R1"

Distance		Actual	Average speed
miles		min. sec.	m.p.h.
0·0	NEWCASTLE	0 00	—
16·6	Morpeth	22 00	45·2
34·8	Alnmouth	40 39	58·5
46·0	Chathill	54 00	50·4
65·7	Tweedmouth	75 05	56·1
66·9	BERWICK	77 00	37·6
83·2	Grantshouse	103 45	36·6
87·9	Cockburnspath	109 15	51·3
95·3	DUNBAR	115 55	66·7
117·9	Inveresk	139 45	56·8
121·4	Portobello	143 15	60·0
124·4	WAVERLEY	148 30	—

This was a good run. The start was excellent, and the time out to Alnmouth is just nine seconds *faster* than my last footplate journey on "The North Briton", with a 365-ton load and an "A4" to haul it! After that the driver of No. 1237 had no need to hurry, and his average speed of 56 m.p.h. over the 19·7 miles from Chathill to Tweedmouth does not compare with the fast running regularly made over this stretch today. The tendency now is rather the reverse of that when the "R1s" were first introduced, and a run on the "Flying Scotsman" made just at the time this chapter was being written gave me times of 43½ min. to Alnmouth, 55½ min. to Chathill, and 74 min. 37 sec. to Tweedmouth—this with an "A3" and 500 tons. In North Eastern days, however, the slack through Berwick was very severe, to about 10 m.p.h., and the tractive ability of the "R1s" was amply needed in getting on the move again up the long bank to Burnmouth. That slack would be worth quite 3 to 4 min. compared with present running conditions, when I recently clocked an *average* speed of 56·7 m.p.h. over the 2·3 miles from Tweedmouth, through Berwick, to Marshall Meadows! Another fine run was made with engine 1237 on a dynamometer car test with the East Coast Royal Train. Starting from York, with 302 tons Sessay (18·0 miles) was passed in 21 min., speed having been sustained at 62 to 65 m.p.h. since Tollerton. The details of this trial show that no difficulty was experienced in maintaining the high boiler pressure of 225 lb. per sq. in. Further details of this run are included in Chapter Eleven, which is devoted to locomotive running in the 1900-1914 period.

Wilson Worsdell's last locomotive class, the "V1" Atlantic, actually appeared after his retirement, and considered by dimensions alone it exhibits some rather curious points. Presumably with a view to reducing maintenance costs the boiler pressure was no more than 180 lb. per sq. in., so that the basic comparative dimensions of the three two-cylinder "big engine" classes were:

Class		V	R1	V1
Cylinders	dia. by stroke in.	20 × 28	19 × 26	19½ × 28
Coupled wheel dia.	ft. in.	6 10	6 10	6 10
Boiler pressure	lb. per sq. in.	200	225	180
Grate Area	sq. ft.	27	27	27
Nominal Tractive Effort	lb.	23,200	21,900	19,870

But although the "V1" was the least powerful, on the above basis, it was nevertheless the heaviest, as some strengthening and deepening of the frames was made at the fore end. Both the original "V" Class and the "R1s" had the pressure lowered to 180 lb. per sq. in. when they were superheated, but that change was yet to come. The "V1" series was distinguishable from Class "V" not only by the deeper framing at the front end but also by the narrow splashers, following the style of the later "S" 4-6-0s. There were ten "V1s", numbered 696 to 705. Like the original "Vs" they were capable of hard work on the road, and they survived until after the second world war. In their original non-superheated condition they ran well, but somewhat naturally, due to their low tractive effort, they could not make much of a show on heavy banks. This characteristic is clearly shown in a run on the 2.20 p.m. up afternoon "Scotsman" from Edinburgh, timed by Mr. Cecil J. Allen and tabulated opposite.

It will be seen from the log that time was gained to Dunbar, but the ascent of Cockburnspath bank was very laboured, with an average of no more than 24·5 m.p.h. up the 4·7 miles to Grantshouse. A fast descent to Berwick followed, with a maximum speed of 72½ m.p.h., and the finest running on the second stage came after the maximum of 76½ m.p.h. down the Longhoughton bank, and a fast passage through Alnmouth Junction.

Wilson Worsdell retired on 31st May, 1910, and was succeeded by Vincent L. Raven, who had been Chief Assistant Mechanical Engineer for some 15 years. The new C.M.E. was an out-and-out North Eastern man, and one moreover who had taken the widest interest in all mechanical and electrical engineering activities. He had been prominent in developing the art of cab signalling to assist drivers in running their trains in fog; he had already been closely

N.E.R.: 2.20 p.m. WAVERLEY—NEWCASTLE

Load: 350 tons gross
Engine: 4-4-2 No. 697 Class "VI"

Distance		Schedule	Actual	Average speed
miles		min.	min. sec.	m.p.h.
0·0	WAVERLEY	0	0 00	—
3·0	Portobello	6	5 10	34·9
9·5	Prestonpans	—	12 45	51·4
17·8	Drem	24	22 00	53·8
29·1	DUNBAR	36	33 20	59·3
36·5	Cockburnspath	—	42 05	50·7
41·2	Grantshouse	53	53 35	24·5
46·3	Reston Junct.	59	59 05	55·6
51·9	Burnmouth	—	64 00	68·4
57·5	BERWICK	73	69 50	—
0·0		0	0 00	—
1·3	Tweedmouth	—	3 15	24·0
6·1	Goswick	—	9 10	48·7
15·3	Belford	18	19 05	55·7
23·9	Christon Bank	—	28 25	55·3
32·1	Alnmouth	36	36 50	58·4
41·3	Chevington	—	45 30	63·7
50·3	Morpeth	56	54 10	62·3
			sig. stops	
66·9	NEWCASTLE	78	75 30 NET	—

associated with the introduction of electric traction on Tyneside, and was later to be responsible for the electrification of the Newport-Shildon mineral line, which proved invaluable during the war years. Above all he was a strong and brilliant administrator. From the outset he established his headquarters at Darlington, using offices at North Road works until the magnificent new building on the Stooperdale estate was ready. Known locally as "Buckingham Palace" and standing well back from the Brinkburn Road, this remarkable edifice might well pass as one of the "stately homes of England". Everything that careful expenditure, architectural skill and good taste could do was done in its construction, and it remains a monument to the princely status of the North Eastern Railway and to the genius of its architect, Mr. W. Bell, of York. In the new organisation set up at Darlington Mr. A. C. Stamer, another 100 per cent. North Eastern man, was appointed Assistant Mechanical Engineer.

There were no immediate changes in policy, regarding locomotive design. The modern passenger and freight engines had their work well in hand, and the task of the C.M.E.'s department was to keep the motive power stud ahead of traffic requirements, instead of in a state of "catching up". The first new design to appear was the Class "Y" three-cylinder 4-6-2 tank engine. Arising from the success of the Class "X" humping engines, the three cylinder principle was now applied to a tank engine designed for the shorter coal-train hauls from the collieries to the ports. Since these were intended for work on the road rather than shunting the boiler was considerably larger than that of Class "X", with 1,648 sq. ft. of heating surface, and the cylinders were smaller—16½ in. against 18 in. on the Class "X". With a boiler pressure of 180 lb. per sq. in. the nominal tractive effort was 29,405 lb. They had all the traditional North Eastern external characteristics, including the huge polished safety valve casing, and on their side tanks they carried the large crest, as used on the tenders of the express passenger engines. Twenty of these fine engines were built as follows: (1910 batch) 1113, 1114, 1126, 1129, 1136, 1170; (1911 batch) 1174, 1175, 1176, 1179, 1180, 1181, 1182, 1183, 1190, 1191, 1192, 1193, 1195. Seventeen of them are still in service on British Railways, the majority working from Hull, Dairycoates shed.

The adhesion weight is 55½ tons and with very heavy trains sanding proved an important factor. At slow speeds below 10 m.p.h. engines of this class could sustain drawbar pulls of over 10 tons with efficient sanding; but on some tests made near Shildon with No. 1126, the engine slipped to a standstill on a bad rail when hauling a load of 864 tons up a gradient of 1 in 185 due to a defect in the sanding gear. One of the original requirements was an ability to haul loads of 1,000 tons at 20 m.p.h. on level track; this, the Class "Y" engines could accomplish comfortably. On the Shildon tests previously mentioned No. 1126 started a load of 864 tons from rest on a gradient of 1 in 148, and accelerated to 10 m.p.h. in just over half a mile.

In making provision for new express passenger motive power the relative merits of the existing large engines were considered, particularly with regard to the dynamometer car trials of 1906, referred to elsewhere; and on almost every count the compound Atlantics stood supreme. I have good reason to believe that matters went so far as the placing of orders for ten more of those engines, but that representations made at the very last minute led to a change, and eventually resulted in a three-cylinder simple being chosen instead. Engine building capacity at Darlington works was very fully booked up for the year 1911, for in addition to fourteen Class "Y" 4-6-2 tanks, there was an order for twenty more "T1" 0-8-0s, and the first of the new mixed traffic 4-6-0s were to follow. So, for the first time since the McDonnell régime, orders for North Eastern express passenger engines were placed with outside contractors. During 1911 the North British Locomotive Company built the first twenty of the new Atlantics, ten of Class "Z" using saturated steam, and ten of Class "Z1" with Schmidt superheaters. There were certain points of similarity in the chassis and the wheelbase dimension between the new "Zs" and the four-cylinder compounds; but these arose no doubt from the basic arrangement of having all three cylinders driving on to the leading coupled axle. The distance from the bogie centre to this leading coupled axle was 10 ft. 8 in. against 10 ft. 6 in. on the compounds. The three cylinders were $15\frac{1}{2}$ in. dia. on the saturated engines and $16\frac{1}{2}$ in. on the superheated ones, the stroke in each case being 26 in. The boiler pressures were 180 lb. per sq. in. for Class "Z" and 160 for the superheated "Z1s".

The saturated, or "Z" Class, had boilers similar to those of Class "V", but the tubes were not quite so closely packed. Instead of 268 tubes the "Zs" had 254, as in Class "R1", and so the total heating surface was reduced as compared with Class "V"—a total of 2,340 sq. ft. against 2,455. As in the Class "X" and "Y" three-cylinder tank engines the three cylinders and their valve chests were carried in a single steel casting; the piston valves were $7\frac{1}{2}$ in. dia., and the valve details were: $1\frac{3}{8}$ in. lap, $\frac{1}{16}$ in. lead, and the valve travel in full gear was $4\frac{19}{32}$ in. for the inside cylinder and $4\frac{15}{32}$ in. for the outside. The diameter of the exhaust nozzle was at first $4\frac{3}{4}$ in., but with a three-cylinder engine having six exhausts per revolution the capacity for steam flow through the blastpipe is greater so that direct comparison cannot be made with the two-cylinder engines preceding the "Zs". In the "Z1" engines a high degree of superheat was aimed at, giving a steam temperature of 640 deg. Fahr, at a working pressure of 160 lb. per sq. in. A large heating surface in the superheater was needed, 530 sq. ft., but despite this the ordinary tubes were so packed that the total heating surface, including superheater, was actually greater than that of the saturated engines. The boiler proportions, and the degree of superheat attained, were the subjects of experiments on the "S2" 4-6-0 engines, in 1912 and as the "Z1s" were modified as a result of these trials I will defer reference to the subsequent developments until the "S2s" have been introduced. In the meantime some interesting trials had been conducted with the second of the non-superheater "Zs", No. 709. The numbering of these engines, by the way, was not consecutive, the two original batches being as follows:

Class "Z"				Class "Z1"			
706 709 710	714 716 717	718 719	720 721	722 727 728	729 732 733	734 735	736 737

The valve motion was designed for a maximum cut-off in full gear of 65 per cent., as compared with 75 per cent. in Class "V1", and the first indicator trials of 709 showed that the engine could be worked in 15 per cent. cut-off (notch 1). It will have been noticed that the steam lap is longer on the "Zs" than on previous North Eastern engines, and the full gear valve travel of about $4\frac{1}{2}$ in., would be equivalent to something like $5\frac{1}{2}$ in. with a maximum cut-off of

75 per cent. A good port opening was obtained in 15 per cent., and after certain experiments with the valve setting a drawbar pull of 1·3 tons at 60 m.p.h. was obtained with this setting on the reverser. Some experiments were made with higher boiler pressure, 200 lb. per sq. in. and on one particular occasion the down "Flying Scotsman" was specially made up to a tare load of 536 tons for test purposes. This, however, required a coal consumption of 85 lb. per mile in working to a booked average speed of 51·2 m.p.h. from York to Newcastle. In general the performance of the engine may be judged from the average coal consumption of about 5½ lb. per drawbar horsepower hour. By present standards this would be considered high, but the working of the "Zs" was greatly improved by superheating. As a result of the trials of engine No. 709 it was considered that the coal consumption of non-superheated "Zs" would be, in general, slightly above that of the "V1" Class, which averaged 53 lb. per mile. It was expected, however, that the three-cylinder engines would show an over-riding advantage in repair costs.

Some thirteen years later, it was shown by some dynamometer car trials between Newcastle and Edinburgh that the "Zs" were considerably superior on all counts. This was a comparison of superheater engines of both the two- and three-cylinder type—701 versus 729. Sir Nigel Gresley gave very complete details in a paper read before the Institution of Mechanical Engineers in July, 1925, and supplemented this by certain details of mileages between repairs, and the effects of three-cylinder propulsion upon tyre-wear. Although they had three sets of Stephenson's link motion between the frames the "Zs" were popular at sheds with those responsible for maintenance, though in their mechanical simplicity and straightforwardness they were very free from troubles.

N.E.R.: ATLANTIC COMPARISONS

Class ... ... Type	"VI" 2-cylinder	"Z"* 3-cylinder
Average coal per D.H.P. hour on 1924 trials, lb.	6·15	4·6
Average water per D.H.P. hour on 1924 trials, lb.	4·52	3·73
Average mileage between repairs (whole class)	58,000	73,000
Average mileage before renewal of coupled wheel tyres	252,256	333,673

*When all three-cylinder engines were superheated the distinction "ZI" was dropped.

For superheater engines of 1912 vintage the above coal consumption figures are high—that of the "V1" exceptionally so. The original "Z1" Class, of which No. 729 was a member, had the Schmidt superheater, and the Schmidt type of piston valve ring may have been retained. The two engines in the 1924 trials had each run some 18,000 miles since last general overhaul at the time of the tests, and the results may have been affected by steam leakage past the valve rings. In any event, a sister engine, No. 733, gave some distinctly better results in comparative trials with Great Northern and North British Atlantics in 1923. Coal consumption or not, the three-cylinder Atlantics proved a magnificent investment to the North Eastern Railway. As revenue earners the work they came to do was prodigious; they were no trouble to maintain, steamed well, and rode luxuriously, so that it was not surprising they became universal favourites. They were faster engines than the "V" and "V1" Classes, and when the famous 43-min. timing from Darlington to York was revived in 1922 they did some most spectacular work on it. In 1935, prior to the introduction of the "Silver Jubilee" streamlined train, some high speed braking trials were carried out between Darlington and York; very rapid acceleration was needed to obtain the test speeds required, and a "Z" was attached to assist the Gresley Pacific concerned. Assist she certainly did, for the speed on certain sections reached 100 m.p.h.!

But when they were first introduced, in 1911, such speeding was a long way ahead, and the gruelling experience of the first World War had yet to be endured. So far as loads were concerned the Coal Strike of 1912 provided something of a curtain raiser. During that emergency, to reduce engine mileage the down "Flying Scotsman" incorporated the 2.5 p.m. from York to Newcastle, and called additionally at Darlington; the resulting loads were some of the heaviest that had then been witnessed in this country and on one occasion when Mr. Cecil J. Allen was fortunate enough to be a passenger, a "Z1", No. 732, made the magnificent run tabulated herewith:

N.E.R.: THE "FLYING SCOTSMAN"

Load: 77 axles, 502 tons tare, 550 tons full
Engine: Superheater 4-4-2 No. 732 Class "Z1"

Distance		Actual	Speeds *
miles		min. sec.	m.p.h.
0·0	YORK	0 00	—
1·6	Poppleton Junct.	4 25	—
5·5	Beningbrough	9 45	—
11·2	Alne	16 05	60
13·4	Raskelf	18 20	58½
18·0	Sessay	23 15	55½
22·2	Thirsk	27 30	62½
30·0	Northallerton	35 20	57½
33·7	Danby Wiske	39 15	61½
38·9	Eryholme	44 25	57½
41·5	Croft Spa	47 25	64½
44·1	DARLINGTON	50 15	—

*Maximum and minimum speeds by stop watch

At the close of 1911 Darlington works completed the first engine of the new superheated mixed traffic 4-6-0 type, Class "S2", No. 782. This was an enlarged version of the non-superheated Class "S", with a 5 ft. 6 in. diameter boiler, and the advantage of high degree superheating. The cylinders were 20 in. by 26 in. and the coupled wheels 6 ft. 1 in., but the boiler proportions were the subject of extended tests with engine No. 797 in 1912. The boiler pressure was at first only 160 lb. per sq. in. Like H. A. Ivatt on the Great Northern, Vincent Raven adopted superheating as a means of obtaining an engine of equivalent power with a lower boiler pressure than previously. At the same time he aimed at a high degree of superheat, and the "S2" engines were originally provided with no less than 545 sq. ft. of heating surface in the superheater elements. As originally designed superheat temperatures of about 575 deg. Fahr. were obtained on tests with engine No. 797; but better results were obtained after a number of the small tubes had been blocked up and the steaming of the engine was if anything improved. The desired superheat temperature of 640 deg. was obtained by this revised proportioning of the evaporation and superheating surfaces, and some modifications were afterwards made not only to the "S2" boilers but also to those of the superheater "Zs". The grate area on the "S2s" was 23 sq. ft., and the weight of the engine in working order 70¾ tons.

The "S2" Class was intended for true mixed traffic duty, and the rosters included cases of passenger working in one direction, and fast freight trains in the other. A favourite round trip from Newcastle was on the 12.30 p.m. Liverpool express as far as York, returning with the 3.50 p.m. Scotch goods. The last engine of the "S2" Class, No. 825, was selected for a trial of the "Stumpf" uniflow system of steam distribution. The object of this system was to avoid the reversal of direction of the steam flow in the cylinders, and to obviate the condensation that tends to occur. In the ordinary locomotive cylinder the steam enters and is exhausted through the same ports, whereas in the "Stumpf" layout exhaust takes place through ports in the middle of a long cylinder. The cylinder body needed to be nearly twice the length of a standard cylinder and the appearance of engine No. 825, as shown in the colour plate facing page 141, was highly unconventional for the year 1913, though it would cause little comment today, so far as exposure of "the works" is concerned. In 1913 comparative trials were run between engines 825 and 797 between Newcastle and York, but on the basis of these trials there appears to have been little to choose between the two engines. Both were completely master of the duties assigned to them, though it will be seen from the table overleaf that the coal rates were much better in hard slogging freight service than when running express passenger trains.

In ordinary service the "S2" engines steamed well, and handled loads in excess of 400 tons on trains like the down "Flying Scotsman". On one occasion No. 797 made a net time of 94 min. from York to Newcastle with a load of 440 tons. The fastest run I

TRIALS OF ENGINES 797 AND 825

Train	12.31 p.m. Newcastle to York		10.28 a.m. Newcastle to York		3.50 p.m. York to Darlington		1.52 p.m. York to Newcastle	
Engine	797	825	797	825	797	825	797	825
Average load, tons tare ...	223	262	339	341	791	800	376	396
Booked speed, m.p.h.	51·2	51·2	51·8	51·8	24·0	24·0	51·2	51·2
Average I.H.P.	698	733	801	726	640	581	798	757
Coal per mile, lb.	40·9	39·3	45·6	37·2	74	69·5	46·3	41·7
Coal per D.H.P., hr. lb. ...	5·35	4·6	4·65	4·02	3·26	3·28	4·5	4·2
Water per D.H.P., hr. lb. ...	32·8	31·4	31·4	30·1	23·6	23·8	29·2	29·3

have ever seen with one of them was made some years after the first World War when No. 798 made almost "even time" between Darlington and York with a load of 350 tons. The following is a log of the journey:

N.E.R.: DARLINGTON TO YORK

Load: 46 axles, 330 tons tare, 350 tons full
Engine: Class "S2" 4-6-0 No. 798

Distance		Actual	Speed *
Miles		min. sec.	m.p.h.
0·0	DARLINGTON	0 00	—
2·6	Croft Spa	4 55	53½
5·2	Eryholme	7 55	55
10·4	Danby Wiske	13 05	66
14·1	Northallerton	16 50	61
17·5	Otterington	20 05	—
21·9	Thirsk	24 15	66
26·1	Sessay	28 15	—
28·0	Pilmoor	30 00	67
30·7	Raskelf	32 25	70½
32·9	Alne	34 15	74
34·4	Tollerton	35 30	—
38·6	Beningbrough	39 20	68
42·5	Poppleton Junct.	43 00	
—		p.w. slack	
44·1	YORK	46 25	

Net time 45¾ min.
*Max. and min. speeds by stop watch.

In 1913 the first thirty engines of the new superheater 0-8-0 goods class were completed at Darlington, but I am leaving consideration of these willing, hardworking machines to the chapter concerned mainly with the war period, and I will conclude the present chapter by reference to Raven's new 4-4-4 passenger tank engines of 1913. They were designed to replace the four-coupled passenger tender engines on the longer distance branch trains radiating from Darlington. The 4-4-4 wheel arrangement was chosen to provide equally good riding qualities in both directions of running, and the cab was designed to give good protection to the men when running bunker first. It was originally intended to use them on the Stainmore route, but so far as I know they never worked regularly to Kirkby Stephen or Tebay. The Class lettering having reached "Z", these new engines took the vacant letter "D", previously used for the Worsdell compound 2-4-0s. In the 4-4-4 tanks the three cylinders were 16½ in. by 26 in.; coupled wheels 5 ft. 9 in.; the relatively small boiler provided a total heating surface of 1,332 sq. ft. and the working pressure was the usual 160 lb. per sq. in. The total weight in working order was 84¾ tons, of which 39¾ tons were available for adhesion. They were free-running engines, though rather prone to roll at times. They made short work of the gradients on the coastal route from Saltburn to Whitby, and also did excellent work on the residential trains from Leeds. Twenty of them were built in 1913-4 numbered 2143 to 2162, and another 25 followed in 1920-2. During L.N.E.R. days they were converted to 4-6-2s (Class "A8"); they are all still in service, and are doing excellent work. The rebuilds are among the smoothest riding engines I have ever travelled on.

Chapter Eleven

LOCOMOTIVE PERFORMANCE, 1900-1914

IN studying the day-to-day running of North Eastern locomotives between 1900 and 1914, and comparing the standards then maintained with those of today, certain operational factors must be taken into account quite apart from the changes that have taken place in locomotive design. It is not my own intention to make any such comparisons, but those readers who are familiar with present-day running will inevitably make comparisons of their own. First of all as to speed, the wheel had certainly come full circle since Professor Foxwell chided the North Eastern for leaving the hardest work of the East Coast service to the Great Northern. In 1900 the North Eastern pressed for an acceleration of the "Flying Scotsman", and when the Great Northern and North British refused, the North Eastern referred the dispute to the Board of Trade. Judgment was made in favour of acceleration, and from November of that year the "Flying Scotsman" was booked into Edinburgh at 6.15 p.m. instead of the previous 6.30 p.m. While this judgment was a triumph for the North Eastern it was also significant of the way things had changed at Kings Cross since the days of F. P. Cockshott.

Apart from this, from 1902 onwards, the fastest North Eastern running was made on trains apart from the East Coast partnership, such as the forerunner of the present "North Briton", which was booked to run the 80·6 miles from York to Newcastle, via the High Level Bridge, in 82 min. start-to-stop. Then, in 1904, came the 44-min. run from York to Darlington of the 5.30 p.m. from Kings Cross. The fastest running on the East Coast service was with the night expresses including some from York to Newcastle in 90 min. with heavy sleeping car trains. In general locomotive performance could be described as steady rather than spectacular. No official encouragement was given to drivers to make up lost time, indeed, any attempt to do so over the North British section of the route would probably have led to a reprimand. In presenting this general survey of running I am much indebted to the kindness and enthusiasm of Mr. J. Mawson Rounthwaite, of Belford, Northumberland, who has put at my disposal a magnificent collection of logs that he compiled while in the service of the North Eastern Railway. To these I have added some notable journeys clocked by Messrs. Rous-Marten, Cecil J. Allen, and R. J. Purves, while to these details of running are added those of engine performance recorded in the North Eastern dynamometer car, including some remarkable work by the 4-cylinder compound Atlantic No. 730.

North Eastern engine performance in that period was characterised generally by vigorous starts and rapid approaches to stopping stations. Drivers appear to have relied on the superior power of the Westinghouse brake, as compared with that of the vacuum brake, and such a time as 4 min. 55 sec. over the 5·5 miles from Beningbrough to the stop in York station would nowadays be regarded as somewhat venturesome. Even on leisurely schedules like that of the down "Flying Scotsman" from York to Newcastle—97 min.—the starts would be vigorous, even though subsequent speeds over the level stretches of the line did not greatly exceed 55 m.p.h. Over the North British line maximum speeds on the Cockburnspath bank were usually restrained to about 70 m.p.h. and the work over this section was greatly hampered by comparison with present-day practice by the exceptionally severe slack to 5 m.p.h. through Berwick station. In the earlier years of this review the main line north of Ferryhill was free from colliery troubles; but the first occurrence of the subsidences that were to be such a handicap for nearly thirty years between Ferryhill and Newcastle came just before the outbreak of the first World War. The older approach to Newcastle involved no more than the handicap of longer mileage; the slack through Gateshead was no more severe than the present one over King Edward Bridge Junction. The new bridge itself was opened in 1906.

Vincent Raven was responsible for locomotive running, and as early as 1896 he was giving very serious attention to cab signalling apparatus to assist drivers in foggy weather. The earliest arrangement provided an audible indication only when the signal was at danger. It consisted of a trip arm, after the style of the modern automatic train stops on London Transport lines, but mounted in the "four-foot", and connected to the gear for actuating the semaphore signals. One of these stops was installed at *every* signal along the line, "distants" and "homes" alike, and when the signal was in the warning, or danger position the stop was raised. In this position it struck a pendulum lever carried on the locomotive and the movement of this lever caused a warning whistle to sound in the cab. It was open to criticism that the lever, or stop might be broken by the force of the impact at high speed, and that if from any cause the trip device in the track had been broken no warning signal would be received. No indication was given when the signal was clear. In actual practice, however, the stops had been so carefully and successfully designed that breakages were practically unknown, and the enginemen came to place complete trust in the integrity of the apparatus. Long stretches of the main line were equipped, and many express passenger and fast freight engines had the warning gear in their cabs. In later years Raven developed an electrical system using ramps which gave a most elaborate system of visual signals in the cab, even to the extent of indicating the route to be taken at junctions. It appears to have been very successful, but its use was discontinued soon after

[*Courtesy: H. W. Davis*

Wilson Worsdell:
C.M.E. 1890-1910.

[*British Railways*

Sir Vincent Raven:
C.M.E. 1910-1922.

[*British Railways*

A. C. Stamer:
Acting C.M.E. 1915-1919.

[*British Railways*

J. H. Smeddle:
Loco. Running Superintendent.

[R. J. Purves

The down Flying Scotsman exchanging mailbags at Lamesley: engine No. 1680 Class "V".

[R. J. Purves

12.30 p.m. Liverpool-Newcastle express passing Low Fell, hauled by "S2" class 4-6-0 No. 797.

No. 2259: Class "T2" 0-8-0. [*Locomotive Publishing Co.*

No. 911: Class "S3" 3-cylinder 4-6-0. [*O. S. Nock*

No. 901: Class "T3" 3-cylinder 0-8-0. [*Locomotive Publishing Co.*

2.20 p.m. ex-Waverley, up "Scotsman" passing King Edward Bridge Junction, hauled by engine No. 728 Class "Z1".

[*R. J. Purves*

TABLE I. N.E.R.: 9.38 a.m. YORK—NEWCASTLE

Engine No. ... / Engine Class ... / Load tons E/F ...		1523 "J" 100/105		1870 "Q1" 100/105	
Distance		Actual	Speeds *	Actual	Speeds *
miles		min. sec.	m.p.h.	min. sec.	m.p.h.
0·0	YORK ...	0 00	—	0 00	—
1·6	*Poppleton Junct.* ...	3 35	26·9	3 27	27·8
5·5	Beningbrough ...	8 04	52·1	7 37	54·8
11·2	Alne ...	13 34	62·2	12 53	65·1
13·4	Raskelf ...	15 37	64·3	14 47	69·5
16·1	Pilmoor...	18 17	60·8	17 26	61·2
18·0	Sessay ...	20 13	59·0	19 15	62·8
22·2	Thirsk ...	24 19	61·5	23 07	65·3
26·6	Otterington ...	28 35	62·0	27 07	66·0
30·0	NORTHALLERTON ...	31 52	62·0	30 20	63·5
33·7	Danby Wiske ...	35 22	63·5	33 45	64·9
38·9	Eryholme ...	40 18	63·2	38 27	66·4
41·5	Croft Spa ...	42 37	67·6	40 47	67·0
44·1	DARLINGTON ...	44 59	66·2	43 18	62·2
49·5	Aycliffe ...	50 27	59·3	48 52	58·3
54·3	Bradbury ...	55 00	63·4	53 33	61·4
57·0	Ferryhill ...	57 38	61·4	56 18	58·9
61·9	Croxdale ...	62 10	64·8	61 10	60·5
66·1	DURHAM ...	66 45	54·9	65 44	55·3
70·0	Plawsworth ...	71 10	53·0	70 19	51·1
71·9	Chester-le-Street ...	72 49	69·1	72 00	67·5
74·7	Birtley ...	75 14	69·6	74 39	63·5
76·3	Lamesley ...	76 36	70·5	76 14	60·6
77·6	Low Fell ...	77 38	75·4	77 23	67·8
78·9	Bensham ...	78 55	60·8	78 46	56·3
		p.w. slack		p.w. slack	
80·0	Gateshead ...	80 39	—	80 24	—
80·6	NEWCASTLE ...	82 06	—	82 05	—

*Average speeds station-to-station

grouping. So we come to the runs themselves, most of which were timed by Mr. J. Mawson Rounthwaite.

To open the ball, there are firstly two runs on the train we now know so well as the "North Briton". Then, as now, it was timed fast, but in those earlier days the restaurant car was not attached until Newcastle and the load from York was correspondingly lighter. It was an ideal job for a "single"; in studying the log in Table I it will be seen that the start was brisk, and that a steady and uniform speed was maintained north of Beningbrough until there came a fast concluding run down into the Team Valley with an average speed of 75·4 m.p.h. between Lamesley and Low Fell. The driver had time in hand to offset the engineering slack near Bensham and reached Newcastle "on the dot". Rous-Marten timed a run that was considerably faster in the earlier stages, with engine No. 1517, and the same load. The start was brilliant, passing Beningbrough in 7 min. 11 sec., and speed then averaged 68·4 m.p.h. throughout to Darlington. Adverse signals slowed them down passing Darlington itself, where the time was 41 min. 3 sec. from the start at York, and with easy running afterwards the total time to Newcastle was 80 min. 48 sec. On another trip with a "single", engine No. 1521 with a load of 130 tons, dense fog prevailed; yet with the Raven cab signalling apparatus in action this second driver ran with such confidence as to pass Raskelf in 14 min. 19 sec. from York, and after a signal stop at Sessay Wood Junction recovered to make an average speed of 66·3 m.p.h. from Thirsk to passing Darlington. In the companion log in Table I the big 7 ft. 7 in. coupled engine had an easy task, and kept the precise time that was characteristic of the train of that period. At that time it did not originate at Leeds, as it has done for so long now; it ran in connection with the 5.15 a.m. newspaper express from Kings Cross and provided an 8¼-hour service from London to Edinburgh.

Details of some contemporary runs with heavy East Coast expresses are given in Table 2. The "Flying Scotsman", leaving York at 2.3 p.m., was then allowed 97 min. to Newcastle, and the "Q" Class engine No. 1929, in the first column, produced the usual excellent start. Moderate speed followed over the faintly adverse stretch to Darlington; but after the signal check near that station some brisk running was made from Durham down into the Team Valley, with an average speed of 66 m.p.h. from Plawsworth to Low Fell. There were no troubles from colliery subsidences at that time, and maximum speeds in the neighbourhood of Lamesley often reached nearly 80

TABLE 2. N.E.R.: YORK—NEWCASTLE

Train		2.3 p.m.	11.57 p.m.	2.3 p.m.
Engine No.		1929	1680	2013
Engine Class		Q	V	R
Load tons tare		308	325	355
Load tons full		330	345	375
Distance		Actual	Actual	Actual
miles		min. sec.	min. sec.	min. sec.
0·0	YORK	0 00	0 00	0 00
1·6	Poppleton Junct.	—	5 24	—
5·5	Beningbrough	9 28	10 29	9 10
11·2	Alne	15 28	16 40	15 10
16·1	Pilmoor	21 27	21 45	20 14
22·2	Thirsk	28 16	27 58	26 35
30·0	NORTHALLERTON	37 00	35 45	34 36
33·7	Danby Wiske	41 05	39 26	38 22
38·9	Eryholme	46 38	44 36	43 42
41·5	Croft Spa	49 23	47 08	46 20
		sigs.		
44·1	DARLINGTON	52 20	49 41	48 56
				sigs.
49·5	Aycliffe	59 37	55 51	56 20
57·0	Ferryhill	69 33	64 04	66 55
61·9	Croxdale	75 00	68 50	72 13
66·1	DURHAM	79 51	73 18	77 10
				sigs.
70·0	Plawsworth	84 40	78 23	82 20
71·9	Chester-le-street	86 28	80 08	—
74·7	Birtley	89 04	82 36	88 07
77·6	Low Fell	91 35	85 02	91 06
78·9	Bensham	92 52	86 18	92 36
		sigs.		sigs.
80·6	NEWCASTLE	96 42	89 33	97 15
Booked time	min.	97	90	97
Net time	min.	94½	89½	91¾
Average speed Alne to Croft Spa		54·4	59·7	58·4

m.p.h. The second run in Table 2 was on the 8.15 p.m. Aberdeen "sleeper", and hoar frost on the rails caused serious slipping in the first mile or so out of York. After that the big Atlantic got away well, and made the fastest time of all three runs between Alne and Croft Spa. There was some free running north of Durham on this trip with an average speed of 68·6 m.p.h. from Plawsworth to Low Fell, and the 90-minute timing was in the end maintained. The third run was a grand effort by an "R" Class 4-4-0 on the "Flying Scotsman", with a load of 375 tons. Although in contemporary writings these engines received most attention from their running on the fast 1.9 p.m. express from Darlington to York they really bore the brunt of the East Coast workings for many years, and as dividend-earners on those heavy, well-patronised trains they can have had few rivals. On the journey detailed in Table 2, No. 2013, despite two signal checks, was so comfortably on time that no unduly high speed was necessary in the concluding stages.

We now come to the very interesting stretch of line north of Newcastle, and in Table 3 are set out details of eight non-stop runs to Edinburgh. While these include a variety of engines one could not say that they present a comparison between the capacities of the locomotives in question, as the Atlantics and the 4-6-0s were no more than lightly loaded. Runs 1, 2, 4 and 5 were on the fast morning express from York, at different periods in its history when changes in the timing will be noted. In passing it is interesing to note that on the present 132-min. schedule of this service the load is strictly limited to a maximum of 350 tons, even though such large and modern locomotives as the "A1" and "A4" Pacifics are used for its haulage. On run No. 1 in Table 3 the driver of No. 2115 was the great Tom Blades, of Gateshead, who had fired No. 1620 on the last night of the Race to Aberdeen, and who drove No. 2400 *City of Newcastle* on the dynamometer car trials between Kings Cross and Doncaster in 1923. His run with No. 2115 was made in 1905, and with so light a load the effort needed was small. Speed averaged 64 m.p.h. along the undulating road from Longhirst to Alnmouth, and the racing stretch from Christon Bank to Beal was taken at 67·2 m.p.h With 72 min. left for the 57·5 miles from Berwick to Waverley there was no need for hurry, and the relatively easy time of 6 min. 53 sec. for the 5·1 miles from Reston up to Grantshouse will be noted.

A run with a Class "R" engine appears in the next column; it was very similar except that some rather faster work was done after the Ayton slack. There is, also, a very close similarity to be seen in the running times made by the smaller-wheeled 4-6-0, No. 2006 of Class "S", on the night express in column 3, though again such a relatively light load would not be likely to test the capacity of the engine seriously. The fourth run, with a non-superheater "Z" Class engine, was timed at a later date by Mr. Cecil J. Allen. It shows

TABLE 3.

N.E.R.: NEWCASTLE—EDINBURGH

Run No.		1	2	3	4	5	6	7	8
Train		11.18 a.m.	11.10 a.m.	4.47 a.m.	11.14 a.m.	11.18 a.m.	4.47 a.m.	3.41 p.m.	3.48 p.m.
Engine No.		2115	2027	2006	721	532	730	1232	2017
Engine class		S1	R	S	Z (NS)	V	4CC	R	R
Load tons E/F		165/175	170/180	180/190	208/220	242/260	250/265	297/315	315/335
Distance miles		min. sec.	min. sec.	min. sec.	min. sec.	min. sec.	min. sec.	min. sec.	min. sec.
0·0	NEWCASTLE	0 00	0 00	0 00	0 00	0 00	0 00	0 00	0 00
1·7	Heaton	3 53	3 52	3 50	—	4 48	4 00	4 20	4 02
5·0	Forest Hall	8 33	8 30	8 25	—	10 45	8 47	9 27	9 17
9·9	Cramlington	14 19	14 35	14 15	14 05	16 55	14 38	15 45	16 02
—		—	p.w.s.	—		—	—	—	—
13·9	Stannington	18 19	19 22	18 24	—	20 53	18 18	20 00	20 47
16·6	MORPETH.	21 03	22 25	21 20	20 30	23 37	21 18	22 53	24 02
20·2	Longhirst	24 59	26 31	25 05	—	27 22	—	—	28 14
25·6	Chevington	30 10	31 56	30 15	30 05	32 32	32 10	32 30	34 12
31·9	Warkworth	35 56	38 02	36 00	—	38 20	38 45	38 35	40 57
34·8	ALNMOUTH	38 36	40 47	38 45	38 20	40 57	41 50	41 20	43 57
37·5	Longhoughton	41 14	43 23	41 25	—	43 30	44 35	43 52	46 49
39·4	Little Mill	43 33	45 42	43 50	—	45 44	47 22	46 11	49 52
43·0	Christon Bank	47 09	49 25	47 40	46 50	49 17	—	—	54 06
46·0	Chathill	49 41	51 50	50 18	—	51 43	54 10	52 35	56 52
51·6	Belford	54 56	56 57	55 50	54 55	56 33	59 35	57 56	62 42
58·6	Beal	61 04	62 56	62 25	—	62 12	66 00	64 02	69 16
65·7	Tweedmouth	68 17	69 57	70 20	67 50	68 56	73 55	71 15	77 07
66·9	BERWICK	69 49	71 17	71 55	69 30	70 25	76 07	73 10	78 40
72·5	Burnmouth	79 04	79 50	80 57	78 00	79 38	86 32	84 08	89 17
74·1	Ayton	80 59	81 40	82 52	—	81 40	88 40	86 13	91 34
—		—	p.w.s.	—	—	—	—	—	—
78·1	Reston	85 13	86 30	87 00	83 50	85 58	93 01	90 43	96 06
83·2	Grantshouse	92 06	93 02	93 20	89 45	93 00	99 32	97 34	102 57
87·9	Cockburnspath	97 19	97 45	98 15	94 40	98 19	—	—	108 03
90·6	Innerwick	99 51	100 02	—	—	100 35	—	—	110 20
—					—	p.w.s.	—	—	—
95·2	DUNBAR	104 18	104 25	105 17	101 25	105 37	112 08	108 22	115 00
106·6	DREM	116 23	115 45	—	113 20	116 17	123 54	119 26	128 19
111·2	Longniddry	121 26	120 32	123 05	—	120 47	128 47	124 22	133 52
—		p.w.s.	—	—	—	p.w.s.	—	sigs.	—
117·9	Inveresk	130 11	127 10	—	—	128 00	p.w.s.	133 13	141 17
—		sigs.	—	—	sigs.	—	—	sigs.	—
121·4	Portobello	139 51	130 30	133 40	130 20	131 52	142 34	138 13	145 04
—		sigs.	p.w.s.	p.w.s.	—	p.w.s.	—	sigs.	—
124·4	WAVERLEY	149 30	135 39	139 23	134 45	137 02	148 14	162 33	149 57
	Booked time min.	142	140	143	138	142	148	149	152
	Net time min.	136½	133	138½	133¼	134	144	140	150

the fastest climbing out of Berwick, which, in company with all the other runs in this table followed the 5 m.p.h. slack then enforced through Berwick itself. Speed was worked up to 43½ m.p.h. on the 1 in 190 leading to Burnmouth, though even this would provide no great tax with a load of 220 tons. The times made by two further Atlantics may be compared in columns 5 and 6: a "V", No. 532, on the fast morning express, and the Smith compound No. 730 on the 4.47 a.m. sleeper. The compound made a good start, but afterwards the driver spun out the longer time allowance, which was scheduled with this train in 1907, to reach Waverley within a few seconds of exact punctuality, albeit after a somewhat dull run. The "V" was, for some reason, very slow in starting out of Newcastle; but after Morpeth normal speed was run, and some really fast running followed after the ascent of Longhoughton bank. Speed averaged 72½ m.p.h. from Christon Bank to Beal, and Mr. Rounthwaite tells me that the maximum speed was almost 80 m.p.h. on the descent from Belford. After passing Berwick practically on time nothing exceptional was needed to Edinburgh.

Lastly, there are two runs with "R" Class engines on the "Flying Scotsman". Mr. Rounthwaite was on the footplate of No. 1232; that engine was then relatively new from the shops and in magnificent form. The train was 7 min. late from Newcastle, but the driver was keen to make up time, and eventually made a net time practically equal to the fastest pre-1914 schedules of the 11.18 a.m.. Even the "Scotsman", with its heavy load, was allowed no more than 21 min. to pass Morpeth and although 40 per cent. cut-off was used up Forest Hall bank nearly 2 min. were dropped. Excellent running followed, with an average of all but 60 m.p.h. from Morpeth to Berwick, even though the approach to Berwick was very slow due to fog. The engine was pounded hard up the 1 in 190 following the 5 m.p.h. slack, again on 40 per cent. cut-off, and then after a minimum speed of 41 m.p.h. at Grantshouse the Cockburnspath bank was descended more freely than usual, without brake applications. Passing Longniddry, 111·2 miles, in the excellent time of 124 min. 22 sec. a punctual arrival in Waverley seemed almost certain; but a series of checks followed culminating in a dead stand at Abbeyhill Junction for 12 min. Although having to restart this heavy train on the 1 in 78 gradient into Calton Tunnel Mr. Rounthwaite tells me that No. 1232 lifted her load cleanly away. It would be difficult to find a better example of heavy load haulage by a Class "R" engine than this fine run.

The comparison trip in Column 8 was made in 1906 in conditions as unfavourable as could be imagined. The driver had not got his regular engine; the substitute was not in the best of condition, and there was a very strong north-west wind going, which naturally hampered the running right through Northumberland. An extremely vigorous start was made out to Forest Hall—too vigorous indeed, as pressure dropped back and the boiler had to be nursed. But the nursing was to some purpose, for after Berwick the climbing to Grantshouse was slightly faster than that of No. 1232, and with a clear road time was comfortably in hand from Dunbar onwards. In the adverse circumstances, this again was a very good run.

Table 4 includes details of some further journeys north of Berwick. No. 2022, another "R", was working the *fourth* part of the 8.15 p.m. from Kings Cross in August, 1905, just prior to "The Twelfth". The preceding train had left Newcastle only 4 min. previously so, and the start was somewhat delayed. But from a signal stop at Killingworth No. 2022 ran the 61 miles to Berwick in 60 min. 25 sec. start-to-stop, having averaged 71 m.p.h. over the 17¾ miles from Christon Bank to Goswick. The train ahead must also have been running extremely well, for the total time to Berwick by this fourth section was only 74 min., or 69 min. net. The two trains were running so close together that No. 2022 got practically no water at Lucker troughs, and had to stop at Berwick in consequence. But the crew meant real business; water was taken in 3¾ min. and the restart was magnificent, with speed rising to 53 m.p.h. before Burnmouth. There was a slight signal check at Reston, but down Cockburnspath bank for once really high speed was run, with a maximum of 82 m.p.h. near Innerwick, and an average of 67·8 was made onwards to Longniddry. No. 2022 was still close on the heels of the preceding train and slight checks followed; but after going through

TABLE 4. N.E.R.: BERWICK—EDINBURGH

Train, ex Newcastle		1.32 a.m.	8.10 p.m.	3.28 p.m.
Engine No.		2022	1878	1619
Engine Class		R	Q	3CC
Load tons E/F		205/215	230/245	265/280
Distance		Actual	Aetual	Actual
miles		min. sec.	min. sec.	min. sec.
0·0	BERWICK	0 00	0 00	0 00
5·6	Burnmouth	10 16	12 37	11 55
7·2	Ayton	12 01	14 49	14 04
		sigs.		
11·2	Reston	16 11	19 22	18 40
16·3	Grantshouse	23 19	26 40	26 10
21·0	Cockburnspath	27 47	31 52	31 05
23·7	Innerwick	29 47	34 20	33 30
28·3	DUNBAR	34 02	39 00	37 42
39·7	Drem	45 57	—	49 15
44·3	Longniddry	50 22	56 50	54 40
		sigs.	p.w. slack	
51·0	Inveresk	58 05	64 07	62 04
				sigs.
54·5	Portobello	61 23	68 23	66 32
			p.w. slack	sigs.
57·5	WAVERLEY	64 57	73 54	74 21
Booked time min.		*	80	74
Net time		62	72	70½

*From special stop for water

Portobello at fully double the prescribed 20 m.p.h. (!) the engine was opened right out and made the amazing concluding time of 3 min. 34 sec. to the Waverley stop. Shades of 1895! Speed limits or not, however, the total time from Newcastle was no more than 142 min. 42 sec., just *inside* schedule, and the net time was no more than 130 min.

The other two runs in Table 4 are slow by comparison, but they show the work of a "Q" Class 4-4-0 on the down afternoon "Scotsman", and that of the 3-cylinder compound No. 1619 on the "Flying Scotsman". The afternoon "Scotsmen", by the way, were always known in the service as the "Diners", and the name, like the West Coast soubriquet "The Corridor" persists to the present day. The 2 p.m. ex-Waverley may be officially named "The Heart of Midlothian", but to railwaymen she is still "The Diner". Both 1878 and 1619 had their respective tasks well in hand; the uphill average speeds were 42 and 40¾ m.p.h. between Reston and Grantshouse, while the 23·3 miles from Cockburnspath to Longniddry were run at average speeds of 56·2 and 59·2 m.p.h. respectively. The Class "Q" engines were not often used on the best expresses north of Newcastle, but this run of No. 1878 shows entirely adequate performance, and followed a run from Newcastle to Berwick in exactly the 78 min. booked.

A still finer run with a Class "Q" engine appears in Table 5 on the up Diner, leaving Waverley at 2.20 p.m. The train was badly delayed at the start by engineering slacks, and lost 6 or 7 minutes in consequence; but really excellent work followed from Dunbar to Grantshouse, and the time of 17 min. 46 sec. for this distance of 12 miles was the best in the table. On a good recent trip with the up "Night Scotsman" we took 17 min. 20 sec. for the same stretch, with an "A2" Pacific having more than double the tractive effort, 50 sq. ft. of grate area, and hauling a load of 545 tons. The performance of No. 1873 does appear to have been exceptional, as Mr. Rounthwaite had not, in his most extensive experience, noted better work on this incline with Class "R" engines similarly loaded. The run with No. 2018 was timed by Mr. John S. MacLean and shows what could be done out to Dunbar with a clear road. It was chiefly in the immediate start that this engine gained the advantage, as the average speed from Longniddry to Dunbar was no more than 60 m.p.h. In the third column of Table 5, No. 2013 had the heaviest load Mr. Rounthwaite noted taken up Cockburnspath bank unassisted by an "R" Class engine. Exact time was maintained to Berwick, though the uphill work from Dunbar was inferior to that of the "Q" Class engine No. 1873. The last run tabulated was clocked by Mr. Cecil J. Allen soon after the introduction of the superheater "Z1" engines; it was an excellent performance, with a minimum speed of 23 m.p.h. on the Cockburnspath bank.

TABLE 5. N.E.R.: EDINBURGH—BERWICK

Train ...		2 p.m.	2.20 p.m.	2.20 p.m.	10 a.m.
Engine No.		2018	1873	2013	735
Engine Class		R	Q	R	Z1
Load tons E/F		240/255	290/310	312/335	350/375
Distance		Actual	Actual	Actual	Actual
miles		min. sec.	min. sec.	min. sec.	min. sec.
0·0	WAVERLEY	0 00	0 00	0 00	0 00
			p.w. slack	sigs.	
3·0	Portobello	5 00	7 55	7 50	6 20
6·5	Inveresk	9 15	13 26	12 36	—
			p.w. slack		
13·2	Longniddry	16 59	23 26	20 49	—
17·8	Drem	21 43	28 48	25 40	24 45
29·2	DUNBAR	33 01	40 40	37 17	36 10
33·8	Innerwick	38 17	45 50	42 40	—
36·5	Cockburnspath	41 32	49 12	46 05	44 25
41·2	Gransthouse	50 51	58 26	57 20	54 05
46·3	Reston	56 04	63 38	63 02	59 20
50·3	Ayton	59 39	67 10	66 34	—
51·9	Burnmouth	61 16	68 50	68 27	64 20
57·5	BERWICK	67 24	75 05	74 58	71 30
Booked time ... min.		70	75	75	71
Net time ... min.		67½	69	72½	70¾

Table 6 sets out details of two smart runs south of Berwick. The "M" Class engine No. 1632 was clocked by Mr. John S. MacLean, and put up a good steady performance with a moderate train. No. 2015, on the other hand, had taken pilot assistance from Edinburgh to Grantshouse with this heavy train, and most justifiably so. Very

TABLE 6. N.E.R.: BERWICK—NEWCASTLE

Engine No.		1632		2015	
Engine Class		M		R	
Load tons E/F		180/190		338/355	
Distance		Actual	Speeds	Actual	Speed
miles		min. sec.	m.p.h.*	min. sec.	m.p.h.*
0·0	BERWICK	0 00	—	0 00	—
1·2	Tweedmouth	2 37	27·6	3 17	21·9
8·3	Beal	10 10	56·4	10 37	58·3
15·3	Belford	17 36	56·5	18 00	56·8
20·9	Chathill	23 35	56·1	24 30	51·7
23·9	Christon Bank	26 35	60·0	27 45	55·4
27·5	Little Mill	30 56	49·7	32 38	44·2
29·4	Longhoughton	32 59	55·6	34 50	51·8
32·1	ALNMOUTH	35 18	70·2	37 09	70·2
35·0	Warkworth	38 16	58·7	40 00	61·0
41·3	Chevington	44 36	59·8	46 45	56·0
46·7	Longhirst...	49 52	61·9	52 44	54·2
50·3	MORPETH	53 28	60·0	56 52	52·2
53·0	Stannington	57 11	43·6	60 22	46·2
57·0	Cramlington	61 26	56·5	65 02	51·4
				sigs.	
61·9	Forest Hall	66 08	62·5	70 43	51·7
65·2	Heaton	69 22	61·1	74 58	46·6
66·9	NEWCASTLE	72 36	—	77 56	—
Booked time ... min.		74		78	
Net time ... min.		72½		76½	

*Averages from station to station

fine work followed. After a rapid start, and good going over the rise from Beal to Chathill, the incline past Christon Bank was climbed at a minimum speed of 39 m.p.h. and a speed of 72 m.p.h. was sustained down Longhoughton bank. By Cramlington the driver had sufficient time in hand to offset the effect of a signal check at Forest Hall, and Newcastle was reached dead on time.

We come next to the high speed stretch from Darlington to York, with three runs on the 43-min. "flyer", and two on the "Flying Scotsman". The runs of 1872 and 2013 were clocked by Mr. Rous-Marten, and that of 1672 by Mr. R. J. Purves. On the first two runs the acceleration from rest must have been terrific, to pass Croft Spa in such times as 3 min. 23 and 24 sec.; but by Danby Wiske

TABLE 7. N.E.R.: DARLINGTON—YORK

Run No. ...		1	2	3	4	5
Engine No.		1872	2013	1672	1244	1238
Engine Class		Q	R	R	R1	R1
Load tons E/F		152/170	152/170	152/170	348/365	377/405
Distance		Actual	Actual	Actual	Actual	Actual
miles		min. sec.	min. sec.	min. sec.	min. sec.	min. sec.
0·0	DARLINGTON	0 00	0 00	0 00	0 00	0 00
2·6	Croft Spa	3 24	3 23	3 54	5 15	5 05
5·2	Eryholme	5 55	5 59	6 14	8 15	8 05
10·4	Danby Wiske	10 35	10 38	10 33	13 25	13 35
14·1	NORTHALLERTON	13 51	13 58	13 46	16 50	17 10
17·5	Otterington	16 57	17 05	16 36	20 05	20 30
21·9	Thirsk	20 53	20 49	20 04	23 50	24 30
26·1	Sessay	24 40	24 36	23 33	27 35	28 25
28·0	Pilmoor	26 20	26 17	25 09	29 20	31 00
30·7	Raskelf	28 31	28 39	27 23	31 45	32 35
32·9	Alne	30 21	30 33	29 09	33 30	34 35
38·6	Beningbrough	35 05	35 30	33 45	38 30	39 45
42·5	Poppleton Junct.	—	—	37 00	41 45	43 05
44·1	YORK	40 00	42 53	39 34	44 40	46 00
Average Speed Otterington to Beningbrough m.p.h.		69·7	68·7	73·7	68·7	65·8

the third run had taken the lead, chiefly through the uphill acceleration to 69 m.p.h. as early as Eryholme. Apart from the starts, "even time" running between Darlington and York is so frequent today as to be a commonplace even with the heaviest trains, and while this chapter was being written I clocked an "A1" to pass Beningbrough in 34 min. 58 sec. with 475 tons, on the up "Heart of Midlothian". The time of No. 1672, however, remained the record throughout North Eastern days, and included what was then considered a high maximum speed for almost level track of 78 m.p.h. Columns 4 and 5 of Table 7 shows the large "R1" Class engines at their best in heavy load haulage at high speed. Both these runs were timed by Mr. Cecil J. Allen. They really belong to a later period than the majority of journeys detailed in this chapter, as both engines had, by the time concerned, been superheated. The well-sustained running with these heavy trains, at 68·7 m.p.h. from Otterington to Beningbrough by No. 1244 and at 65·8 m.p.h. by No. 1238 is particularly interesting in view of the special runs to be considered next, and set out in Table 8.

In 1906 a series of dynamometer car tests were carried out between Newcastle and York to determine the relative load hauling capacities of the various large passenger locomotives. By the courtesy of the Railway Executive I have been privileged to study this report. From the reproductions of the actual dynamometer car charts I have been able to reconstruct the log of each trip, and Table 8 sets out details of three journeys from Darlington to York, including maximum and minimum speeds. The Class "R" engine No. 2028 was in average condition; she was worked in 40 per cent. cut-off throughout from Milepost 43½ to Milepost 7. Steam chest pressure was 150 lb. per

TABLE 8.

N.E.R.: DYNAMOMETER CAR RUNS, DARLINGTON—YORK

Engine No. ...		2028		784		730	
Engine Class		R		V		4CC	
Load tons empty/full		343/365		373/395		435/455	
Distance		Actual	Speeds	Actual	Speeds	Actual	Speeds
miles		min. sec.	m.p.h.	min. sec.	m.p.h.	min. sec.	m.p.h.
0·0	DARLINGTON	0 00	—	0 00	—	0 00	—
1·2	*Black Banks Box* * ...	2 35	—	2 50	—	2 37	—
2·6	Croft Spa	4 47	51	5 02	52	4 42	55½
5·2	Eryholme	7 52	50	8 03	51	7 34	54½
10·4	Danby Wiske	13 16	63	13 22	65	12 39	66
14·1	NORTHALLERTON ...	16 54	60	16 55	60	16 09	60½
17·5	Otterington	20 15	62½	20 09	66	19 25	65
21·9	Thirsk	24 22	65	24 02	69	23 29	67
26·1	Sessay	28 28	60	27 46	67	27 24	63½
28·0	Pilmoor	30 21	61	29 26	69	29 11	64½
30·7	Raskelf	32 56	64	31 44	72	31 39	66½
32·9	Alne	35 01	62	33 34	71	33 38	67
34·4	Tollerton	36 28	61	34 50	71	35 00	65
38·6	Beningbrough	40 37	60	38 26	70	38 58	62
42·5	*Poppleton Junct.*† ...	44 32	58½	41 51	68	42 48	58
44·1	YORK	45 56	—	44 15	—	45 33	—

*Now abolished †Now Skelton

sq. in. going up to Eryholme, and between 130 and 140 onwards to Thirsk, where a slight easing took place. The vigorous start, and subsequent running were characteristic of the class with heavy trains. The "V" Class engine, with a heavier train, made closely similar times to Northallerton but then got away to a fine burst of speed. The report contains no mention of the cut-off used, but steam chest pressure was maintained between 160 and 170 lb. per sq. in. throughout from Northallerton to Beningbrough. Over the 21·1 miles from Otterington to Beningbrough, where speed averaged 69·2 m.p.h., the drawbar pull averaged 1·75 tons—within measurable distance of Churchward's famous target of 2 tons at 70 m.p.h.

The run with the compound Atlantic No. 730 is of exceptional interest, not only in view of the heavy load but for details of the working. To save a good deal of description I have set out details of steam chests pressures, cut-offs, etc., in a separate table, but I can add that the steaming of the engine during the rapid start up to Eryholme, and throughout to York, was excellent, with pressure maintained between 215 and 225 lb. per sq. in., until the firing was eased south of Tollerton. These are the figures:

Distance miles	Cut-offs		Boiler pressure	High pressure steam chest
	H.P.	B.P.		
	per cent.	per cent.	lb. per sq. in.	lb. per sq. in.
0·0	75	80	220	160
0·2	53	63	220	160
0·5	53	63	222	220
1·5	53	63	220	200
3·0	53	63	220	190
5·2	53	63	215	155
23·0	59	66	220	135
29·0	63	70	220	125
30·0	53	63	220	150

The above mileages are the distances from Darlington at which changes were made in either the regulator opening or the cut-off, or in some cases to both controls. After the very fine start to Croft speed was held steadily at $54\frac{1}{2}$ m.p.h. on the 1 in 391 to Eryholme, involving a drawbar pull of 2·9 tons, and a drawbar horsepower, corrected for gradient, of 1,030. South of Northallerton, due to the lower speed, the drawbar pull was not quite so high as that of No. 784; it was sustained very evenly at 1·7 tons. But for a non-superheater Atlantic of 1906 vintage this was a remarkable performance with a load of 455 tons, and a triumph for Walter Smith's masterpiece. But if this run was a triumph how shall I describe the second of the journeys set out in Table 9? For, on a northbound trip with the "Flying Scotsman" the load was made up to no less than 456 tons *tare,* and No. 730 handled it quite comfortably within schedule time. By comparison there is a run with No. 2114, also with the dynamometer car attached, and while this 4-6-0 did quite adequately with a normal "Flying Scotsman" load of those days, the superiority of the compound Atlantic was absolute.

In starting from York No. 2114 was linked up as follows:

Distance (miles)	Cut-off %
0·0	70
0·1	62
0·55	55
1·2	45
1·7	40

Afterwards 40 per cent. was maintained throughout to Newcastle, except when the regulator was closed while coasting downhill from Relly Mill Junction through Durham. Steam chest pressure was between 140 and 155 lb. per sq. in. from York to Eryholme; between 115 and 130 onwards to Tursdale Junction, and 125 downhill through the Team Valley. It will be seen that the running times are very similar to those made in ordinary service, and set out in Table 2. There were no checks at all until after Bensham.

TABLE 9.

N.E.R.: DYNAMOMETER CAR RUNS, YORK—NEWCASTLE

Engine No. ...		2114		730	
Engine Class ...		S1		4CC	
Load, tons, empty/full ...		365/385		456/475	
Distance		Actual	Speeds	Actual	Speeds
miles		min. sec.	m.p.h.	min. sec.	m.p.h.
0·0	YORK ...	0 00	—	0 00	—
1·0	*Milepost 1* ...	2 51	—	2 30	—
3·0	*Milepost 3* ...	5 53	—	5 11	50
5·5	Beningbrough ...	9 07	49	8 02	54
9·7	Tollerton ...	13 57	54	12 39	55¼
11·2	Alne ...	15 36	55	14 16	56
13·4	Raskelf ...	18 00	54	16 39	55
16·1	Pilmoor ...	21 02	53	19 38	53¼
18·0	Sessay ...	23 11	53	21 46	54
22·2	Thirsk ...	27 49	57	26 16	58
26·6	Otterington ...	32 29	56	31 07	52
30·0	NORTHALLERTON ...	36 16	52	34 54	56
33·7	Danby Wiske ...	40 13	60½	38 39	61
38·9	Eryholme ...	45 46	51½	44 00	56½
41·5	Croft Spa ...	48 33	59½	46 32	64
44·1	DARLINGTON ...	51 19	52½	49 07	57
49·5	Aycliffe ...	58 28	43½	55 11	51½
54·3	Bradbury ...	64 28	53	60 30	57½
			44		50½
57·0	Ferryhill ...	67 46	51	63 42	54
61·9	Croxdale ...	73 01	64	68 51	66½
65·1	*Relly Mill Junct.* ...	76 30	46½	72 11	50
66·1	DURHAM ...	77 52	41½ *	73 38	31 *
67·5	*Newton Hall Junct.* ...	79 49	48	75 44	48
70·0	Plawsworth ...	82 42	58½	78 31	61
71·9	Chester-le-Street ...	84 30	68	80 15	72/69
74·7	Birtley ...	86 57	69	82 39	71
76·3	Lamesley ...	88 25	69½	84 00	71½
77·6	Low Fell ...	89 38	66	85 14	70
78·9	Bensham ...	91 13	—	86 39	—
		sigs.		sigs.	
80·1	NEWCASTLE ...	94 20	—	90 35	

*Speed restriction

ENGINE WORKING DETAILS OF No. 730's RUN (*ABOVE*)

Distance miles	Cut-offs		Boiler pressure	Low pressure steam chest
	H.P.	L.P.		
	per cent.	per cent.	lb. per sq. in.	lb. per sq. in.
0·0	75	80	220	125
0·5	63	70	217	70
1·7	53	63	210	60
4·0	53	63	190	45
10·0	41	54	200	40

The compound, with her 475-ton load, made a brilliant start out of York, reaching 50 m.p.h. in 3 miles from rest, and passing Beningbrough in 8 min. 2 sec.

The vigorous start brought the boiler pressure down a little—as well it might! But by Alne it was back to 200 lb. per sq. in. and it was mostly kept around that figure onwards to Ferryhill. Cut-off was advanced to 47 per cent. H.P. and 58 per cent. L.P. just after Thirsk, and no further changes were made, save when the engine was put into full gear while coasting down from Relly Mill Junction to Durham. The drawbar pull was 1·8 tons steadily between Tollerton and Alne, while after the engine was opened out a little at Otterington it was sustained at 2·6 tons up to Northallerton while running at 55 m.p.h. The minimum speed of 56½ m.p.h. at Eryholme was excellent with this enormous train, but no less so was the lowest speed of 51½ m.p.h. on the rise from Darlington to Aycliffe. For the year 1906 this was, taken all round, a magnificent piece of running.

As a result of these trials the relative capacities of the various express engines were established as follows:

Engine class	Relative Capacity	Drawbar pull at 55 m.p.h. (tons)
R	100	1·3
SI	105	1·38
V	128	1·66
4CC	145	1·88

It will be seen that although the "V" and the "4CC" exceeded the above figures of drawbar pull considerably at times during the trials the official figures were fixed somewhat lower, to allow no doubt for adverse conditions in running.

Lastly among details of main line running come a series northbound from York on trains stopping at Darlington, as set out in Table 10. The first four are on the 5.30 p.m. from Kings Cross, originally timed in 44 min. from York to Darlington, and the run tabulated in the first column is that of the inaugural trip on October 1st, 1904. It was timed by Mr. Rounthwaite. The start was brilliant, so much so that no particular effort was needed afterwards, and the average speed from Alne to Croft Spa was the lowest of the four runs with this train. The second run, timed by Mr. Cecil J. Allen, was excellent, showing a high sustained average speed with a 200-ton load. I should explain also that all the runs with "R" Class engines included in this chapter were made before superheaters were added. Run No. 3, the fastest of the whole series, was timed by Mr. R. J. Purves, and was the work of that fine driver Johnson, of Gateshead. The overall time of 42 min. 8 sec., start-to-stop, made with a "V1"

TABLE 10.

N.E.R.: YORK—DARLINGTON

Run No.		1	2	3	4	5	6	7	8
Engine No.		2102	2102	696	1237	1237	1908	2112	710
Engine class		R	R	V1	R1	R1	Q	S1	Z (S)
Load tons E/F		140/150	187/200	210/225	236/250	302/305	297/320	317/335	292/315
Distance		Actual	Actual	Actual	Actual	Actual	Actual	Actual	Actual
miles		min. sec.	min. sec.	min. sec.	min. sec.	min. sec.	min. sec.	min. sec.	min. sec.
0·0	YORK	0 00	0 00	0 00	0 00	0 00	0 00	0 00	0 00
5·5	Beningbrough	7 11	7 55	7 33	8 10	8 53	8 55	9 02	8 22
11·2	Alne	12 24	12 55	12 45	13 35	14 33	14 59	15 12	13 38
13·4	Raskelf	14 19	14 40	14 38	15 35	16 40	17 13	17 30	15 34
16·1	Pilmoor	16 50	17 10	17 01	18 10	19 18	20 06	20 25	17 58
18·0	Sessay	18 37	18 50	18 41	20 00	21 07	22 11	22 30	19 40
—		—	—	—	—	sigs.	—	—	—
22·2	Thirsk	22 29	22 35	22 13	23 40	25 33	26 38	27 00	23 18
26·6	Otterington	26 34	26 30	25 52	27 30	30 35	31 12	31 30	27 00
30·0	NORTHALLERTON	29 52	29 30	28 50	30 40	34 14	35 00	35 27	30 02
33·7	Danby Wiske	33 20	32 50	32 02	34 00	37 58	39 02	39 32	33 20
38·9	Eryholme	38 23	37 15	36 26	38 35	43 34	44 32	45 24	37 46
41·5	Croft Spa	40 57	39 30	38 41	40 55	46 18	47 17	48 20	39 59
—		sigs.	—	—	sigs.	—	—	—	sig. stop
44·1	DARLINGTON	44 50	42 50	42 08	44 20	49 07	50 40	52 25	49 30
	Schedule time ... min.	44	44	45	45	—	52	53	46
	Average speed Alne to Croft Spa ... m.p.h.	63·5	68·3	70·0	66·5	60 (net)	56·2	54·8	68·9

engine against the gradually rising character of the road, was fully equal to the times of 40 and 41 min. made by "Z" Class engines with similar loads in the reverse direction. With a heavier train, in column 4, the "R1" Class engine made a good run, though she was not pushed so hard in starting out of York.

Run No. 5 is of unusual interest, as it was a dynamometer trial with the Royal Train made on February 18th, 1909, made with none but railway staff on board. In starting from York the cut-off on No. 1237 was reduced to 35 per cent. in just over a ¼-mile from the start, and to 27 per cent. in one mile. As to the regulator, from a wide initial opening, giving 175 lb. steam chest pressure, it was eased back to about 140 at Beningbrough, and varied between 130 and 170 until the check approaching Thirsk. Speed had reached 59 m.p.h. by Beningbrough, touched 63½ at Alne, and was steady at 65 m.p.h. after Sessay. After the check the engine was worked under slightly easier steam. Boiler pressure was well maintained between 215 and 225 lb. per sq. in., except for a brief drop to 210 near Tollerton. After the check, which was to 40 m.p.h., speed was worked up to 57 m.p.h. on passing Northallerton, but then the regulator was eased so as to reduce steam chest pressure to the 100-130 lb. per sq. in. range, and with 25 per cent. cut-off the speeds were 59 m.p.h. at Danby Wiske, 54 at Eryholme, and 59 again at Croft Spa.

Runs 6 and 7 timed by Mr. Rounthwaite show characteristic work with the down afternoon Scotsman, showing a "Q" and an "S1" keeping closely to the moderate schedules then laid down. The last run is included for comparison purposes, as it is right outside the period under review; it is my fastest personal experience with a North Eastern engine over this route, and was timed in 1933 on the 1.55 p.m. out of York. No. 710 was originally a non-superheater engine, but by that time she had been brought into line with the later engines of the class. The running was magnificent, with maximum speeds of 72 m.p.h. at Thirsk, 73 at Danby, and 75 at Croft Spa, and in consideration of the load of 315 tons the engine performance was probably the finest of the whole series.

* * * *

On the secondary routes, in the same period, a great deal of excellent work was being done by the older express engines. The 8.55 a.m. from Scarborough to York was a smartly timed train, with allowances of 24 min. for the 20·9 miles from Scarborough to Malton, and 28 min. onwards to York, 21·2 miles. The Fletcher "901" Class engine No. 329 was at one time a favourite engine on the job, and on one occasion, noted by Mr. Cecil J. Allen, she took 23 min. 38 sec. to Malton, and 27 min. 5 sec. to York. The load was 120 tons, and speed was sustained at 68 m.p.h. on the level between Heslerton and Rillington. On the 6.3 p.m. non-stop from York to

TABLE 11. N.E.R.: CARLISLE—NEWCASTLE (BLAYDON)

Load: 132 tons tare, 140 tons full
Engine: McDonnell type 4-4-0 No. 1494

Distance		Actual	Speeds*
miles		min. sec.	m.p.h.
0.0	CARLISLE	0 00	—
2.5	Scotby	5 15	28.5
4.3	Wetherall	7 17	52.9
6.0	Heads Nook	9 35	44.4
7.4	How Mill	12 01	34.5
10.8	Brampton Junct.	18 57	—
1.6	Naworth	4 12	22.9
3.1	Low Row	6 17	43.2
6.9	Gilsland	10 57	48.9
5.3	HALTWHISTLE	8 20	—
4.7	Barden Mill	6 40	—
8.8	Haydon Bridge	10 50	—
3.6	Fourstones	5 45	—
7.6	HEXHAM	10 43	—
3.1	Corbridge	5 33	33.5
5.4	Riding Mill	8 18	50.2
7.7	Stocksfield	11 28	44.0
10.2	Prudhoe	14 38	47.3
12.4	Wylam	17 18	49.6
14.6	Ryton	19 29	60.3
16.7	BLAYDON	22 58	

*Average Speeds

Scarborough, engines of the "901" Class also made some good runs. No. 329 with 105 tons passed Malton in 25¼ min. and completed the run of 42·1 miles in 48 min. 55 sec., while No. 925 hauling 175 tons did extremely well to pass Malton in 25 min. 5 sec. and to complete the run in exactly 48 min. This was running well above the standards required of the "901" Class in their hey-day on the main line.

Mr. Cecil J. Allen clocked a number of runs on the 10.40 a.m. through train from Middlesbrough to York, which ran non-stop from Northallerton. 2-4-0 engines were invariably used, and with a load of 140 tons, the 30 miles from Northallerton to York were regularly covered in about 33½ to 34½ min. start-to-stop. Engines responsible for this kind of work were "901" Class Nos. 53 and 827, and the "Tennant" No. 1479. Mr. Rounthwaite has given me details of a run with a McDonnell 4-4-0 on the Carlisle road; the speed is nothing very wonderful, with a light train, but in view of the peculiar interest attached to the McDonnell engines I have tabulated the log in full. The start from Carlisle up to Wetherall must have been excellent, with an average speed of over 50 m.p.h. from Scotby, and there was some smart work between stops on the gradual descent from Haltwhistle. Full use can hardly be made of the final stretch east of Hexham, as there is a good deal of curvature and some pronounced slacks, as it Wylam Junction. Nevertheless there was some 60 m.p.h. running on the last stage before the Blaydon stop.

[R. J. Purves

The 12.20 p.m. Newcastle-Sheffield express near Low Fell, hauled by Class "R" 4-4-0 engine No. 1232.

[R. J. Purves

The down "Flying Scotsman" on Lucker troughs hauled by non-superheater "Z" 4-4-2 No. 718. (Note T.P.O. van next to engine.)

Up mineral train on Deepdale Viaduct, hauled by a superheater Class "C" 0-6-0. [Ian S. Pearsall

[*W. J. Reynolds*

The Raven Pacific No. 2400 (later named *City of Newcastle*) at Kings Cross during dynamometer car trials in 1923.

[Courtesy: M. W. Earley

[illegible] at York: a Leeds train leaving hauled by a "Q1" 7 ft. 7 in. 4-4-0 No. 1869

Some of the most interesting of the secondary workings on the North Eastern were the evening "residential" expresses to Scarborough and Bridlington run during the summer months. There were non-stop trains to Bridlington from both Leeds and Sheffield and, in addition, the celebrated 75-min. run from Leeds to Scarborough. The Sheffield train included a restaurant car. The timings of these trains were:

Route	Distance miles	Time min.	Average speed m.p.h.
Rotherham—Bridlington *	76·0	94	48·5
Leeds—Bridlington	63·4	73	52·2
Leeds—Bridlington	67·6	75	54·0

*The Sheffield—Bridlington service

Although the Sheffield train had the disadvantage of a more difficult route, the most exacting work was required on the Scarborough "Limited", since the prolonged slack through York has to be taken into account, as well as the need for reduced speed over the curving stretch in the Derwent Valley. The "J" Class 4-2-2 locomotives were used on these trains, and with loads of 90 to 100 tons the performance was often sparkling. Logs of all three trains are tabulated from details recorded by Mr. Cecil J. Allen. On the Sheffield service, providing good time was made to Selby no higher speeds than 60 to 62 m.p.h. were needed on the level stretches between Selby and Market Weighton, and again between Driffield and Bridlington. On the 3½-mile ascent over the Wolds, from Market Weighton to Enthorpe, where the gradient is 1 in 95-100 continuously, the lowest

TABLE 12.

N.E.R.: ROTHERHAM (MIDLAND)—BRIDLINGTON

Load: 4 coaches, 105 tons gross
Engine: Class J 4-2-2 No. 1521

Distance		Actual	Speeds *
miles		min. sec.	m.p.h.
0·0	ROTHERHAM	0 00	
5·1	Swinton	7 45	—
10·5	Frickley	16 05	62½ max.
19·6	Pontefract	26 25	—
25·5	Monk Fryston	33 30	—
26·2	*Milford Junct.*	slack	20
32·7	*Wistow Junct.*	43 15	
		sig. stop mom.	
33·3	SELBY	45 55	
	Foggathorpe...	—	61½
50·8	Market Weighton	65 25	(slack)
54·4	Enthorpe	71 10	36½
		—	71½
64·6	DRIFFIELD	81 30	(slack)
		—	61½
76·0	BRIDLINGTON	94 35	

Net time 93 min.
*Max. and min. speeds by stop watch

TABLE 13. N.E.R.: 4.47 p.m. LEEDS—BRIDLINGTON

Load: 4 coaches, 105 tons gross
Engine: Class "J" 4-2-2 No. 1524

Distance		Actual	Speeds *
miles		min. sec.	m.p.h.
0·0	LEEDS	0 00	
		sigs. severe	—
4·4	Cross Gates	8 25	—
9·7	Micklefield	14 15	67
16·5	Hambleton	20 50	easy
—	*Wistow Junct.*	sigs. stop 25 seconds	
20·7	SELBY	27 50	(slack)
—	Foggathorpe...	—	64½
38·2	Market Weighton	46 05	25 (slack)
41·8	Enthorpe	51 20	41½
49·0	Southburn	57 55	72½
52·0	DRIFFIELD	61 10	—
		sigs. stop 15 seconds	
54·1	Nafferton	66 00	60
61·2	Carnaby	72 40	68
63·4	BRIDLINGTON	75 50	—

Net time 70½ min.
*Max. and min. speeds by stop watch

speed on the run tabulated was 36½ m.p.h. Considerably faster work was done by engine No. 1524 on the Leeds-Bridlington express. On the Scarborough "Limited", however, a really brilliant piece of work was recorded by Mr. Cecil J. Allen, in the year 1913, and a reference to this will aptly conclude the chapter. As with the "Tennants" and the "Fletchers", which in their secondary days were regularly

TABLE 14. N.E.R.: LEEDS—SCARBOROUGH

Load: 3 coaches, 85 tons gross
Engine: Class "J" 4-2-2 No. 1523

Distance		Actual	Speeds *
miles		min. sec.	m.p.h.
0·0	LEEDS	0 00	—
4·4	Cross Gates	6 50	53
9·7	Micklefield	12 10	74
		sigs.	85
14·8	Church Fenton	17 00	30
17·9	Bolton Percy	20 30	64
23·6	*Chaloners Whin Junct.*	25 25	74
25·5	YORK	27 55	10 (slack)
29·7	Haxby	33 35	—
34·7	Flaxton	38 00	71½
37·0	Barton Hill	40 00	68
41·3	Castle Howard	44 40	slack
46·7	MALTON	50 55	—
51·1	Rillington	55 25	—
55·0	Heslerton	58 50	74
60·0	Ganton	63 05	76½
64·7	Seamer Junct.	67 15	—
		sigs.	—
67·6	SCARBOROUGH	71 40	—

Net time 69½ min.
*Max. and min. speeds by stop watch

called upon to run trains of 100 to 150 tons at speeds sustained over 65 m.p.h. on level road, so this run of No. 1523 included some very much faster work on level track than ever the "J" Class engines were called upon to perform when they ran the 9.38 a.m. from York to Newcastle. For, on this Scarborough "Limited", here was No. 1523 accelerating to 74 m.p.h. before Chaloners Whin Junction, and to 76½ m.p.h. after Malton, to say nothing of what Mr. Allen in his original description of the run called "the terrific maximum" of 85 m.p.h. down the Micklefield bank. It was a grand effort.

OLDER N.E.R. ENGINES—SUPERHEATER EQUIPPED

N.E.R. Class Letter Type	F 4-4-0	G 4-4-0	M 4-4-0	Q 4-4-0	R 4-4-0	R1 4-4-0	S1 4-6-0	4CC 4-4-2
Cylinders: dia.	18 in.	18 in.	19 in.	19 in.	19 in.	19 in.	20 in.	14¼ in./22 in.
stroke	24 in.	24 in.	26 in.	26 in.	26 in.	26 in.	26 in.	26 in.
Piston valve dia.	7½ in.	7½ in.	8¾ in.	8¾ in.	8¾ in.	10 in.	8¾ in.	7½ in./10 in.
Boiler:								
small tubes: Number	105	96	89	89	126	90	126	124
small tubes: O/dia.	1¾ in.	1¾ in.	1¾ in.	1¾ in.	1¾ in.	2 in.	1¾ in.	2 in.
length between tube plates	10 ft. 11⅛ in.	10 ft. 7⅛ in.	11 ft. 10⅛ in.	11 ft. 10⅛ in.	11 ft. 10⅛ in.	11 ft. 3⅛ in.	15 ft. 4⅛ in.	15 ft. 0 in.
Superheater flues								
Number of tubes	18	18	18	18	18	24	18	18
O/dia.	5¼ in.	5¼ in.	5¼ in.	5¼ in.	5¼ in.	5¼ in.	5¼ in.	5¼ in.
Heating surface:								
small tubes	525 sq. ft.	466 sq. ft.	482·4 sq. ft.	482·4 sq. ft.	683·6 sq. ft.	529·8 sq. ft.	936·6 sq. ft.	974 sq. ft.
superheater flues	270 ,, ,,	262 ,, ,,	293 ,, ,,	293 ,, ,,	292·7 ,, ,,	371 ,, ,,	401 ,, ,,	371 ,, ,,
firebox	112 ,, ,,	98 ,, ,,	123 ,, ,,	123 ,, ,,	144 ,, ,,	158 ,, ,,	130 ,, ,,	180 ,, ,,
superheater elements	263 ,, ,,	270 ,, ,,	288 ,, ,,	288 ,, ,,	306 ,, ,,	371·5 ,, ,,	390 ,, ,,	368 ,, ,,
Grate area	17·3 ,, ,,	15·16 ,, ,,	19·8 ,, ,,	19·8 ,, ,,	20 ,, ,,	27 ,, ,,	23 ,, ,,	29 ,, ,,

Chapter Twelve

THE WAR AND THE CHANGING SCENE

WHEN the emergency of the first World War broke upon Britain in 1914, the North Eastern Railway was at the very zenith of its strength, financially and otherwise. The virile organisation built up by Sir George Gibb had proved a training ground for some outstanding young railway administrators. As the scale and intensity of the war effort increased one after another of the senior North Eastern officers were called to fill posts of high responsibility in the national service. The General Manager, Sir Alexander Butterworth, played a leading part in the work of the Railway Executive Committee in London; Sir Eric Geddes, as he afterwards became, was made Deputy Director General of Munitions Supply, in May, 1915, and from September of that year Vincent Raven was acting as Chief Superintendent of the Royal Ordnance Factories, Woolwich. In addition, J. H. Smeddle, Divisional Locomotive Superintendent, York, who was a Major in the Territorials, was immediately called to the colours, and went to France in 1915. In this book we are concerned with the impact of the war upon the Locomotive Department, and there the North Eastern was extremely fortunate in having Raven's assistant to carry on at Darlington. Mr. R. Bell has written: "A. C. Stamer acted as Chief Mechanical Engineer with a resource and urbanity that combined to secure a large output of both Government and North Eastern Railway work. His popularity with the workmen was a valuable asset for the Company during the difficult war years. He understood the men's ways of looking at things and having been a good cricketer in his younger days, took a genuine interest in their games and hobbies".

New construction at Darlington never entirely ceased in the war years, though in 1916 no more than two new locomotives were completed, the "Z" Atlantics, 2205 and 2206. But one extremely interesting feature of this period, a feature that was first manifested just before the war, was the programme of modernising older engines by the fitting of superheaters. All the Worsdell express engines with the exception of the 4-2-2 singles were so treated, and 4-4-0s of the "F", "M" and "Q" Classes continued to render excellent and relatively economical service on secondary main lines, and on the longer branches. The boiler dimensions of eight older classes, as superheater equipped, is given in the accompanying table. It was a remarkable programme; and one without parallel anywhere in the country. I saw a good deal of the working of the superheater Class "F" and "G" 4-4-0s working between Leeds, Hull and Bridlington in 1919 and 1920, and they always seemed very smart-running and lively engines. It would have been interesting to see the effects of superheating upon the four-cylinder compound Atlantics examined in some tests with the dynamometer car; but during the war years the emphasis was naturally upon freight, and indeed the Atlantics, both compound and simple, took a share in the working of heavy through goods trains on the main line.

But with this mention of freight I must now come to the "T2" superheater 0-8-0s, referred to in Chapter Ten, and first constructed in 1913. These engines had wheels 4 ft. 7¼ in. dia.; cylinders 20 in. dia. by 26 in. stroke, and a boiler pressure of 160 lb. per sq. in. The boiler and firebox dimensions were:

Small tubes
number 90
outside diameter... ... ... 2 in.

Superheater flues
number 24
outside diameter... ... ... 5¼ in.

Heating surfaces (sq. ft.)
small tubes ... ... 722·2
superheater flues... ... ... 504·0
firebox ... ... 144·0
superheater elements ... ... 544·8
total ... ... 1,915·0

Grate area (sq. ft.) 23

In Class "T2" Raven produced an engine that could be driven "all-out" for indefinite periods at anything up to maximum mineral train speeds. Working in 72 per cent. cut-off (full fore gear) and with full regulator these engines would develop 1,000 drawbar horse-power at 19 m.p.h., and this maximum capacity was ably demonstrated in some dynamometer car trials carried out between Newport and Shildon in 1915 over the heavily worked mineral line on which electric traction was inaugurated in that same year. The results of these trials, with engine No. 1250, can be summarised as set out in the accompanying table:

TESTS OF "T2" ENGINE BETWEEN ERIMUS AND SHILDON

Test ref.	Load tons	Dist. miles	Total time min.	Running time min.	Time with steam on min.	Average D.B. Pull tons	Average speed m.p.h.	Average D.B. Horse power
A	651	16·6	66½	60	55½	6·86	16·6	736
B	700	16·6	73	70½	66	7·64	14·2	690
C	703	16·6	84½	75	70	7·06	13·3	602

On certain of these tests the engine was stopped specially on gradients to observe the restart. On a grade of 1 in 103, on Test A, the engine got away cleanly and sustained a drawbar pull of 10½ to 11 tons for some 5 minutes while accelerating its load to 12 m.p.h.

From the dynamometer car records which I have been privileged to examine some examples of sustained performance on the rising gradients have been tablulated separately herewith:

ENGINE PERFORMANCE, "T2" CLASS

Load tons	Speed m.p.h.	Gradient	D.B. Pull tons	D.B. Horse power	Cut-off per cent.
651	27	1 in 230	6·3	1020	72
651	28½	1 in 450	5·4	920	68
700	7	1 in 103	11·7	500	72
700	14·3	1 in 147	10	860	72
700	22·3	1 in 235	7·5	1000	72
700	28·5	1 in 450	6	1060	68
703	23·7	1 in 235	6·7	950	68

A further test was made down the same stretch of line with a loaded train of 1,466 tons. The engine regulator was opened only for three very brief periods, in restarting from signal stops; otherwise the train was coasting throughout. The average speed between Shildon and Erimus was no more than 10·5 m.p.h. since every care had to be taken to avoid getting this huge load out of control on the descending gradients.

The runs made with engine No. 1250 were to ascertain maximum power. The driver was instructed exactly how to work the engine, and for the most part the going was absolutely "all-out"—full open regulator, full forward gear. But a test was taken with a "P3" engine No. 1225 on which the handling of the engine was left entirely to the driver, to work as he would have done in ordinary rather than test conditions. Although the "P3" has a potential capacity that was some 75 per cent. of that of a "T2" the performance was as follows:

Average speed ... ... 9·9 m.p.h.
Average pull ... ... 5·2 tons
Average D.H.P. 315

The average drawbar horsepower of the "T2", with its crew working under strictly supervised conditions, showed an output nearly 2½ times greater than that of the "P3", though the latter engine was apparently working well within its maximum capacity.

Thirty "T2" engines had been built at Darlington in 1913, and with the introduction of electric traction on this same line in 1915 and the successful performance of the ten electric locomotives built specially at Darlington in 1914 the traffic operating situation on this heavily worked line between Newport and Shildon was maintained in a healthy state through the war. In maximum output the electric locomotives were not greatly superior to the "T2" Class; they took trains of empties totalling some 800 tons behind the tender up the grade, against 700 with the steam 0-8-0s, and they worked at much the same speeds. A further batch of 40 engines of Class "T2" was built at Darlington Nos. 2213-2252: 19 in the year 1917, 8 in 1918, and 13 in 1919, while after the end of the war an order was placed with Armstrong-Whitworths for another 50 of these engines. They were numbered 2253 to 2302 inclusive, and were delivered between November, 1919 and April, 1921. Altogether the "T2s", or the "Q6" Class as they became known in L.N.E.R. days, were extremely successful. They carried on the North Eastern tradition of heavy freight and mineral haulage, not only in 1914-1918 and beyond, but during a second and more desperate national emergency. As recently as 1951 I heard the "Q6s" referred to as "the engines that won the war"! I rode on one of them on a characteristic duty in the early spring of 1953, on a heavy train from Blackhill, down the Derwent Valley line into Blaydon. We ran tender first, and from the high stance in the cab one could look out and get an excellent view of the line ahead, as we eased our way down the grade.

Reverting to the time of the first World War the North Eastern, in company with most British Railways was asked to send locomotives to France to work with the Railway Operating Division. The North Eastern contribution was to send the entire strength of Class "T1", the 50 non-superheater 0-8-0s with slide valves. It was no small sacrifice, for the "T1s" were relatively new engines. In any case they won golden opinions from the British Army operating men in France. My own chief, Mr. Kenneth H. Leech, who was a locomotive officer in the R.O.D., had some of them in his charge and gives them absolutely full marks for their solid reliability, and their willingness in slogging up heavy grades. In the meantime on the North Eastern itself, Atlantic express engines were often pressed into freight duties on the main line, and construction of the "Z" Class engines continued as follows:

Year	Number of engines	Running numbers
1914	11	2163—2172, 2193
1915	11	2194—2204
1916	2	2205, 2206
1917	5	2207—2211

An important addition to North Eastern strength on the personnel side was that the Company secured the release of Mr. Smeddle from the forces, and he thereupon became assistant to Mr. Stamer, with particular responsibility for locomotive running. The partnership proved a very happy one in every way, and despite the stress of wartime conditions North Eastern locomotive affairs were maintained in very good order. It is perhaps no more than a small point, but it was never found necessary to abandon the beautiful express engine livery, and it was still found possible to keep the majority of engines looking smart and clean.

N.E.R.: WARTIME LOADS—YORK TO DARLINGTON

Engine No.		649	2172	2165	2172	2195	2197
Engine Class		V	Z	Z	Z	Z	Z
Load tons gross		425	460	470	540	560	600
Distance		Actual	Actual	Actual	Actual	Actual	Actual
miles		min. sec.	min. sec.	min. sec.	min. sec.	min. sec.	min. sec.
0·0	York	0 00	0 00	0 00	0 00	0 00	0 00
5·5	Beningbrough ...	—	—	9 25	10 10	11 35	11 25
11·2	Alne	16 00	15 20	15 25	16 20	18 25	18 00
16·1	Pilmoor	—	20 25	20 25	21 20	24 00	23 30
					sigs.		
22·2	Thirsk	27 50	26 35	26 40	28 15	30 40	30 25
30·0	NORTHALLERTON	37 15	35 00	35 30	12 35†	40 20	40 30
3·7	Danby Wiske ...	—		6 55	7 00	7 20	7 40
8·9	Eryholme	13 00	*	13 00	12 45	13 40	14 30
14·1	DARLINGTON ...	19 45	17 50	19 25	18 50	20 50	21 35
Max speed at Thirsk	m.p.h.	62	64	61	61	55½	55½

*68 m.p.h. at Croft Spa †Net time from York 36 min.

On the main line, the dynamometer car trials in pre-war days of the Atlantic engines 730 and 709 were in some way dress rehearsals for the regular working of colossal loads towards the end of the war. Early in 1919 in *The Railway Magazine*, Mr. Cecil J. Allen recorded that on the 6.25 p.m. down express from York six successive runs had been made with gross loads behind the tender of 560, 615, 600, 510, 465 and 625 tons; while some contemporary runs on the 9.38 p.m. gave loads of 485, 470, 455, 575, 470 and 425 tons. Each one of these enormous trains was taken single headed by a "Z" Atlantic. Amid all the difficulties of wartime conditions the operating department had evidently found no opportunity to adjust timetables to the loading conditions, and the 9.38 p.m. in particular was still expected to run the 30 miles from York to Northallerton in the optimistic time of 32 min. start-to-stop! The 6.25 p.m. was allowed 38 min. for the same run. I have tabulated details of some of the runs actually made, and although time was almost invariably lost the actual work of the locomotives was excellent.

If comparison is made with the tables 2, 9 and 10 in Chapter Eleven, in which pre-war running is discussed, it will be seen that the normal passing times with East Coast expresses was 35 to 36 min. at Northallerton, after starting times of 9 to 10 min. from York to Beningbrough. Atlantics obviously had to be handled with some care in starting such colossal loads as 550 to 600 tons over the curves out of York, and the maximum speeds subsequently reached were in most cases actually *higher* than the general standards of pre-war days with East Coast trains. For example, on the three runs in Table 2 (Chapter Eleven) the average speeds between Pilmoor and Thirsk are 53·7, 59·0 and 57·7 m.p.h. whereas in the wartime load table on page 177 the averages on runs 2, 3, 5 and 6 are 59·5, 58·6, 55·0 and 53·0 m.p.h. respectively. Two of the best runs of all stand to the credit of engine No. 2172, and with the 11.10 a.m. up from Darlington to York this same engine not only took, single-handed, a train of *twenty-three* coaches 638 tons tare and 700 tons gross, but kept time—44·1 miles in 59 min. start-to-stop! The North Eastern Railway may well have been proud of such performances as these; not only so, but the moment time-table reconstruction began after the war, and loads were lightened, the "Z" Atlantics and their drivers notched straight back into "top gear". As early after the Armistice as the spring of 1920, engine No. 718 on the 5.30 p.m. from Kings Cross, with a load of 255 tons, passed Northallerton in 31¾ min. from the start at Clifton Junction, 29·8 miles, and reached Darlington in 47 min. As to speed achievements the most brilliant days of the "Z" Atlantics were still to come, though in the immediate post-war years the emphasis on locomotive design at Darlington was once again upon freight. The last "Z", No. 2212, was built experimentally on a modified arrangement of the "uniflow" system; but development work on this engine does not seem to have progressed far when grouping took place.

Vincent Raven returned from his distinguished war service honoured with a knighthood and the K.B.E. So far as main line motive power was concerned he began, at once, to work upon the project of electrification between York and Newcastle, but in the meantime two new types of large 3-cylinder main line locomotives were turned out from Darlington works in 1919: the "T3" heavy mineral 0-8-0, and the "S3" mixed traffic 4-6-0. Five "T3" engines were built as a first trial, whereas with Class "S3", after a first batch of five was completed in December, 1919, construction proceeded steadily with further engines. In contrast, it was not until 1924 that further engines of Class "T3" were built. In dealing with design and performance, however, I will take Class "T3" first. The boiler was somewhat larger than that of the "T2"; as originally built the heating surfaces were as follows:

102	Small tubes (2 in. outside dia.) ...	866	sq. ft.
24	Superheater flues (5¼ in. outside dia.)...	531·9	"
24	Superheater elements	530·1	"
	Firebox	166	"
	Total	2,094	"
	Grate area	27	"

With three cylinders 18½ in. by 26 in., 4 ft. 7¼ in. wheels and 180 lb. per sq. in. boiler pressure the nominal tractive effort at 85 per cent. boiler pressure was 36,963 lb. With the boiler pitched higher than on the "T2" engines, the "T3s" with their shorter chimneys were much finer-looking; they very soon showed, too, that their higher tractive effort was no mere academic figure. Very soon after its construction the first engine, No. 901, was put through some dynamometer car trials on the Carlisle road. Westbound she took, on one of these trials, a load of 1,402 tons, and was master of it at all points on the route. The gradients, however, are not severe in the westbound direction; the worst stretches are from Haydon Bridge, where there were lengths of 1 in 221, 279, 243, 291 and 293, with some short easier stretches intermediately. On the trip with the 1,400 tons load the train was stopped at Haydon Bridge. An excellent restart was made on a gradient of 1 in 298, and the speed then averaged 17·35 m.p.h. to a test stop at Low Row, 17·9 miles in 62 min. start-to-stop. The average drawbar pull during this run was 8·2 tons, and the engine steamed freely when working with regulator full open and cut-off 74 per cent. On the return journey loads of up to 800 tons were handled successfully on the heavy grade up to Naworth. For test purposes a stop was made on the 4-mile grade of 1 in 107 east of Wetherall; with a load of 784 tons the engine started easily on the grade, and a drawbar pull of 12½ tons was registered in the process. No. 901, indeed, pulled the dynamometer car spring out to its maximum extent, 16¼ tons, on one special occasion, when, in addition to the train load, the car brakes were applied to try and ascertain the maximum pull of which the engine was capable.

The gradients quoted in the foregoing are taken from the report of the trials. The latest profile shows some variation at certain points.

As at present running the boiler dimensions of these engines differ from those of the original design, as follows:

156	Small tubes (2 in. outside dia.) ...	1,293·3 sq. ft.
24	Superheater flues (5¼ in. outside dia.)	518·2 ,,
24	Superheater elements...	446·4 ,,
	Firebox	169·4 ,,
	Total heating surface...	2,427·3 ,,
	Grate area	26·7 ,,

The fifteen engines of this Class, L.N.E.R. "Q7", are now stationed at Tyne Dock for working the iron ore trains up to Consett, and on this most interesting duty I was privileged to ride on No. 63465, old 624 and one of the batch built by the L.N.E.R. after grouping. We had a maximum load train, 22 hopper wagons and a brake van, representing an estimated load of about 690 tons behind the tender, and after taking banking assistance up the sharp grade from Tyne Dock, No. 63465 took this heavy train single-headed to Stella Gill; then, of course, we were banked in rear up the tremendous climb to Annfield Plain. We were stopped by signal at Pontop Crossing to allow two passenger trains on the Sunderland-Newcastle line to cross, after which we got away in fine style over the gradually rising gradients. We covered the 9 miles from Pontop Crossing to a stop abreast of Milepost 11½ in 47 min. inclusive of a 7 min. stop for water at Washington, and a signal stop just prior to this junction. Our running average speed was 14 m.p.h., with a maximum of 23 m.p.h. on level track. The engine was in very good trim, steaming freely, and with a good even beat. She was worked in one notch from full gear, 65 per cent. cut-off, and between Pontop Crossing and Stella Gill the first port of the regulator sufficed, except for a short spell on the 1 in 135-104 gradient near Harraton.

But it was on restarting from Pelaw Junction, with another "Q7", No. 63471, in rear, that the really thrilling part of the journey began. From this point up to Annfield East the ruling gradient is 1 in 50; there are short stretches of 1 in 35 and 1 in 42, and for 35 minutes on end we blazed away with the main regulator practically full open, and the cut-off in 65 per cent. Against this hard slogging the boiler steamed magnificently. Pressure was never below 160 lb. per sq. in. and for the most part it was above 170, and sometimes blowing-off. We maintained a full glass of water, and indeed it seemed as though the engine could have sustained the effort indefinitely. The mileposts on this line relate to a zero at Ouston Junction, on the Team Valley line, and between Posts 1 and 7¼ we averaged 11·7 m.p.h. on these terrific gradients. There was one especially thrilling piece on the climb; we had been pounding up the 1 in 52 above Beamish station at 9 to 10 m.p.h. where we came to a pronounced easing of the gradient for nearly half a mile at West Stanley. But there was no easing. Both engines were allowed to charge away, "flat-out", to nearly 30 m.p.h. and the roar of the three-cylinder exhaust was indescribable. There was good reason for such tactics for a stretch of 1 in 35 follows, and we climbed it without falling below 14 m.p.h. It was also at this precise moment that the engine blew off! But by now Annfield was in sight; the worst of the climbing would soon be at an end, and the bank engine would drop off. Over the easier gradients onwards to Leadgate we averaged 18 m.p.h., and finally came to a stand at Carr House East Box, just short of Consett station in 51½ min. from South Pelaw Junction, 11·3 miles. In this book I have often written about the hard work demanded from North Eastern freight engines; I could not have wished for a finer example than this trip from Tyne Dock to Consett.

The "S3" engines (L.N.E.R. Class "B16") had the same boiler, cylinders and motion as Class "T3" but they were 4-6-0s with 5 ft. 8 in. coupled wheels, and a nominal tractive effort of 30,032 lb. The weight of the engine alone, in working order, is 77¾ tons, against the 72½ tons of Class "T3". But these new 4-6-0s constituted another thoroughly successful design, in which all the earlier North Eastern characteristics were perpetuated: Stephenson's link motion, three sets of valve gear, outside admission. A high degree of superheat was obtained, and Raven used a higher boiler pressure than with his earlier superheater engines. Seventy engines of Class "S3" were built at Darlington, as follows:

Year	1919	1920	1921	1922	1923	1924
Number built	1	21	13	5	28	2

As to their work on the road, I have recently described in very full detail* an excellent round trip I made on the footplate of No. 61426 (old 931) from York to Wath, and back; but for easy reference I am including here a log of the outward journey.

N.E.R.: 8 a.m. GOODS, YORK—MEXBOROUGH WEST

Load: 43 wagons, "equal to 58"; Approx. 750 tons
Engine: ex-N.E.R. 3-cylinder 4-6-0 No. 61426 (Class "B16")
Driver: F.W. Marshall; Fireman: R. Doughty (York shed)

Distance		Actual	Speeds
miles		min. sec.	m.p.h.
0·0	Dringhouses Yard	0 00	
1·0	*Chaloners Whin Junct.*	4 30	—
2·7	Copmanthorpe	9 42	27
6·6	Bolton Percy	18 00	30½
7·8	Ulleskelf	20 32	30
9·7	Church Fenton	24 30	27
11·8	Sherburn-in-Elmet	29 27	23
13·6	*Milford Junct.*	33 47	26
14·3	Monk Fryston	35 33	22
15·6	Burton Salmon	38 55	27
		sigs.	5
18·2	FERRYBRIDGE	46 50	—
20·2	PONTEFRACT	54 15	20½
			17½
22·9	Ackworth	61 45	34
			18½
26·4	Moorthorpe	71 51	33½
29·3	Frickley	76 42	16½
32·5	Bolton-on-Dearne	84 05	29
33·2	*Dearne Junct.*	85 37	15 (slack)
34·1	*Mexborough West Junct.*	90 20	

By the time the "S3" 4-6-0s were getting into their stride the whole railway scene in Great Britain was changing. Sir Eric Geddes had been appointed as the first Minister of Transport, and it was ironical that this brilliant ex-N.E.R. man was to sponsor the scheme that struck so deeply at the individualism of the old North Eastern Railway. But there was a "something" about the line itself and its men that helped many of the old traditions to survive. In its development and in its prosperity the N.E.R. was in its own district, in many ways an industrial epitome of the times. Its roots were deep down in some of the most ancient cities of England; at its board meetings

* In *4,000 Miles on the Footplate* (Ian Allan).

great landed proprietors sat side by side with self-made men from the Newcastle quayside; eminent public men like Sir Edward Grey took genuine pleasure in the affairs of the railway that served their countryside. Grey—Viscount Grey of Fallodon as he became after the war—was not merely a director, and a former chairman; he was an enthusiast. Guests at his house in Northumberland would often be taken to the lineside in the afternoons to see the down "Flying Scotsman" come sweeping down Christon Bank. But the story of North Eastern locomotive development is not quite ended. Almost at the moment of grouping Sir Vincent Raven's Pacific engine No. 2400 was completed at Darlington—obviously a counterblast to Gresley's 1470 and 1471 turned out at Doncaster earlier in 1922. But the Raven Pacifics, North Eastern though they were in every detail, belong more to the transition years, and their design and work will be discussed in the next chapter. With his Pacifics on the road Sir Vincent Raven retired, though his greatest ambition, the electrification of the main line between York and Newcastle, remained unfulfilled.

Chapter Thirteen

ANOTHER TRANSITION: N.E.R. TO L.N.E.R.

WITH the appointment of Mr. Gresley as Chief Mechanical Engineer of the Eastern Group it was only natural that before long there would be an infiltration of Great Northern ideas into the locomotive practice of the enlarged system. But there was never any definite attempt to obliterate the individuality of the other constituent companies. It is true that new engines of alien design came to be built at Darlington, but the older classes lived on, and except on the Great Central they retained their own lineaments inviolate. Stamer was appointed Assistant Chief Mechanical Engineer of the L.N.E.R., and while he remained at Stooperdale, the North Eastern traditions were nobly upheld. Construction of the former standard locomotive types was allowed to continue for a time, and the following additions were made to the stock, from 1922 onwards:

Year	Engine class	Number built
1922	D	6
	P3	19
	S3	5
	4-6-2	1
1923	4-6-2	1
	P3	10
	H	5
	S3	28
1924	S3	2
	4-6-2	3
	T3	10

I should add that 19 further Class "D" 4-4-4 tank engines had been built in 1920-1, bringing the total of that class up to 45. Also, the total post-war construction of "P3" engines was 35. In 1924 Darlington began building the Gresley "K3" Moguls in large numbers, and apart from the "J72" 0-6-0 shunting engines in 1949-51, as previously mentioned, the last purely North Eastern locomotives to be constructed were five Class "X" 4-8-0s, 1656-1660, in 1925.

So we come to the Raven Pacifics. The completion of the first Gresley Pacific in the early spring of 1922 created extreme interest, particularly in the comparisons to be made with *The Great Bear*. It was, however, surely without precedent that *The Railway Magazine* of July, 1922, was able to publish an outline drawing and full dimensional details of the North Eastern Pacific then under construction at Darlington, five months before the actual engine appeared. From the drawing it was seen that she was a much enlarged and elongated

"Z". The only noticeable difference was the provision of a wide firebox. The cylinders were 19 in. dia. by 26 in. stroke; piston valves 8¾ in. dia.; three sets of Stephenson link motion; coupled wheels 6 ft. 8 in. dia. and boiler pressure 200 lb. per sq. in. The nominal tractive effort at 85 per cent. boiler pressure was 29,918 lb., much the same as that of the Gresley Pacifics. The proportions of the boiler and heating surfaces were as follows:

Small tubes
- Number 119
- Outside dia. ... ... 2¼ in.
- Distance between tubeplates ... ... 21 ft.

Superheater flues
- Number 24
- Outside dia. ... ... 5¼ in.

Heating surfaces
- Small tubes ... ... 1,472 sq. ft.
- Superheater flues... ... ... 692·7 „
- Superheater elements ... ... 509·9 „
- Firebox ... ... 200·0 „
- Total ... ... 2,874·6 „

Grate area ... ... 41·5 „

The boiler was very long, and some trouble might have been expected with the steaming; but to judge from those who worked on No. 2400 in her early days there was no difficulty at all. She was entrusted to Driver Blades, of Gateshead, and it was he who worked her in the dynamometer car trials against a Gresley Pacific, between Kings Cross and Doncaster in the early summer of 1923. Very little definite information emerged about those trials; no logs were ever published and no technical details were released, but one gathers that No. 2400 was fully equal to the Gresley "A1", then in its original condition with short travel valves. The fireman on those trials was C. Fisher, now a Locomotive Inspector at York, and in this latter capacity he has accompanied me on several recent footplate trips. The hardest train to work in those trials of 1923 was the 5.40 p.m. down from Kings Cross. The load was usually well over 500 tons and the timings were then:

Section	Distance	Time
	miles	min.
Kings Cross to Peterborough...	76·4	87
Peterborough to Grantham	29·1	37
Grantham to Doncaster	50·5	55

In those years we younger enthusiasts were not so well informed as the enthusiasts of today, and it so happened that I had occasion to travel to Leeds at the time of those trials. I was living on the other side of London, and when invited to visit an old school friend, at Leeds, I chose to travel by the 4 p.m. train, in preference to the 5.40 p.m., so as not to be late in arriving at the home of my hosts. It was a decision that I shall never cease to regret. Little did I know that on that very evening the 5.40 p.m. was being worked by the N.E.R. engine No. 2400!

In later years I was never fortunate enough to clock anything outstanding with these engines, let alone the equal of the best work of the Gresley "A1s" after those engines were fitted with long travel valves. My best run was with No. 2401, on the up "Flying Scotsman" in 1932, though I fancy a "Z" could have done equally well if really put to it. The log is tabulated herewith:

L.N.E.R.: BERWICK—NEWCASTLE "FLYING SCOTSMAN"

Load: 392 tons tare, 415 tons full
Engine: Raven 4-6-2 No. 2401 *City of Kingston-upon-Hull*

Distance		Actual	Speeds *
miles		min. sec.	m.p.h.
0·0	BERWICK	0 00	—
1·2	Tweedmouth	3 20	—
6·1	Goswick	9 00	72
8·3	Beal	10 50	69
15·3	Belford	17 30	56
20·9	Chathill	23 07	65
23·9	Christon Bank	25 57	61½
25·9	*Milepost* 41	28 15	49
27·5	Little Mill	30 00	56
29·4	Longhoughton	31 52	69
32·1	ALNMOUTH	34 15	65½
35·0	Warkworth	37 18	54½
38·4	Acklington	40 42	65
43·7	Widdrington	45 55	60
		pitfall slack	20
50·3	MORPETH	56 10	—
57·0	Cramlington	65 20	54½/47
61·9	Forest Hall	70 25	61½
65·2	Heaton	74 05	—
66·9	NEWCASTLE	78 10†	—

*Max. and min. speeds by stop watch
†Schedule 80 min.

Three more of these engines were built at Darlington in 1924 and, at the same time as the Gresley "A1s" 4473-4481 and 2543-2572 were named, these five North Eastern Pacifics became:

2400 *City of Newcastle*
2401 *City of Kingston-upon-Hull*
2402 *City of York*
2403 *City of Durham*
2404 *City of Ripon.*

It was the Atlantics, however, that stole the limelight in the first years after the grouping. The famous timing of 43 min., start-to-stop, from Darlington to York was restored on the evening Glasgow-Leeds dining car express, now "The North Briton", and early in 1923 No. 2163 made the fine run tabulated herewith. Running at over 80 m.p.h. on dead level track was then something of a novelty, and in publishing the run in *The Railway Magazine*, Mr. Cecil J. Allen remarked: "Thus these North Eastern 3-cylinder Atlantics yield but little, if at all, to the Great Western 4-6-0s in the matter of sustained high speed on the level". One could not wish for higher praise than that. In explanation of the leisurely start I should add that delays were sometimes experienced from the 7.15 p.m. mail train from Newcastle, which was due at York only 8 min. ahead of the Glasgow-Leeds "diner"; drivers tended to run easily at the start, and then to open out after Northallerton.

N.E.R.: 8.49 p.m. DARLINGTON—YORK

Load: 7 cars, 211 tons tare, 220 tons full
Engine: Class "Z" 4-4-2 No. 2163

Distance		Schedule	Actual	Speeds *
miles		min.	min. sec.	m.p.h.
0·0	DARLINGTON	0	0 00	—
2·6	Croft Spa		4 55	31·8
5·2	Eryholme		7 50	54·5
10·4	Danby Wiske		12 50	62·4
14·1	NORTHALLERTON	15	16 15	65·0
17·6	Otterington		19 15	70·0
21·9	Thirsk	23	22 45	73·7
26·1	Sessay		26 09	74·2
28·0	Pilmoor		27 38	76·7
30·7	Raskelf		29 40	79·6
32·9	Alne	32	31 17	81·7
38·6	Beningbrough		35 28	81·6
41·0	*Skelton Bridge Box* ...		37 16	80·0
42·5	*Poppleton Junct.*		38 35	68·5
			sigs.	
44·1	YORK	43	42 55	

*Average speeds, station to station

In the early days of grouping interchange between locomotives of the various constituent companies were generally popular, and on the L.N.E.R. comparative tests were carried out between Atlantics of Great Northern, North Eastern and North British design between Newcastle and Edinburgh. No. 733 represented the N.E.R. and No. 878 *Hazeldean*, the N.B.R. For the Great Northern, a piston-valve engine with 32-element superheater was naturally chosen, but to clear the Scottish loading gauge her chimney and dome had to be cut down. This engine was No. 1447. Each locomotive was worked by men from its own line, and in running the trains they were allowed full discretion as to how they worked the engines in their charge. Each engine made five return trips with ordinary service trains, taking whatever loads were offered, and in addition three special runs were made, one with each engine, on trains made up to maximum tonnage. The service trains were the 3.26 p.m. relief to the down "Flying Scotsman", allowed 154 min. for the 124·4 miles from Newcastle to Edinburgh, and the 10.35 p.m. up "Night Scotsman", booked in 151 min. Both trains were non-stop. The special trains worked on October 16th, 17th and 18th, 1923, were allowed 154 min., non-stop, in each direction.

COMPARATIVE TESTS WITH ATLANTIC ENGINES MADE BETWEEN NEWCASTLE AND EDINBURGH, 1923

LEADING PARTICULARS OF ENGINES

Particulars	N.E.R.	G.N.R.	N.B.R.
Weight in working trim tons			
Engine ...	77·1	69·6	76·7
Tender ...	45·6	43·1	45·4
Total ...	122·7	112·7	122·1
Heating Surface, square feet			
Firebox ...	185	141	184·8
Tubes ...	1298	1824	1619·0
Total water heating surface ...	1483	1965	1803·8
Superheater ...	392	568	263·0
Boiler pressure lb. per sq. in. ...	175	170	180
Grate Area sq. ft. ...	27	31	28·5
Cylinders			
Number ...	3	2	2
Diameter, in. ...	16½	20⅛	21
Stroke, in. ...	26·0	24	28
Driving wheels, diameter, in. ...	82	80	81
Adhesive weight, lb. ...	88,700	89,600	89,600
Tractive effort at 85% boiler pressure, lb. ...	19,300	17,580	23,324
RATIOS			
Adhesive weight / Tractive effort = ...	4·6	5·1	3·84
Tractive effort / Heating surface = ...	10·2	6·9	11·3
Heating surface / Grate area = ...	69·4	81·8	72·4

RESULTS OF THE TESTS

Railway ... Engine No. ...	G.N.R. 1447	N.E.R. 733	N.B.R. 878
Average Load, tons tare			
Service Trains ...	307	311	345
Special Trains ...	406	406	406
Average Speed, m.p.h. * ...			
Service Trains ...	49·3	49·0	48·8
Special Trains ...	46·0	47·2	47·5
Average D.B.H.P.			
Service Trains ...	393	391	529
Special Trains ...	527	529	525
Average Steam Chest Pressure lb. per sq. in.			
Special Trains ...	97	132	138
Average Cut-Off			
Special Trains % ...	40	42	38
Coal per D.H.P. hour lb.			
Service Trains ...	5·08	4·45	4·12
Special Trains ...	4·42	3·63	4·15
Average Superheat temp. in deg. Fah. ...	624	577	520
Evaporation, lb. of water per lb. of coal ...	7·2	8·6	8·2

*Inclusive of various checks on most runs.

PERFORMANCE ON COCKBURNSPATH BANK

Railway ... Engine ...	G.N.R. 1447	N.E.R. 733	N.B.R. 878
Load, tons ...	406·5	406·5	366
Average boiler pressure, lb. per sq. in. ...	162	175	175
Steam chest pressure lb. per sq. in. ...	140	147	138
Average cut-off % ...	40	56	52
Speed on bank m.p.h.			
at foot ...	47·5	50·5	44·0
minimum...	20	22·5	21·5
Drawbar pull, tons			
at foot ...	2·45	2·20	2·35
maximum actual ...	4·75	4·80	4·70
„ corrected for gradient ...	5·92	6·08	5·97

The results which are tabulated overleaf will come as a joy to the Scots, and something of a shock to Great Northern enthusiasts. They certainly blow sky-high the idea, frequently expressed in post-grouping days, that the North British Atlantics were extravagant on coal. With the service trains *Hazeldean* was the most economical of all in the vital quantity of coal per drawbar horsepower hour, though in haulage of the 400-ton special trains the North Eastern "Z" moves into the first place.

The performance of the North British Atlantic was uniformly good, and her coal consumption generally below the best North Eastern standards; but in working the heavy special trains the "Z" appears to have been operating nearer to her optimum efficiency and gave the commendable average of 3·63 lb. of coal per D.H.P. hour. Throughout the tests the Great Northern engine was much the heaviest on coal, and on the 400-ton train trials her consumption was 54 lb. per mile against 49 lb. by *Hazeldean* and only 43½ lb. by the "Z" No. 733. These results are extremely interesting in view of the comparative dimensions of the three engines; it will be noted in particular that in heavy working the engine with the *smallest* grate area was the most economical. The dimensions of the engines, as tested, are given in the accompanying table. A further table gives some details of work on the Cockburnspath bank, on the south-bound runs with the 400-ton special trains.

The North British trip included above was on the heaviest of the "service" runs. On the 400-ton special train a signal check was experienced at Cockburnspath station, and ready comparison in the performance cannot be made with the other runs. An interesting development soon after grouping, which gave the North Eastern enginemen an excellent chance to show what they could do, was an alteration in the working of the 5.30 p.m. express from Kings Cross whereby the York stop was omitted, and a non-stop run made from Grantham to Darlington, 126·8 miles in 142 min. It was not a very economical arrangement. The engine worked down on the 8 a.m. from Newcastle and stood idle at Grantham for nearly 8 hours, while different crews were needed for the up and down trains. Be that as it may, the North Eastern men seemed to delight in showing off the paces of their engines, doubtless for the edification of the Great Northern pilotmen who rode with them as far as York. Night after night Doncaster was passed well ahead of time, but after slowing down to walking pace through York to set down the pilotmen the running over the N.E. line never seemed to be very enterprising, even when running late. Four runs, all timed by Mr. Cecil J. Allen, are tabulated herewith, all included most exhuberant starts, while the second effort of engine No. 721, in Colume 4, continued in terrific style right through to Selby. At this point the train was 12 min.

L.N.E.R. GRANTHAM—DARLINGTON: RUNS WITH N.E.R. "Z" ATLANTICS

Run No. ...	... ...		1	2	3	4
Engine No.	... ...		721	736	727	721
Load tons gross	... ...		280	280	280	280
Distance		Schedule	Actual	Actual	Actual	Actual
miles		min.	min. sec.	min. sec.	min. sec.	min. sec.
0·0	GRANTHAM	0	0 00	0 00	0 00	0 00
4·2	Barkston		7 00	6 55	7 00	6 40
9·9	Claypole		11 40	11 40	11 45	11 20
14·6	NEWARK	16	15 25	15 30	15 35	15 15
20·9	Carlton		21 05	20 50	20 55	20 20
28·2	*Markham Box*		28 35	28 20	28 15	27 20
33·1	Retford	36	33 15	33 00	32 45	32 00
			p.w. slack	—	—	—
38·4	Ranskill		40 40	38 10	37 40	37 00
42·2	Bawtry		44 30	41 50	40 55	40 10
					sigs.	
45·6	Rossington		48 35	45 55	45 30	43 30
					sigs.	
50·5	DONCASTER	54	53 30	50 35	52 45	47 30
				sigs.		
54·7	*Shaftholme Junct.* ...	59	58 10	61 50	57 40	51 25
60·5	Balne		64 00	68 05	63 20	56 55
64·3	Templehirst		68 00	72 20	66 55	60 20
				sigs.		
68·9	SELBY	77	73 25	78 15	72 00	65 05
73·0	Riccall		79 15	85 20	78 30	70 40
						sigs.
80·7	*Chaloners Whin Junct.* ...		88 00	93 25	86 55	80 45
			sigs.	sigs.	sigs.	sigs.
82·7	YORK	94	92 15	98 30	92 30	86 25*
126·8	DARLINGTON ...	142	142 20	144 30	139 35	—
Net time (equivalent) to stop at York			88½	88½	87	82
Maximum speeds m.p.h.						
near Claypole			79	77½	77½	77½
„ Retford			71½	71½	75	67
„ Ranskill			—	—	70½	75
„ Templehirst			—	—	69	71½

*Stop in York station

early! But the engine unfortunately ran hot that night, and had to come off the train at York.

In the meantime North British Atlantic drivers were working down to Newcastle, and they, too, were "showing off", with some most brilliant starts from Edinburgh towards Dunbar. Some years later, and in the hands of Scottish crews, the "Zs" did their very last regular work on East Coast expresses with the 1.20 p.m. from Kings Cross, as between Newcastle and Edinburgh. In 1933 during the period of the summer service, Haymarket shed had their two star Pacifics, 2795 and 2796, earmarked for the non-stop "Flying Scotsman", and it was something of a paradox that during this time, while the 1.20 p.m. Scotsman was loaded daily to 10 coaches north of Newcastle, it was Atlantic-hauled, whereas on the winter service, when Pacifics were available, the load was usually no more than eight. I spent a holiday at Berwick in the late summer of that year, and was able to travel on the down afternoon "Scotsman" on several occasions. There did not appear to be any difficulties in keeping time between

L.N.E.R.—THE 1.20 p.m. ex KINGS CROSS : ALNMOUTH—BERWICK

Run No. ...			1		2		3		4	
Engine No.			2196		734		729		2401	
Engine class			"Z"		"Z"		"Z"		4-6-2	
Load, tons tare/full			318/340		317/340		319/340		335/360	
Distance		Schedule	Actual	Speeds	Aetual	Speeds	Actual	Speeds	Actual	Speeds
miles		min.	min. sec.	m.p.h. *	min. sec.	m.p.h. *	min. sec.	m.p.h. *	min. sec.	m.p.h. *
0·0	ALNMOUTH	0	0 00		0 00		0 00	—	0 00	—
2·7	Longhoughton		6 14	33	6 26	32½	6 10	33¼	6 27	33
4·6	Little Mill		9 39	34½	9 56	33¼	9 31	35¼	9 52	35½
8·2	Christon Bank		13 55	64½	14 16	64½	13 38	66½	13 55	69
11·2	Chathill		16 35	71	16 55	69	16 15	71½	16 25	75
14·4	Lucker		19 40	62½	19 54	66	19 08	66	19 10	69
16·8	Belford	20	22 03	60	22 07	62½	21 20	64½	21 20	64½
20·1	Smeafield		25 05	71	25 08	72½	24 18	74	24 18	74
23·8	Beal		28 13	73	28 08	75	27 12	76½	27 15	75
26·0	Goswick		30 08	68½	29 59	70½	29 00	72½	29 10	69
29·7	*Milepost 64½*		34 02	51	33 42	52½	32 36	57	33 01	53
30·9	Tweedmouth		35 23	57½	35 03	59	33 50	60	34 20	58
32·1	BERWICK	36	37 30	—	37 00	—	35 43	—	36 40	—

*Maximum and minimum speeds by stop watch.

Newcastle and Alnmouth—34·8 miles in 45 min. start-to-stop—even though there was a troublesome pitfall slack at Annitsford; but the next stage on to Berwick, at an average speed of 53·4 m.p.h. was a stiff job with a load of 340 tons. I was able to clock this train on three occasions in the summer of 1933, and once at an earlier date with a Raven Pacific. On only one run out of the four was strict time kept, by the Atlantic 729, and the speeds made, as shown in Column 3 of the accompanying table, testify to the nature of this schedule.

Up the continuous 1 in 170 of Longhoughton bank speed rose to 35¼ m.p.h., and then some very fast running followed, with an average speed of 67·4 m.p.h. from Christon bank to Tweedmouth. As evidence of the work the "Z" Atlantics were required to do in their declining years it is interesting to compare this fast average of engine No. 729 with those of the pre-1914 runs in Table 3 of Chapter Eleven. There, it was only on one run, with a "V" hauling no more than 260 tons, that the 1933 effort of No. 729 was beaten. Otherwise the average speeds between Christon and Tweedmouth lay between 59 and 66½ m.p.h. On passing Goswick No.

729 was a minute ahead of the other two "Zs", and her driver pressed his advantage home with a remarkable ascent of Scremerston bank. Here the 3¾ miles at 1 in 230-190 were cleared at a minimum speed of 57 m.p.h. The other two "Zs" did good work, though it was not fast enough for timekeeping, while the Pacific in the fourth column did little better through a rather feeble start.

This chapter is bound to concern the express engines to the virtual exclusion of all others, since it was always the express engines that seem to take the first onslaught of any amalgamation, or change in policy. And so I pass on to a few more personal notes on the Atlantics. In the summer of 1934 I was travelling by the 2.5 p.m. from Waverley to Kings Cross, on which one Pacific engine usually worked through from Edinburgh to York. We had an "A1", No. 2569 *Gladiateur,* and with a load of 475 tons she seemed a bit lifeless even from the start. Soon it was evident she was in trouble for steam and we stopped at Tweedmouth for assistance. There was always an East Coast "standing pilot" at that depôt, as at Darlington, and a "Z", No. 2203, was quickly attached. The two engines ran the 65·2 miles to Newcastle in 71¼ min. regaining 6¾ min. and bringing the train in only 11 min. late. The Pacific was in no state to continue with the diagrammed working and the train was handed over to two fresh "Zs", Nos. 2171 and 2193. They continued to Darlington in 44¾ min. (6¼ min. gain) and finally ran the 44·1 miles on to York in 43 min. 54 sec. start-to-stop. We passed Poppleton Junction, 42·5 miles, in 40 min. 8 sec., and but for a slow finish could easily have kept the 43-min. booking of the 8.49 p.m. up. As it was we regained a further 3 min., and handed over the train only 3 min. late. A fresh "A1", No. 2575 *Galopin,* then took over, and the train was on time by Shaftholme Junction—an excellent recovery.

The very last time I travelled in an East Coast express behind North Eastern engines came in the following year, on no less a train than the down "Aberdonian". I was going north to do some footplate work on the Gresley 2-8-2s. Partly due, no doubt, to the eagerness with which I was anticipating those journeys, and partly due to the heat of that August night, I slept fitfully; at Newcastle I gave it up altogether and clocked the speeds instead. We made a good run, with our 515-ton train, passing Berwick (66·9 miles) in 73¾ min., and after a permanent way check we cleared Grantshouse in 96 min. 40 sec. We did some smart work through the Lothian country, averaging 63 m.p.h. from Dunbar to Portobello, and with a quick run in reached Edinburgh in 139 min. 55 sec. When I got down on to the dark, chilly platform, ready to ride the relieving engine forward to Dundee, I was delighted to find that our motive power from Newcastle had not been a modern Pacific, but two old

North Easterns—an original "V", No. 1794 leading, and an "R", No. 2025 next to the train.

The old N.E.R. engines were certainly putting up some spirited work in the middle " 'thirties", where they had the opportunities, but they were rather depressing to see. Many of the Atlantics were just covered in grime, and when a considerable proportion of the top-link Pacifics were in a similar state one could hardly expect otherwise. In the last years before the second World War, however, Darlington running shed became a literally shining example to the rest, and the two East Coast pilots, and Atlantics engaged on other duties, were once again in the state of spotless cleanliness that one took for granted on the old N.E.R. Those Darlington engines were mostly "Vs" of the second batch, but 1680 of the original series was among their number, when I spent some time at the shed taking photographs in the autumn of 1938. My last run behind a North Eastern Atlantic was made that same day, on the 10.5 a.m. from York; No. 705 (Class "V1") was the engine and with 310 tons she ran to Northallerton in much the same style as was needed on the "Flying Scotsman" and the "Diner" in days before the first World War. Thirsk was passed in 25½ min. and Northallerton reached, after a signal check, in 34¾ min. The second World War dealt heavily with these engines, and the "Zs", too, and when I went north again in 1945 and 1946, the survivors were in a state of decrepitude that does not bear thinking about. Of their later days I like to remember them best as I saw them frequently in 1938 and 1939, when I was often at Darlington and Northallerton on signalling work; though one missed the huge polished safety valve covers on the "Vs", on the "V1s" and the earlier "Zs", in their regained splendour these Atlantics revived a pleasing link with the old North Eastern Railway.

Epilogue

THE NEW N.E.R.

IN times when surviving links with the old companies are becoming fewer and further between, it was pleasant to ride the engine of the "Flying Scotsman", in 1952, southbound from Edinburgh, on a locomotive named *Edward Fletcher* and to witness a run that would surely have delighted "The Old Man", in its economy and the sweetness of running. At Newcastle the shed master from Gateshead came across to the Central station to wish me "Bon Voyage", and in the few minutes before the fresh engine backed down he said: "We've got 'one-four-seven' for you. She's always been rather a favourite of mine". "One-four-seven"—60147 that was, of course—*North Eastern,* and when she came down he showed me, with pride, the old N.E.R. crest carried above the nameplate.

Edward Fletcher, and then *North Eastern*! Can I be forgiven for having a few nostalgic memories as we pulled out over the King Edward Bridge? But a non-stop run to Grantham, many stretches of flat-bottomed rail, and colour-light signals right through York all belonged to the new "N.E.R." rather than the old one. So far as equipment goes, the old and the new are still very much mixed, and in this book particular reference has been made to the present-day work of the old North Eastern Railway engines. I shall remember for many a day those tough little "J77s" at Blyth, thundering up on to the staiths; then there was the "J21", climbing over the moorland from Kirkby Stephen, over Belah viaduct to Stainmore; the "G5" tanks on the Sunderland locals; the 4-8-0s at Erimus yard, and those unforgettable "Q7s" blasting their way up to Consett. But nostalgic memories of the old N.E.R., and its engines are not confined to non-railwaymen like myself. When this book was in its earlier stages the Motive Power Superintendent went to considerable trouble to work out for me a number of trips that would show the old engines at work; but with the time factor in mind I queried whether a run with an old Class "R" 4-4-0 (L.N.E.R. "D20") would yield any useful data, having regard to the light nature of their duties in comparison with their grand running on the East Coast trains of forty to fifty years ago. "Oh, but you *must*", came the reply; and it was intimated smilingly, but none the less firmly, that whatever else I did in the way of North Eastern footplate work I must not exclude the "D20" Class, if for no other reason than that of "auld lang syne"!

This was easier said than done. It was not as though the N.E.R. was close at hand; for me, a journey to York alone meant 300 miles of travelling before I could set foot on a North Eastern engine, and another 300 miles to get back home afterwards. But such was the programme of runs mapped out, and such was the compelling interest of each successive journey, at it came to be made, that distance became no obstacle, and I fitted in many trips amid lecturing and other engagements. Even so the Class "R" got left until the summer service had started—until, indeed the bulk of the book had been sent to the publishers. Then one Saturday in mid-June I travelled to Scarborough to pick up the 11.25 a.m. Liverpool express, which travels via the coastal route; it calls at Filey and Bridlington, and then runs non-stop to Gascoigne Wood, where it is handed over to the London Midland Region. Selby shed is quite a stronghold of the remaining "D20s". During the winter they work on main line locals, and other light duties; but in the summer they are mostly earmarked for assisting on the heavy holiday trains to and from Bridlington and Scarborough. So it turned out that I was privileged to spend two hours on the footplate of No. 62384 (old 1184) on an express passenger job that included a fair amount of 60 m.p.h. running.

It was a light duty for the engine, with a "D49" ahead of us, and only 270 tons between them; but that was not the point. Bowling along, under easy steam it is true, I experienced what I was never fortunate enough to do in their prime—the "feel" of a North Eastern express engine at speed. It is not enough to say she rode beautifully, because many good riding engines are unkind and harsh to those in their cabs. Old 62384 was wonderfully smooth and steady, but I could also sit down indefinitely. There was no jarring to the body, no jolting, and the little noise there was came from the cab roof. Many years ago Rous-Marten remarked upon the exceptional riding qualities of the "Q1" 4-4-0s when they were new; if 62384 was still so good when demoted to the status of a local train "hack" I can well believe what these North Eastern 4-4-0s were like in their prime. She was very nicely handled by Driver Horsman and Fireman Holmes, of Selby; the reverser was mostly in the first notch (out of four) from mid-gear, about 25 per cent. cut-off. Both when steaming and coasting the action at the front-end was sweet, and entirely free from any "kicking".

When we left Scarborough, the day promised to be sweltering hot. A sea mist was lifting, and the sun beat down upon the open platform at Londesborough Road. But after we had turned south from the main line at Seamer the mist came down again, and on the high ground behind the sea cliffs of Speeton and Bempton we seemed to be right in the clouds. Personal memories came crowding in as we coasted down through Flamborough and past Sewerby Crossing, where I took some of my earliest railway photographs and snapped a "J" single toiling up the bank with a Hull to Scarborough train. But at Bridlington, where we made out last stop, the new order was very much in evidence at the running shed; where in those far off days of 1919 and 1920 I used to see "Tennants", "Singles", Class "F" 4-4-0s,

"Waterbury's", and nothing bigger than a Class "Q", there were now "B1s", L.M.S. Class "4" 2-6-0s, and only a solitary "B16". Nostalgic memories again!

On this recent trip, in which No. 62384 participated, we did our fastest running along the level between Bridlington and Driffield, sustaining 61 m.p.h. for about 4 miles, and we followed this with a brisk ascent ever the Wolds. At Enthorpe, the summit point, we were stopped by signal, and held for 5 min. but time was well in hand, and after descending to Market Weighton and slacking heavily through the junctions we had another pleasant gallop over the level to Selby, covering the 10·6 miles from Everingham to Cliff Common at an average speed of 55 m.p.h. We had clear signals right through Selby and, after observing a permanent-way caution, worked up to 50 m.p.h. at Hambleton before slowing for the final stop. The last 6·3 miles from Selby to Gascoigne Wood Junction took 10¾ min. Here a Stanier Class "5" 4-6-0 was waiting to take on the train, and after uncoupling we returned tender first, and light engine to Selby.

The Class "R" 4-4-0s now stationed at Selby are still doing quite first class work, on occasions. They work the 11 a.m. semi-fast from Doncaster, and this train runs non-stop from Selby to York. In Chapter Eleven I included details of the brilliant start made out of York by No. 2102 on the first night of the 44 min. Darlington timing of the 5.30 p.m. from Kings Cross. On that night, with a load of 140 tons the 5·5 level miles out to Beningbrough were covered in 7 min. 11 sec. On the 8th day of May, 1952, No. 62378 (old 724) had the 11 a.m. down from Doncaster, with a load of 160 tons, and in starting from Selby she made times that fully equal the spectacular 1904 effort of 2102; for she passed Escrick—6·7 miles including some rising gradients—in the astonishing time of 8 min. 18 sec. The speed did not exceed 63 m.p.h. but the time was made possible by a phenomenal acceleration from Selby whereby Riccall, 4·1 miles, was passed in 5 min. 43 sec. at 59 m.p.h. York was reached in 17 min. 4 sec., start-to-stop, after a slow approach from Chaloners Whin Junction. I may add that the crew were quite unaware that anyone was clocking them in detail.

In a book of this kind one tends to think wholly in the past, and to write in the past tense; but in turning back through these pages—to the "P3" thundering up the grade past Ashington Colliery, to the Tyne Dock "T3s", to the "S3s" and to the Erimus hump yard tanks—one realises that the many surviving engines of North Eastern build still have a vital rôle in the massed array of British railway motive power. Now, to the hard slogging of massively-built freight engines, these recent experiences with the "R" Class add a touch of old-time express passenger elegance to the picture of present-day N.E.R. power, and they enable me to end on that cheerful note, instead of one of mere nostalgia.

Index

Boilers: *Page*
- On "1001" class 42
- On "901" class 72
- Tennant 2-4-0 72
- Non-standard 115
- T2 class 0-8-0 174
- T3 class 0-8-0 178
- 4-6-2 express engines ... 184

Brake Trials 51

Bramhope Tunnel Accident 7

Bury Engines 35

Cab Signalling ... 134, 144

Coal Consumption:
- "C" class engine No. 107 79
- Class "M" 94
- Interchange trials 187–8
- "901" class 55
- V1 and Z class 138

Constituent Companies:
- Locomotive stock 2, 3
- York, Newcastle & Berwick 2
- York & North Midland ... 2, 8
- Leeds Northern 2, 13
- South Durham & Lancs. Union 4, 5
- Derwent Valley 5
- Newcastle and Carlisle ... 15

Compound Locomotives:
- T. W. Worsdell's ... 74 *et seq.*
- No. 1619 Class 3CC ... 103
- No. 730 and 731 121

Cross-water Tubes ... 104

Cylinder Construction:
- 3-cylinder engines 130

Darlington Works:
- S. & D. Locomotives ... 29
- First engine built 40
- Building of Tennant class ... 43, 63
- Building of "R1" class ... 132

Death of W. M. Smith ... 121

Dynamometer Car Tests: *Page*
- 901 and Tennant (Tweedmouth) 70
- J, M, and Q1 (Tweedmouth) 99, 100
- T & T1 0-8-0 (Tebay) 116, 117
- S2 engines 141
- R, V, and 4CC Newcastle-York 158
- S1 and 4CC York-Newcastle 160
- T2—Simpasture branch ... 174
- T3—Carlisle road 179
- Pacifics: Kings Cross to Doncaster 184

Dynamometer Cars:
- Great Western 119
- North Eastern 119
- L. & N.W.R. 70

Engineers (N.E.R.):
- E. Fletcher 2, 18, 23–30, 44 *et seq.*
- T. E. Harrison 2
- W. Bouch ... ... 18, 34 *et seq.*
- J. Kitching 43
- J. A. Haswell 51
- A. McDonnell ... 58 *et seq.*
- John Stephenson 58
- George Graham 58
- Wilson Worsdell ... 58, 73, 84
- W. M. Smith ... 69, 78, 84
- T. W. Worsdell ... 73 *et seq.*
- V. L. Raven ... 84, 134, 173
- A. C. Stamer 135, 173, 176, 183
- J. H. Smeddle ... 173, 176

Engineers (other railways):
- Aspinall, J. A. F. 58
- Churchward, G. J. 119
- Drummond, D. 104
- Holt (ex M.R.) 79
- Ivatt, H. A. 58, 119
- Johnson, S. W. 79, 89, 99, 104
- Maunsell, R. E. L. 42, 58

Engine Capacity:
- R. S1. V. & 4CC compared 161

Engine Classes (N.E.R.):
- Early singles 19, 21
- "220" class 22
- "Jenny Lind" (Y. & N.M.) 22
- Early 2-4-0s 23
- "390" class 23
- "13" class 24
- Fletcher types 1854–70 ... 24

Page

" 544 " class 30
Whitby bogies 31
S & D types ... ... 34 *et seq.*
" Woodlands " class ... 36
" Saltburn " 36
" Ginx's babies " 38
" 1001 " class 39
" Gamecocks " 43
" 708 " class 44
" 398 " class 49
B.T.P. class 49
" 901 " class 50–54
" 1440 " class 56
McDonnell 4-4-0 60
,, 0-6-0 61
Tennant 2-4-0 63
Class A 74
,, B 76
,, B1 76
,, C 74
,, C1 75
,, D (2-4-0) 77
,, E 82
,, E1 82
,, F 78
,, F1 78
,, G 82
,, H 83
,, I 79
,, J 80
,, K 89
,, L 89
,, M 89–92
,, N 89
,, O 91
,, P 90
,, P1 103
,, P2 120
,, P3 120
,, Q 97
,, Q1 97
,, 3CC 103
,, 4CC 121
,, 290 101
,, R 109–124
,, R1 132
,, S 112–124
,, S1 114
,, S2 140
Stumpf 4-6-0 No. 825 ... 140
Class S3 180
,, T 114
,, T1 116
,, T2 173
,, T3 178
,, U 120
,, V 119
,, V1 134

Page

Class W 129
,, X 129
,, Y 135
,, Z 136
,, D (4-4-4T) 142
4-6-2 express passenger ... 183

ENGINE CLASSES (OTHER COMPANIES):
L.N.W.R. 18 in, 0-6-0 ... 76
G.N.R. " 251 " class 119, 186
G.W.R. " 28XX " 2-8-0 ... 115
G.C.R. 0-8-4 Humping tank 129
Southern class " Z " 0-8-0T 42
N.B.R. 4-4-2 *Hazeldean* ... 186

ENGINES, L.N.E.R. CLASSES:
Class J72 102
,, J77 102
,, A1 4-6-2 (Peppercorn) 193
,, A4 *Mallard* 119
,, A8 4-6-2 tank ... 142

ENGINE DIAGRAMS:
3-cyl. 2-2-2 No. 77 19
3-cyl. 2-2-2 No. 77 rebuilt 20
2-2-2 No. 212 " Jenny Lind " type 21
2-4-0 No. 545 30

ENGINE LIVERIES:
Styles at Gateshead, Darlington York and Leeds ... 32
On engine 910 (York Museum) 53
Tennant engines 64
Wartime 177

ENGINE MILEAGE: "R" CLASS 109

ENGINE NAME LISTS:
" Woodlands " class ... 36
" Saltburn " class 37
" Towlaw " class 40
" 1001 " class 40–41
Raven Pacifics 185

ERIMUS YARDS 130

FOOTPLATE OBSERVATIONS:
Penrith-Darlington (Class C) 76
Newcastle - Sunderland - Durham (O) 91
Blyth Pilots (290 class) ... 101

Page

Ellington Colliery (P3 class) 120
Consett-Blaydon (T2 class) 176
Tyne Dock-Consett (T3 class) 179
Scarboro'-Selby (R class) 194

FREIGHT TRAFFIC:
Early developments ... 4
On S & D line 39
Longer main line runs ... 44
Stella Gill traffic 115
Wartime work 174

GATESHEAD WORKS:
Fletcher's Headquarters ... 18
Cessation of new work ... 132

HUDSON, GEORGE:
Lines projected 1, 2, 5

INDICATOR TRIALS:
" J " class 4-2-2 81
" Z " class 4-4-2 137

INTERCHANGE TRIALS:
G.N.R. - N.E.R. - N.B.R. engines 186

KING EDWARD BRIDGE, OPENING, 1906 8

LOGS OF RUNS:
McDonnell 4-4-0 164
J Class ... 95, 149, 169, 170
M " 95, 96, 156
Q " 98, 150, 154, 156, 162
Q1 " 98, 149
R " 111, 150, 152, 154, 156, 162
R1 " ... 133, 150, 162
S " 113, 152
S1 " 152
V " 150, 152
V1 " ... 135, 162, 177
Z " 139, 152, 156, 162, 177, 186, 189, 190
3CC " 154
4CC " 152
S2 " 141
S3 " 181
Pacifics 185

MAP OF LINES IN DURHAM ... 12

Page

MCDONNELL'S CHANGES ... 59, 60

PERSONALITIES:
Ackworth, Sir William ... 118
Bell, R. 173
Blades, Driver T. 96
Butterworth, Sir A. K. ... 173
Cockshott, F. P. 143
Foxwell, Professor 143
Geddes, Sir Eric 173
Gibb, Sir George 84, 118, 121, 173
Gresley, Sir Nigel 183
Grey, Viscount 182
Macdonald, N. D. 118
Rounthwaite, J. Mawson ... 143
Tennant, Henry 63, 84

PISTON VALVES:
Smith's original type ... 78
Segmental type 79

RACES TO THE NORTH:
" Tennant " runs in 1888 ... 69
Run of No. 117 (F) in 1888 78
Run of Class " J " engines, 1895 94
Record run of 1895 ... 96

RAVEN, VINCENT L. APPOINTMENT AS C.M.E. 134

ROUTES:
York—Newcastle 9
Leamside 9
Team Valley 10
Bishop Auckland 11
Simpasture branch 11
Pontop and South Shields ... 11
Consett ascents 12
Leeds Northern 13
York—Scarborough ... 14
Selby—Bridlington 14
Newcastle—Carlisle ... 15
Darlington - Penrith - Tebay 15
Newcastle—Edinburgh ... 16

SHILDON WORKS 34

SINGLE-WHEELER TANK ENGINES 50

SPEED:
in 1854 6
in 1876 52

Page

Steam Sanding Gear... ... 79

Stooperdale Offices 135

Superheating:
on Z class 136
on S2 class 140
on older engines 172

" T1 " Engines on R.O.D. Duty 176

Uniflow engines:
825 (Class S2) 140
2212 (Class Z) 178

Page

Valve Gears:
On class J 80
on class G 82
after 1890 89
outside valve chests ... 93
4CC class 122
" Z " class 137

Variable Blastpipe 129

Worsdell:
retirement of T. W. Worsdell 83
retirement of Wilson Worsdell 134

Index to Illustrations

EARLY ENGINES: — Page
2-4-0 No. 75 rebuilt from Y.N. & B. engine 25
0-6-0 No. 527 (Hawthorn's) 26
0-6-0 No. 1326 (ex Blyth & Tyne Rly.) 26
2-2-2 No. 326 (ex Y. & N.M.R.) ... 27
0-6-0 tank No. 519 (Manning Wardle) 28
0-6-0 tank No. 1668 (Stephenson's)... 28

STOCKTON & DARLINGTON ENGINES:
0-6-0 No. 1222 (Hawthorn's) ... 26
4-4-0 *Brougham* 46
4-4-0 *Keswick* 46
4-4-0 No. 1269 (Ginx's Babies) ... 47
2-4-0 No. 1050 (Gamecock) 47
0-6-0 No. 1221 as rebuilt 67

FLETCHER ENGINES:
The *Aerolite* as rebuilt 1869 25
2-2-2 No. 451 (original state) ... 27
2-2-2 No. 450 as rebuilt 27
0-6-0 tank No. 476 28
" 25 " class 2-4-0 passenger type ... 45
" Whitby Bogie " 45
2-4-0 No. 847 (901 class) 45
2-4-0 No. 1268 (a rebuilt Ginx's Baby) 47
" 13 " class 0-6-0 Goods No. 529 ... 48
" 708 " class 0-6-0 Goods No. 717 ... 48
" 93 " class 0-6-0 Goods No. 644 ... 48
" 901 " class 2-4-0 (Gateshead variety) 65
BTP 0-4-4T No. 1033... 86

McDONNELL ENGINES:
4-4-0 No. 112 65

TENNANT 2-4-0 ENGINE No. 1463 65

T. W. WORSDELL ENGINES:
Fletcher 0-6-0s rebuilt 67
Fletcher 2-4-0 No. 367 rebuilt ... 68
" A " class 2-4-2 Tank No. 674 ... 105
" C " class 0-6-0 No. 874 88
" D " class 2-4-0 No. 340 68
" E " class 0-6-0T No. 304 105
" F " class 4-4-0 No. 779 85
" G " class 2-4-0 No. 676 68
" I " class 4-2-2 No. 1531 85
" J " class 4-2-2 No. 1517 85

WILSON WORSDELL ENGINES:
" 290 " class 0-6-0 tank No. 1346 ... 86
No. 957 2-2-4 tank engine 86
" M " class No. 1638 (original state) 87
" M " class No. 1621 (as preserved) 87
" O " class 0-4-4T No. 1779 ... 105
" P " class 0-6-0 No. 1897 88
" P2 " class 0-6-0 No. 1678 88
" Q " class No. 1877 87
" S " class 4-6-0 mixed traffic No. 2003 107
" S1 " class 4-6-0 passenger No. 2113 107
" V " class 4-4-2 passenger No. 532 107
" W " class 4-6-2T tank No. 689 ... 128
" X " class 4-8-0 tank No. 1354 ... 128

RAVEN ENGINES:
" S3 " class 4-6-0 goods No. 911 ... 147
" T2 " class 0-8-0 goods No. 2259 ... 147
" T3 " class 0-8-0 goods No. 901 ... 147
" Y " class 4-6-2 tank No. 1113 ... 128
4-6-2 express passenger No. 2400 ... 167

PORTRAITS OF ENGINEERS:
Fletcher, E. 66
McDonnell, A. 66
Raven, V. L. 145
Smeddle, J. H.... 145
Smith, W. M. 66
Stamer, A. C. 145
Worsdell, T. W. 66
Worsdell, W. 145

SHED SCENES:
Tweedmouth 106
Whitby 106

TRAINS AT SPEED:
" C " class goods on Deepdale viaduct 166
" P1 " class coke empties near Stainmore 126
" Q1 " class post-grouping train at York 168
" R " class 10 a.m. Newcastle—Liverpool 126
" R " class 12.20 p.m. Newcastle—Sheffield 165
" 3CC " class No. 1619; Flying Scotsman near Benton 127
" 4CC " class No. 731; 9.50 a.m. Scotsman near Lucker 125
" S2 " class 12.30 Newcastle—Liverpool 146
" V " class on Flying Scotsman (Lamesley) 146
" V1 " class on 12.30 Newcastle—Liverpool 127
" Z " class on down Flying Scotsman (Lucker) 165
" Z1 " class on 2.20 p.m. up Scotsman 148

YORK STATION, SOUTH END ... 108

COLOURED PLATES: — *Facing*
Class T 0-8-0 Mineral engine... ... 97
Compound Atlantic No. 730 ... 55
" R1 " class 4-4-0 No. 1238 ... Title page
Uniflow 4-6-0 No. 825 Class " S2 " 141